THE CAMBRIDGE COMPANION TO
BENJAMIN FRANKLIN

Comprehensive and accessible, this *Companion* addresses several well-known themes in the study of Franklin and his writings, while also showing Franklin in conversation with his British and European counterparts in science, philosophy, and social theory. Specially commissioned chapters, written by scholars well known in their respective fields, examine Franklin's writings and his life with a new sophistication, placing Franklin in his cultural milieu while revealing the complexities of his intellectual, literary, social, and political views. Individual chapters take up several traditional topics, such as Franklin and the American Dream, Franklin and capitalism, and Franklin's views of American national character. Other chapters delve into Franklin's library and his philosophical views on morality, religion, science, and the Enlightenment and explore his continuing influence in American culture. This *Companion* will be essential reading for students and scholars of American literature, history, and culture.

D0378302

CAMBRIDGE COMPANIONS TO
AMERICAN STUDIES

This series of *Companions* to key figures in American history and culture is aimed at students of American studies, history, and literature. Each volume features newly commissioned essays by experts in the field, with a chronology and guide to further reading.

Volumes published:

The Cambridge Companion to Benjamin Franklin edited by Carla Mulford

The Cambridge Companion to Thomas Jefferson edited by Frank Shuffelton

The Cambridge Companion to W. E. B. Du Bois edited by Shamoon Zamir

Volumes in preparation:

The Cambridge Companion to Bob Dylan edited by Kevin Dettmar

The Cambridge Companion to Frederick Douglass edited by Maurice Lee

The Cambridge Companion to Malcolm X edited by Robert Terrill

THE CAMBRIDGE
COMPANION TO
BENJAMIN FRANKLIN

EDITED BY
CARLA MULFORD

CAMBRIDGE
UNIVERSITY PRESS

CAMBRIDGE UNIVERSITY PRESS
Cambridge, New York, Melbourne, Madrid, Cape Town, Singapore, São Paulo, Delhi

Cambridge University Press
The Edinburgh Building, Cambridge CB2 8RU, UK

Published in the United States of America by Cambridge University Press, New York

www.cambridge.org
Information on this title: www.cambridge.org/9780521691864

First published 2008

Printed in the United Kingdom at the University Press, Cambridge

A catalogue record for this publication is available from the British Library

Library of Congress Cataloguing in Publication data
The Cambridge companion to Benjamin Franklin / edited by Carla Mulford.
p.   cm. – (Cambridge companions to American studies)
Includes bibliographical references and index.
ISBN 978-0-521-87134-1 (hardback)
1. Franklin, Benjamin, 1706–1790 – Political and social views.   2. Franklin, Benjamin,
1706–1790 – Knowledge and learning.   3. Franklin, Benjamin, 1706–1790 – Influence.
4. Statesmen – United States – Biography.   5. Scientists – United States – Biography.
6. United States – Intellectual life – 18th century.   I. Mulford, Carla, 1955–
II. Title: Companion to Benjamin Franklin.   III. Series.
E302.6.F8C218   2008
973.3092 – dc22 [B]   2008033470

ISBN 978-0-521-87134-1 hardback
ISBN 978-0-521-69186-4 paperback

CONTENTS

ILLUSTRATIONS

CONTRIBUTORS

DOUGLAS ANDERSON is Sterling-Goodman Professor of English at the University of Georgia. He is the author of *A House Undivided: Domesticity and Community in American Literature* (1990), *The Radical Enlightenments of Benjamin Franklin* (1997), and *William Bradford's Books: Of Plimmoth Plantation And The Printed Word* (2003), as well as twenty articles and book chapters on major figures in English and American literature from the seventeenth through the twentieth centuries.

STEPHEN CARL ARCH is Professor of English and Chair of the Department of English at Michigan State University. He is the author of two book-length studies, *Authorizing the Past: The Rhetoric of History in Seventeenth-Century New England* (1994) and *After Franklin: The Emergence of Autobiography in Post-Revolutionary America, 1780–1830* (2001), as well as numerous articles on early American literature. He has edited Ethan Allen's *Narrative of Col. Ethan Allen's Captivity* for classroom use, and is currently editing two James Fenimore Cooper novels for The Writings of James Fenimore Cooper series. He is also writing a book tentatively titled *Modes of Excess in the Age of Jackson* and focusing on rhetorical and social violence in the 1830s in the United States.

JAMES CAMPBELL was educated at Temple University and SUNY/Stony Brook and is currently Distinguished University Professor at the University of Toledo. He has been a Fulbright Lecturer at the University of Innsbruck (1990–91), and the University of Munich (2003–04). He is editor of *Selected Writings of James Hayden Tufts* (1992) and co-editor of a collection of forthcoming essays, *Experience as Philosophy: On the Work of John J. McDermott*. He has published *The Community Reconstructs: The Meaning of Pragmatic Social Thought* (1992), *Understanding John Dewey: Nature and Cooperative Intelligence* (1995), *Recovering Benjamin Franklin: An Exploration of a Life of Science and Service* (1999), and *A Thoughtful Profession: The Early Years of the American Philosophical Association* (2006).

JOYCE E. CHAPLIN is James Duncan Phillips Professor of Early American History at Harvard University. She received her BA from Northwestern University and her MA and PhD from the Johns Hopkins University, and has taught at Vanderbilt University, the University of Leeds, and the University of Sydney, in addition to Harvard. She is the author of *An Anxious Pursuit: Agricultural Innovation and Modernity in the Lower South, 1730–1815* (1993), *Subject Matter: Technology, the Body, and Science on the Anglo-American Frontier, 1500–1670* (2001), and *The First Scientific American: Benjamin Franklin and the Pursuit of Genius* (2006), and is the editor of "Benjamin Franklin: A How-to Guide: Catalog of an Exhibition," a special edition of the *Harvard Library Bulletin*, vol. 17 (2006). She is currently working on a history of circumnavigation.

KEVIN J. HAYES, Professor of English at the University of Central Oklahoma, co-authored *The Library of Benjamin Franklin* (2006) with Edwin Wolf 2nd. Professor Hayes has written several other books including *A Colonial Woman's Bookshelf* (1996), *Folklore and Book Culture* (1997), and *The Library of William Byrd of Westover* (1997), for which he was awarded the Virginia Library History Award presented by the Library of Virginia and the Virginia Center for the Book.

NIAN-SHENG HUANG is Professor of History at California State University, Channel Islands. He worked with Professor Michael Kammen at Cornell University, where he obtained the PhD in History in 1990. He is the author of *Benjamin Franklin in American Thought and Culture, 1790–1990* (1994) and *Franklin's Father Josiah: Life of a Colonial Boston Tallow Chandler, 1657–1745* (2000). His article, "From the 'Fur Cap' to Poor Richard: The Chinese Connection," appeared in the *Proceedings of the American Philosophical Society* (June 2006). His new book-length research project, a study of the poor in colonial Massachusetts, has won a Massachusetts Historical Society and National Endowment for the Humanities Fellowship for 2007–08.

FRANK KELLETER is Chair of American Studies at Göttingen University, Germany. His publications include a book on death in modern literature, *Die Moderne und der Tod* (1997), a volume on Louis Farrakhan's Nation of Islam, *Con/Tradition* (2000), and a study of competing discourses and practices of Enlightenment in eighteenth-century America, *Amerikanische Aufklärung* (2002). He is the author of articles on Puritan missionaries, the poetry of the early republic, Herman Melville, Philip Roth, and other American authors.

PAUL E. KERRY, a Visiting Fellow at Princeton University, is Associate Professor of History and member of the European Studies faculty at Brigham Young University. He has published *Enlightenment Thought in the Writings of Goethe* (2001), in addition to collections of essays on Goethe, Schiller, Carlyle, and Mozart's opera *The Magic Flute*. His current projects include a book manuscript on German intellectual history, an edited volume on J. R. R. Tolkien, and a co-edited collection on Benjamin Franklin's intellectual world. He is an associate editor of a University of California critical edition of Carlyle's essays. He has been a Visiting Fellow at the University of Cambridge and affiliated with Pembroke College.

WILSON J. MOSES is Ferree Professor of American History at the Pennsylvania State University. He has held Fulbright Professorships in Berlin and Vienna and has visited Europe and Africa on behalf of the United States Information Agency. He is author of *The Golden Age of Black Nationalism* (1978), *Black Messiahs and Uncle Toms* (1982), *Alexander Crummell* (1989), *The Wings of Ethiopia* (1990), *Afrotopia: Roots of African–American Popular History* (1998), and *Creative Conflict in African American Thought* (2004). He is the editor of three documentary volumes, and over one hundred articles, essays, and reviews. He is currently completing a study of Enlightened Despotism and the American Foundation Myth.

CARLA MULFORD, Founding President of the Society of Early Americanists, is Associate Professor of English at the Pennsylvania State University. She has published seven books and over fifty articles and book chapters, including twelve on Benjamin Franklin. She has received fellowships from the National Endowment for the Humanities, the American Council of Learned Societies, and the Andrew W. Mellon Foundation (through the American Philosophical Society and the Library Company of Philadelphia) to assist her work on her book manuscript, now in its final writing stages, *Benjamin Franklin and the Ends of Empire*.

LESTER C. OLSON is Professor of Communication at the University of Pittsburgh, where he specializes in public address, rhetoric, and visual culture. His books include *Emblems of American Community in the Revolutionary Era: A Study in Rhetorical Iconology* (1991) and *Benjamin Franklin's Vision of American Community: A Study in Rhetorical Iconology* (2004). His book on Franklin was recognized with awards from the Rhetoric Society of America and the National Communication Association, the two largest communication and rhetoric societies in the United States. His essays concerning Franklin's pictorial representations of British America can be found in the *Quarterly Journal of Speech*. He earned his PhD from the University of Wisconsin at Madison in 1984.

DAVID S. SHIELDS, McClintock Professor of Southern Letters at the University of South Carolina, edited the Library of America's anthology *American Poetry: The Seventeenth & Eighteenth Centuries* (2008). He also compiled the web-based Archive of Early Southern Recipes hosted by the Southern Foodways Alliance. Former editor of the journal *Early American Literature*, he directs the Southern Texts Society. He is currently writing a history of photography and silent cinema. His book, *Arrested Beauty: Photography and the American Silent Cinema*, is forthcoming from Harvard University Press.

KERRY WALTERS is William Bittinger Professor of Philosophy at Gettysburg College. He is the author of twenty books, including *Benjamin Franklin and His Gods* (1998), *The American Deists: Voices of Reason and Dissent in the Early Republic* (1992), and *Rational Infidels: The American Deists* (1992).

ROCHELLE RAINERI ZUCK completed her dissertation in American literature under the direction of Carla Mulford at the Pennsylvania State University (PhD, English, May 2008). Her project, "*Imperium in Imperio*: Race, Ethnicity, and Transnational Citizenship in American Culture, 1816–1887," explores competing racial and ethnic nationhoods in nineteenth-century America. She is Assistant Professor of English at the University of Minnesota Duluth, where she teaches undergraduate and graduate courses in American literature.

ACKNOWLEDGMENTS

To this volume's distinguished contributors I owe my sincere gratitude for their promptness, flexibility, and commitment to this important project. Dr. Ray Ryan, Senior Commissioning Editor of the Cambridge University Press, suggested this volume to me and has been a resource and support through the various stages of its proposal and initial editing. At the production stage, this volume significantly benefited from the helpful copy-editing of Margaret Berrill, who saved us many errors, and from the steady production oversight of Joanna Breeze. Both Margaret and Joanna kindly helped me get the volume through the system and Rosemary Smith, the proofreader for the Press, caught many errors that otherwise might have made it into our book. I thank the Pennsylvania State University's College of Liberal Arts for a grant of released time that assisted my completing this manuscript along with my other book manuscript, *Benjamin Franklin and the Ends of Empire*. And I thank Ted H. Conklin, for the generosity of spirit that cheered me on in the work through some unanticipated difficult times.

METHOD OF CITATION

All references to the writings of Benjamin Franklin are to standard editions of his works, unless otherwise noted within chapter notes. Internal parenthetical references identify the standard sources, keyed to the abbreviations below. As Stephen Arch explains in chapter 12, Franklin's personal memoir (now known as his autobiography) was not printed in his lifetime, so the text is referenced in various ways as Franklin's memoir, the autobiography, the Autobiography, and *The Autobiography*. The most exact transcription of Franklin's own manuscript version of his memoir appears in the print versions edited by J. A. Leo Lemay and P. M. Zall and readily available in the Library of America volumes edited by Lemay. See Further Reading.

P   *The Papers of Benjamin Franklin.* 38 vols. to date. Ed. Leonard W. Labaree, *et al.* New Haven and London: Yale University Press, 1959– .

A   *The Autobiography of Benjamin Franklin.* Ed. Leonard W. Labaree, Ralph L. Ketcham, Helen C. Boatfield, Helene H. Fineman. New Haven and London: Yale University Press, 1964.

A, NCE *Benjamin Franklin's Autobiography.* Norton Critical Edition. Ed. J. A. Leo Lemay and P. M. Zall. New York: W. W. Norton, 1986.

Smyth   *The Writings of Benjamin Franklin.* 10 vols. Ed. Albert Henry Smyth. New York and London: Macmillan, 1907.

Compiled by Rochelle Raineri Zuck, this chronology highlights only the more frequently discussed events in the life of Benjamin Franklin, including many of the events Franklin mentions in his autobiography. Most comprehensive biographies listed in Further Reading discuss these events fully.

1706	Born January 17 (January 6, 1705, Old Style) in Boston to Josiah and Abiah Folger Franklin, Josiah's second wife.
1714–16	Attends Boston Grammar School and George Brownell's English school (for one year each) but is withdrawn because of the expense of formal schooling.
1718	Apprenticed to brother James, who owns and operates a printing house in Boston.
1721	James Franklin begins his own newspaper, the *New-England Courant*, and Benjamin continues as apprentice, working on the newspaper among other tasks.
1722	Writes fourteen letters, signed "Silence Dogood," submitted anonymously to the *New-England Courant*. James, imprisoned by the Massachusetts Assembly for using his newspaper to challenge local authority, is forced to have brother Benjamin manage the paper.
1723	Leaves his apprenticeship without permission from James and sets out for other colonial cities, first New York, then Philadelphia. Arrives October 6 and finds employment as a journeyman printer with Samuel Keimer.
1724	Travels to London for the first time with James Ralph and Thomas Denham.
1725	Works as a printer in Palmer's printing house in London. Writes *A Dissertation on Liberty and Necessity, Pleasure and Pain*, a deistical response to William Wollaston's *The Religion of Nature*

Delineated. An admirer of Franklin's work introduces him to Bernard Mandeville, famed deist.

1726 Returns to Philadelphia and is employed by Thomas Denham as clerk, bookkeeper, and shopkeeper.

1727 Seriously ill with pleurisy. In June, returns to work in Keimer's print shop. Forms Junto (the "Leather Apron Club"), a private club aimed at self-improvement, with a cluster of other enterprising young men of the artisan class. Members meet Friday evenings to discuss issues of morality, politics, philosophy, and business.

1728 Starts his own printing business with Hugh Meredith.

1729 Writes the "Busy-Body" essay series, published in Andrew Bradford's *American Weekly Mercury*. Interested in improving economic viability of Pennsylvania in the face of a hard currency shortage, writes and publishes *A Modest Enquiry into the Nature and Necessity of a Paper-Currency*, published in April. Purchases Keimer's failed *Pennsylvania Gazette*. (Within a decade turns the failing newspaper into the most widely read paper in the American colonies.) Son William is born in 1729 or 1730 to a woman whose identity is never revealed.

1730 Becomes Pennsylvania colony's official printer. Enters into a common-law marriage with Deborah Read (Rogers). (They cannot legally wed because Read's former husband's whereabouts are unknown, so divorce or death papers cannot be produced.) Son William joins their household.

1731 Joins the Freemasons and is elected junior warden of St. John's Lodge. Forms the Library Company of Philadelphia, the first subscription library in the United States.

1732 Son Francis Folger is born in October. Begins publishing his own *Poor Richard's Almanack* in December; volumes are published annually until 1757.

1733 Embarks on "the bold and arduous plan of arriving at moral Perfection." Visits family in Boston and James Franklin in Newport, RI.

1734 Elected Grand Master of the Freemasons in Philadelphia. Edits and publishes a reprint of James Anderson's *The Constitutions of the Free-Masons*, the first Masonic book printed in America.

1735 Proposes a fire protection society and a system of paid night watchmen for the city of Philadelphia. Although he has ceased even occasional attendance at church about 1732, attends church in order to hear sermons preached by Rev. Samuel Hemphill.

Hemphill, whose philosophy includes preaching practical moralism, is criticized as unorthodox. Interested in methods to induce improved moral habits, Franklin comes to Hemphill's defense and writes several pamphlets. Leaves church after Hemphill is suspended by the Presbyterian Synod in September but continues, for the sake of his family, to make contributions to the church.

1736   Appointed clerk of Philadelphia Assembly. Son Francis dies of smallpox at age four. Franklin organizes Philadelphia's first fire company (Union Fire Company).

1737   Appointed postmaster of Philadelphia.

1738   A mock Masonic initiation rite goes awry, fatally burning an apprentice, with Franklin accused of having taken part in the spurious events. Denies responsibility for and knowledge of the events surrounding the youth's ordeal.

1739   Meets and gets to know George Whitefield, who is visiting Philadelphia for the first time. So impressed by Whitefield's work, encourages subscriptions for printing Whitefield's writings.

1741   Designs Pennsylvania Fireplace, otherwise known as the Franklin Stove.

1743   Publishes *A Proposal for Promoting Useful Knowledge among the British Plantations in America*, the instrument behind the founding of the American Philosophical Society. Proposes a plan for the Academy and College of Philadelphia (later the University of Pennsylvania). Daughter Sarah ("Sally") Franklin is born in August.

1745   From Peter Collinson, Fellow of the Royal Society (London), receives information about electrical experiments conducted in Germany, along with some experimental apparatus. Fascinated with the information, begins experimenting with problems in electricity.

1747   Publishes pamphlet, *Plain Truth*, calling for Pennsylvania defense against French and Spanish piracy on the Delaware River. Publishes satire, "The Speech of Miss Polly Baker, before a Court of Judicature," in *The General Advertiser*. Reports on progress of his electrical experiments to Peter Collinson, who shows Franklin's accounts to the Royal Society.

1748   Joins the Pennsylvania defense militia as a soldier, having refused to serve at the rank of colonel. Takes on as a printing laborer David Hall, who has arrived from London, and so likes Hall's work that he forms a printing partnership with him. Leaves the print shop in Hall's hands, essentially to retire from printing so as to focus on scientific inquiries and public affairs.

1749   Becomes Justice of the Peace for the city of Philadelphia and is appointed Grand Master of Masons. Writes *Proposals Relating to the Education of Youth in Pensilvania*, which leads to the formation of the Philadelphia Academy (later the University of Pennsylvania).

1751   Assists in funding project and founding the Pennsylvania Hospital. Proposes establishing an English School in Philadelphia. Elected to a seat in the Pennsylvania General Assembly. The Academy and the College of Philadelphia open. Franklin's *Experiments and Observations on Electricity*, Part One, a collection of his scientific letters regarding electricity, is published in London. (Parts Two and Three are published in 1753–54.) Pens tract on population, published in 1755 as *Observations concerning the Increase of Mankind, Peopling of Countries, &c.*, in response to the British Iron Act of 1750 prohibiting colonies' further development of slitting and rolling mills, plating forges, and iron and steel manufacture.

1752   The Pennsylvania Hospital opens. Performs the kite experiment, proving that lightning is composed of positively and negatively charged particles and is thus a form of electricity. Installs a lightning rod on his own home. In a letter to his brother John, who suffers from bladder stones, Franklin proposes a design for a flexible urinary catheter.

1753   Receives honorary graduate degrees from Harvard and Yale. Publishes in London a second set of electrical experiments. Receives appointment as joint Deputy Postmaster General of North America. In November, negotiates a treaty with the Ohio Indians in Carlisle, Pennsylvania.

1754   Attends intercolonial meetings in Albany, NY. In July, the conference votes to form a union among the colonies. Franklin proposes a Plan of Union (also known as the Albany Plan) that is sent to the colonies for ratification. This plan, rejected by the colonies and the British government, nonetheless would later influence decision-making about the colonies' Articles of Confederation and the United States Constitution.

1755   In securing Pennsylvania against French invasions, procures supplies for Major-General Edward Braddock, commander of the British forces in North America, for the siege of Fort Duquesne. Supports the Assembly's request to tax the Lords Proprietors'

(Penn family) landholdings in Pennsylvania so as to raise money for the defense of the frontiers against the French and their Native American allies.

1756   Engages in military expeditions to inspect British strength in Carlisle, Harper's Ferry, and New York, and confers in Easton with a segment of Delaware Indians. Elected a Fellow of the Royal Society of London by unanimous vote. Receives honorary degree from the College of William and Mary. Receives election as corresponding member to the Royal Society of Arts.

1757   Receives appointment as Agent of the Pennsylvania Assembly to England, aiming to settle the taxing status of the estates held by the Lords Proprietor. Completes the writing of "Father Abraham's Speech," famously known as *The Way to Wealth*, which becomes the Preface for his 1758 *Poor Richard's Almanack*.

1758   Joins club culture of London and encounters many of the most important natural and political philosophers, writers, explorers, and scientists of his generation, including Andrew Kippis, Richard Price, Captain James Cook, Joseph Priestley, James Boswell, and David Hume. Invents a damper for stoves and chimneys. On a tour of England, visits ancestral family towns with son William.

1759   Receives honorary degree of Doctor of Laws from University of St. Andrews, Scotland, and is thereafter called "Dr. Franklin." During tours of northern England and Scotland, meets Adam Smith, William Robertson, and Henry Home, Lord Kames.

1760   Publishes third edition of his electrical experiments, along with a pamphlet outlining Great Britain's best cultural and economic strategies in North America, *The Interest of Great Britain Considered with Regard to her Colonies, And the Acquisitions of Canada and Guadaloupe.*

1761   Witnesses the coronation of King George III. Invents glass armonica, which is played for the first time in 1762 by Marianne Davies.

1762   Oxford University awards an honorary degree of Doctor of Civil Law. Returns to Philadelphia. Son William is commissioned Royal Governor of New Jersey.

1763   Britain's war with France in North America, often called the Seven Years' War, ends, with the 1763 Treaty of Paris.

1764   During his campaign for a seat in the Pennsylvania Assembly, is wrongly attacked for reasons of character, fiscal incontinence, and bias against Germans and loses the election. Subsequently elected to serve as the Assembly's Agent and sails for London in November. Charts the Gulf Stream (1764–65).

1765   Stamp Act is passed by the House of Commons and protests occur in the colonies. Aware of the intense problems caused by the measures proposed in the Act, Franklin eventually publishes in London several newspaper articles calling for its repeal and attempting to explain colonists' positions on such matters.

1766   Testifies before the Committee of the Whole House of Commons regarding the Stamp Act. Travels to Germany and is elected to the Royal Academy of Sciences in Göttingen.

1767   Visits Paris, meets Horace Walpole, and is presented to Louis XV.

1768   Continuing to attempt to explain colonists' views regarding British intrusions in colonial affairs, publishes *Causes of the American Discontents before 1768*. Appointed Agent of Georgia Assembly.

1769   Joins the Ohio Company, a cluster of well-placed individuals seeking land grants from George III in order to sell land in the Ohio Valley to those who would settle the territory. Elected president of the American Philosophical Society, a position he would hold until his death. Is appointed Agent by the New Jersey House of Representatives. Issues a corrected and enlarged fourth edition of his *Experiments and Observations on Electricity*. Deborah Franklin suffers a stroke and is plagued by failing health thereafter.

1770   Elected to the Massachusetts House of Representatives and thus becomes Agent for Massachusetts. Serves as Agent in England for four colonies: Pennsylvania, Georgia, New Jersey, and Massachusetts. Drawing attention to parallels between political slavery and chattel slavery, prints "A Conversation on Slavery" in London's *Public Advertiser*.

1771   Batavian Society of Experimental Science, Rotterdam, elects Franklin to membership. Writes first part of his autobiography.

1772   Ohio Company receives charter, but territory is never conveyed. Begins public argumentation against the institution of slavery with publication of "The Sommersett Case and the Slave Trade." Obtains secret letters circulated between Massachusetts Governor Thomas Hutchinson and Lieutenant Governor Andrew Oliver and sends this correspondence to Massachusetts Speaker Thomas Cushing.

1773   Hutchinson letters are presented to the Massachusetts House and denounced as inflammatory and inaccurate representation of situation in Massachusetts. Massachusetts House calls to remove Hutchinson and Oliver from office. In England, stands accused of treason on the basis of a letter sent to Cushing, but a copy of the letter is never produced. Publishes "Rules by Which a Great Empire May Be Reduced to a Small One" and "An Edict by the King of Prussia," challenging British treatment of American colonies.

1774   Upon news of Boston Tea Party in London, Franklin is called before King's Privy Council and dismissed from his position of Deputy Postmaster General for his role in the Hutchinson letters affair. First Continental Congress convenes in Philadelphia. Makes several attempts to mediate tensions between Britain and the colonies, but his "Hints for a Durable Union between England and America" is rejected by court in London. Deborah Franklin suffers another stroke and dies December 19. She and Franklin have not seen each other for ten years.

1775   British and colonial American hostilities break out at Lexington and Concord. Returns to Philadelphia and is elected to the Second Continental Congress. Advocates a paper currency and designs continental bills to serve as colonial money. Drafts the Articles of Confederation, but Congress does not adopt this measure. King George III declares the colonies to be in rebellion. Franklin continues his work with the Congress and composes numerous writings in support of the war.

1776   Son William, Royal Governor of New Jersey, is relieved of his duties by the New Jersey militia and put under house arrest. Opts not to intervene when William is later imprisoned in Connecticut. Resigns from Pennsylvania Assembly and focuses on congressional work. Appointed to a committee (including John Jay and John Adams) to compose the Declaration of Independence, drafted by Thomas Jefferson. Elected Congressional Commissioner to France and sails for France.

1777   Commissioners request French aid in war against Great Britain, and Louis XVI offers financial assistance. Elected to the Royal Medical Society of Paris.

1778   Treaties of Amity and Commerce with France are signed, and France goes to war against Great Britain. Is joined in Paris by John Adams, another newly elected Commissioner, to treat with the French. Is appointed Minister Plenipotentiary to France.

Present at initiation of Voltaire into the Masonic Lodge of the Nine Sisters and officiates at Voltaire's Masonic funeral later that year.

1779   Spain declares war on Great Britain. Compilation of Franklin's writings, *Political, Miscellaneous, and Philosophical Pieces*, is published in London by Benjamin Vaughan.

1781   Along with Jay, Henry Laurens, Jefferson, and Adams, is appointed by Congress to act as Peace Commissioner in war. General Charles Cornwallis surrenders to George Washington at Yorktown, Virginia.

1782   Along with Jay and Adams, negotiates for peace with Great Britain.

1783   Treaty of Paris is signed by Great Britain and the United States, ending the American Revolution against Great Britain. Prints treaty on his own press at Passy. Elected an honorary Fellow of the Royal Society of Edinburgh.

1784   Franklin, Adams, and Jefferson are appointed by Congress to negotiate treaties with European nations and Barbary States. Elected to membership in the Royal Academy of History in Madrid. In a letter to daughter Sarah, makes fun of the new Society of the Cincinnati (honoring wartime veterans in perpetuity) and decries the proposal of the eagle as the symbol of the American nation, instead offering the wild turkey as a more fitting representative. Writes second part of the autobiography.

1785   Congress grants Franklin permission to return to the United States and appoints Jefferson as his replacement as Minister Plenipotentiary to France. Creates plan for bifocal eyeglasses. Returns to Philadelphia on September 14 and is met by enthusiastic crowds. Elected to the Supreme Executive Council of Pennsylvania and subsequently appointed its President. Makes first written reference to the invention of bifocals in a letter to George Whatley.

1786   Invents device for the removal of books from high shelves.

1787   Elected to the Federal Constitutional Convention and named President of the Pennsylvania Society for Promoting the Abolition of Slavery. Suggests that sessions of Congress should be opened with prayer, a controversial motion that is later dropped. Also proposes "Great Compromise" on issue of representation in the House and Senate. This measure is approved, making representation in the House contingent on population and representation in the Senate equal among all states.

1788   Writes will and begins Part Three of autobiography. Ends public career by concluding service as President of the Supreme Executive Council of Pennsylvania.

1789   Writes and signs the first protest against slavery addressed to Congress. Elected to membership in the Russian Imperial Academy of Sciences, St. Petersburg. Makes the now famous remark to Jean Baptiste Le Roy: "in this world, nothing can be said to be certain except death and taxes."

1790   On behalf of the Pennsylvania Abolition Society, Franklin petitions Congress for the abolition of slavery and the slave trade. Writes last essay, an account of Sidi Mehemet Ibrahim on the slave trade, designed for the *Federal Gazette*. Dies April 17 at home and is buried beside wife Deborah and son Francis in Christ Church cemetery, Philadelphia.

CARLA MULFORD

Introduction

Benjamin Franklin is one of the best known but least understood of America's revolutionary generation. He is well known to schoolchildren around the world as one who dabbled in the arts and sciences so as to invent bifocals and glass armonicas, refine the draft pipes and dampers of stoves, and develop and foster public libraries, in addition to savings, insurance, and fire companies. Journalists and those who enjoy the craft of printing honor Franklin as a central figure in the formation of printing and communication networks that afforded communication among the British colonies of the eastern seaboard of North America. Numismatists celebrate Franklin as the first Postmaster General in the colonies. Graphic artists and those who like to collect coins and engravings value Franklin's work as an artist of political satire and an engraver of iconographic emblems representative of American materials and concerns. Indeed, Franklin has great significance in a long tradition, from medieval times, of emblem-makers. Farmers and those who read almanacs recognize Franklin as the founder of an almanac tradition in British North America. And scientists and those who study the thermodynamics of the atmosphere in order to make predictions of significant weather events honor Franklin for making the final determination regarding the positive and negative currents behind electricity, for measuring the ocean temperatures, for determining the impact of volcanic eruptions on the weather patterns in places far distant, and for charting the Gulf Stream.

Most people know Franklin for his individual accomplishments, including the creation of devices such as bifocals, stoves, the "grabber" for reaching objects placed on high shelves, and the flexible catheter for releasing bladder stones. Franklin is also commonly remarked about for his presumed sexual appetite and interest in women, a fallacious impression that comes down to us from several anti-Franklin pamphlets of his own day and from highbrows and anti-utilitarian writers of the nineteenth and twentieth centuries.[1] Readers often know of his autobiography, but most do not know about the range of his writings nor the depth of his inquiries into political, economic, and natural philosophy. Few remember that he was the central diplomat in the 1783 Treaty of Paris that settled the war between Great Britain and the British North American colonies, and fewer still that he printed the original treaty on his own press at Passy, France. Specialists know about aspects of his career, but even scholars of his writings often do not address the plethora of his writings nor the complexity of his thinking. This is to say that despite the several hundred biographies of Franklin that have appeared since his death in 1790, Franklin remains as elusive today as he might have seemed to his associates in the eighteenth century.

Many readers who think they know Franklin tend to equate the speaker of "Father Abraham's Speech" with the "real" Benjamin Franklin. Part of this is Franklin's own doing. Some readers across the centuries have misunderstood Franklin's adoption of pseudonyms, a common practice in the tradition of polite letters in Franklin's day. Many of the speakers in Franklin's writings are pseudonymous "characters" in the splendid eighteenth-century tradition wherein a speaker's name is identified with his or her "kind" of person. Silence Dogood, for instance, the masterful mistress of her own youthful Franklinian prose, is not silent, and she would have us all do better than we currently do in our dealings with the world. Franklin adopted names that sometimes masked the seriousness of his content with a jesting or humorous undercurrent: Abigail Twitterfield (a-twitter over sermons condemning the presumed sin of women who don't bear children), Alice Addertongue (who loves to "exercise [her] Talent at Censure" [P 1: 244]), Ephraim Censorious (who excoriates Silence Dogood for chiding men without attempting to reform women), and thrifty Anthony Afterwit (who, only after he was married, realized he had married a spendthrift) – among many others – offered reasonable advice on myriad topics related to daily living. These characters typically conveyed moral or financial or community-oriented advice, and they often, like Father Abraham, were taken simplistically to represent Franklin's views and his approach to life. For this reason, the folksy, iconic voice of the *Poor Richard* almanacs overrode Franklin's more serious and influential writings known best by the leading writers and philosophers of his day, and Franklin, British North America's greatest, most sophisticated and cosmopolitan writer and political, economic, and natural scientist, paradoxically became the symbol of homespun Americanness.

Franklin's own words from his autobiography indicate his surprising beginnings: he essentially overcame the "Poverty and Obscurity in which I was born and bred" to achieve "a considerable Share of Felicity . . . with the Blessings of God" (A 43). Franklin did indeed overcome obstacles in his youth, not the least being the absence of formal training beyond rudimentary letters and numbers. His educational plans for a school and a college, based on his own regimen of self-teaching, featured both traditional and more modern methods of education and subjects of inquiry. Of interest to us today is Franklin's recognition that students best learned by doing rather than by long recitations in Latin and Greek, "dead" languages. Franklin's plans called for training in contemporary languages – including Spanish, Dutch, German, French, Italian – in addition to English, and they featured contemporary writings by authors admired by the current generation. In the areas of science and mathematics, his plans likewise advocated inquiry into practical and mechanical arts that would complement pure research. This was revolutionary in his own day. Also revolutionary is that he sought education for the most talented people rather than those who could pay the most. His plans revealed his inquiring nature and inexhaustible fund of energy for improving the social, political, economic, and moral lives of everyday people. If Franklin did experience a share of the felicity in life, he wished also to ensure that others might have opportunity to enjoy the same happiness.

On Franklin's life

For our purposes, Franklin's life can be divided into three parts, each part marking a different emphasis of his life's career. Franklin achieved his first successes in Boston and Pennsylvania as a printer, so the first segment of his life, from his birth in 1706 until 1757, can be considered Franklin's major printing years, where his primary endeavor centered around his printing business and the local and regional problems faced in Pennsylvania and its environs. Except for a brief stay in London in 1724, Franklin during these years established himself as Pennsylvania's influential printer and postmaster and an efficient and admired leader in political and civic affairs. During these years, he created the Junto, a working man's intellectual club designed for self- and community improvement. And from the Junto arose many of the improvements he sought to implement for the city of Philadelphia. Also during these years, he began to see the unfair advantages in trade that Great Britain was using to keep the colonies (and colonial production) in check so as to favor the workers and livelihoods of those in England. Among the most important publications emanating from these years are Franklin's *Modest Enquiry into the Nature and Necessity of a Paper-Currency* (1729), a tract speaking to the benefits of moving beyond coinage for local trans-actions, with a money system based on land as collateral; his *Pennsylvania Gazette* and *Poor Richard* almanacs, which featured practical learning amid extracts ranging from politics to polite letters; and his *Observations concerning the Increase of Mankind, Peopling of Countries &c.* (written, 1751;

printed, 1755), which offered strategies for keeping the Pennsylvania colony British in the face of immigrants from many areas, with a preponderance of immigrants from the Palatinate, then the poorest part of the country today called Germany. By 1748, Franklin had secured sufficient income and savings that he could leave his printing business in the able hands of his partner, David Hall, retaining the business in his name and centrally located quarters. At this time, he turned his attention more fully to scientific inquiry, specifically into determining the nature and effects of electrical charges, an inquiry begun much earlier in the decade of the 1740s. By the early 1750s, Franklin's *Experiments and Observations on Electricity* (first published in 1751) would ensure that Franklin's name would become one of the best known in the western world and would mark, for those of his own generation, the pinnacle of his achievements.

From the days when he used Silence Dogood as a mouthpiece to speak about supporting public projects, Franklin considered assisting others in his community one of the highest marks of humanity. His own contributions in this area – the Pennsylvania Hospital; savings, fire, and insurance funds; the English School and the Academy; the American Philosophical Society, for instance – are exemplary instances of public service by an individual who would accrue no personal financial gain from his labors. Among his many other endeavors in public projects from this era, Franklin became a leader who was proactive about the safety and security of the rich cultural and agricultural lands held as Pennsylvania territory. He engaged in treaty-making ceremonies with the Lenapes and Iroquois during these years, seeking a middle course in trade and social relations, and he assisted the British leaders, including General Braddock, by supplying from his own funds and friends' barns the materiel essential to securing western Pennsylvania against incursions from the French and their Indian allies. One of Franklin's favorite plans from his work on colonial unity was the Albany Plan of Union of 1754, a strategy whereby the British colonies could contract with one another for mutual benefit and security. The Plan failed to receive approval in both the colonies and Great Britain, the former conceiving it as smacking too greatly of British imperial prerogative, the latter considering it too permissive in its democratic principles, according to Franklin's account in the autobiography.

Franklin became a leading spokesperson for the party interested in taxing the Pennsylvania Proprietary (the Penn family entity that held the charter for Pennsylvania territories). The Proprietary had claimed that, according to charter, the extensive lands claimed as the Penns' estate were free of taxes for local maintenance. His efforts to secure a better tax arrangement for the colony took him to England, at the Pennsylvania Assembly's request, to attempt to negotiate with the Penn descendants and, failing that, with the Crown, regarding the situation of Pennsylvania. These years in Great Britain, roughly 1757 to 1775 (with a break between 1762 and 1764, when he returned to Pennsylvania) mark the second major part of Franklin's life, when he became the prime negotiator between the colonies and Great Britain. Franklin's return to London in 1764 occurred as Pennsylvania continued to try to find workable solutions for the perpetual problems caused by absence of tax revenues from the Proprietary estates, by lack of hard specie, by increased population (and the problems in infrastructure that increased population causes), and by border difficulties. He remained in London because, eventually on behalf of all the colonies, Franklin entered into protracted negotiations with the Crown and Parliament in an effort to secure an imperial compromise enabling the colonies to develop their own internal and intercolonial systems of trade, taxation, labor, and money.

These years of negotiation and compromise were tense for Franklin in the political arena, but they were enjoyable ones for him, as well, for he began to recognize that all Europe perceived the benefit to humanity of his scientific discoveries, particularly the discovery of the positive and negative charges of electricity. He saw his *Experiments and Observations on Electricity* reach a wider and wider audience of readers, and he was awarded honorary degrees from many major European institutions, thus marking the caliber of his achievement. He joined a number of the chief London clubs, dined with the most renowned philosophers of his day, and generally enjoyed a level of celebrity like none he had known in the colonies. He traveled extensively throughout much of Europe, and he joined several societies that elected him to their prestigious membership.

Yet none of the respect accorded Franklin nor the honors bestowed on him would assist his difficult efforts to secure a lasting imperial agreement between Great Britain and the colonies of North America. Even his most important writings from these years – his long pamphlet, *The Interest of Great Britain Considered with Regard to her Colonies, And the Acquisitions of Canada and Guadaloupe* (1760) and *Causes of the American Discontents before 1768* (1768) – while they worked to inform Britons of the situation in North America, failed to convince those in power that Franklin had developed viable and workable imperial analyses from which Great Britain could profit. Franklin turned his humorous pen of the earlier years into a pen wielding occasionally acerbic wit, satirizing Britain (from Crown to hatmaker) and the obtuseness of Britons, even those in Ireland and Scotland, for refusing to acknowledge the oppressions being foisted on Britons in North America. The Franklin who had published "Rattlesnakes for Felons" in the *Pennsylvania Gazette* in 1751 reemerged with a more sardonic and biting tongue in these years. Several of his most bitter satires – "Rules by

Which a Great Empire May Be Reduced to a Small One" and "An Edict by the King of Prussia" – arose in 1773, the year Franklin faced increasing hostility on both sides of the Atlantic, in North America for seeming to continue to conciliate Great Britain and in Great Britain for being too radically opposed to British imperial prerogative. He even mocked his own troubled situation in the public press, with a letter to London's *Public Advertiser*, berating himself for his own presumed ingratitude to Crown and Parliament. Having to accept that he had finally failed in his mission to convince Britain to change its imperial project and facing potential charges of treason, Franklin sailed for North America, where local skirmishes were breaking out.

In the last period of his life, 1775 through his death in 1790, Franklin was an elder statesman and diplomat, facing some of the most difficult of the many challenges in a long and celebrated life. Upon his arrival back in the colonies, he was elected by the Pennsylvania Assembly to serve as Pennsylvania's representative in the Second Continental Congress. As a result of his many years' diplomatic service in England and Europe, Franklin well understood the political, social, and fiscal means by which the colonies could secure their future: recalling his Albany Plan of 1754, he drafted plans for what later became the Articles of Confederation; he submitted resolutions to Congress for unrestrained and untaxed internal and external trade; and he developed a series of emblems and devices that could be printed on Continental paper bills.

As the central negotiator during the years prior to the war, Franklin was called upon again and again to work on committees public and secret, and he became the chief congressional representative to Great Britain when Britain sought to meet with representatives from the colonies. His existing relationship with French intellectuals and the French court was perceived as a crucial means by which the colonies might gain the support of France in their war against Great Britain, so Franklin was again asked to set sail across the Atlantic, this time for Paris, and to serve as chief negotiator in accords Congress sought with France. Joined by John Adams and several others sent for diplomatic reasons, Franklin was instrumental in securing funding and material support from the French in the delicate negotiations. He drafted the treaty articles securing the peace of 1783 in Paris, and he printed the treaty on his own press at Passy, where he resided during his diplomatic mission to France.

But he was aging, and he appealed to Congress more than once to be relieved of his duties, so that he might sail home one last time. Congress finally granted his appeal in 1785, and he returned to Pennsylvania to found the Society for Political Enquiries and to be named President of the Society for Promoting the Abolition of Slavery. It was Franklin who recommended the representational structures of the House and Senate and Franklin who argued against the traditional property qualification for voting, urging instead that voting be extended to the widest possible number of persons. His last public actions related to chattel slavery, which he sought to have abolished in the new American system. He worked tirelessly in this regard, and was disappointed when Congress determined in 1789 that the federal government had no jurisdiction to authorize abolition in the individual states. His last public writing, a satire, mocks a defense of slavery that, couched as if from a leader in the Middle East, speaks to the problems of slavery around the known world.

Approaching the study of Benjamin Franklin

Beginning in the 1990s, Franklin studies have been undergoing a tremendous reconfiguration. With the exception of a few noted historians and others writing for the popular reading market (and thus offering fairly standard twentieth-century biographical interpretations of Franklin), scholars – including authors of the chapters in this volume – have begun to examine Franklin's writings and his life with a new sophistication, and they are articulating for the first time views of Franklin that reveal the complexities of his intellectual, literary, social, and political views. Such scholarship assures us that the Franklin who is emerging in the twenty-first century will be more cosmopolitan, better informed, more sophisticated, and much more highly articulate than the relatively jingoistic Franklin-the-great-American whose character dominated the twentieth century.

Over the past fifteen years there have been roughly five books on Franklin every four years, biographies mostly. Some studies have examined particular aspects of his life or work, but most have examined the life in the general context of eighteenth-century American politics and culture. The interest in Franklin derives from a sense, among many historians whose interest lies in social history, that this is the one "founder" whose reputation has stood up under scrutiny by a negative press. In addition, compared to other American "founders" such as George Washington and Thomas Jefferson, Franklin is, in effect, less "faulty" with regard to the important question of slavery: although Franklin held slaves, he also by midlife embraced the message of emancipation and eventually became President of the Pennsylvania Abolition Society. The biographies have evoked interest in Franklin among general readers, and they have also prompted a few dissenting opinions. The biographies have also made readers curious about who might be the "real" Franklin behind the mask of the autobiography.

The figure of Franklin in the twentieth century served, to some extent, a nationalist front for international purposes: Franklin became a supreme representative of the greatness of American possibilities in the frenzy of publicity about the proverbial American way shortly after the conclusion of the second world war.[2] This is the era when the Franklin papers project was conceived and later implemented (the first volume was published in 1959) and when the United States Information Agency, an independent agency supported by the US government, began its program of explaining and supporting American foreign policy outside the United States. Franklin, whose life was taken to represent the promise proffered by US culture, would become a staple of the agency.

With the scholarly information offered by the Franklin papers project and the significant new work being done on Franklin as a result, the study of Franklin reached a new level of sophistication during the latter half of the twentieth century. Readers today have available to them much more information and analysis than readers of previous generations. They are fascinated with a number of new qualities of Franklin's life and writing that had been submerged beneath the homespun "patriot" message of the middle twentieth century. Newer studies of Franklin are revealing a number of complicated issues that had before been passed over: the sheer "literariness" of Franklin's writings; Franklin's interest in social matters such as women's education and slavery; Franklin's constructions of personal "virtue" in a culture driven by marketplace inequities fueled by a slave and artisan economy; the political and philosophical matters that this significant natural philosopher debated among many of his generation's major philosophers, including Joseph Priestley, Adam Smith, David Hume, Voltaire, and Rousseau; the art and craft of self-conscious self-reflection evident in his own life-writing; and the sheer range of satiric voices one cosmopolitan Briton in North America could create. Franklin attached himself to the culture of Enlightenment only to invoke enlightened self-consciousness in order to call British imperialism into question. Today we can admire the facility with which Franklin managed to circulate in a global environment while retaining his own core set of values fostering community amid diversity.

The *Cambridge Companion to Benjamin Franklin* offers some of the best existing work on Franklin alongside newer interpretations that take advantage of Franklin's transatlantic engagements with the arts and letters, with natural philosophy, and with politics. The essays in this collection delve into some of the questions that previous generations have asked about Franklin, his "Americanness," his literary talent, and his philosophical views, but they also attempt to reveal Franklin as the world-renowned intellectual figure he was understood to be during his own lifetime. Franklin's world and his intellectual milieu were transatlantic and expansive rather than insularly provincial. In this regard, the essays contained in this volume are restoring Franklin to his just place as a leader in the more globalized study of the British Empire.

The volume's opening series of chapters on Franklin's library (Hayes), his philosophical approach to the concept of virtue (Anderson), his crafting of satire (Kerry), and his circulation in the British and European world of the learned and distinguished (Shields) reveal how the complexity of Franklin's thinking and writing was fashioned from the complexity of his reading and experiences throughout his life. Franklin's library and his writings, especially his public writings in the satiric mode, the mode most popular during the eighteenth century, form a central foundation from which we might best understand his place in British North American and British and European culture of his era. The next sequence of chapters captures the rich intellectual society in which Franklin circulated and made his greatest contributions in the contemplative and hard sciences. These chapters provide a conversation about the many different facets of Franklin's beliefs regarding the natural and supernatural worlds of his day. Whether Franklin believed in the Christian God or not, to what extent he might have believed in a supreme being, how his interest in science and Enlightenment might have contradicted any religious impulses, leading instead to philosophical pragmatism – all are questions that these chapters fruitfully explore.

Franklin's views on the events taking place at the conclusion of the American Revolution are highlighted next (Olson), because his mature views on the revolutionary events and their aftermath evince a depth and perspective that few today acknowledge or attempt to understand. Franklin was pro-colonist, finally, in his revolutionary endeavors, and once he turned against the aristocracy in Britain, he would work tirelessly to keep such static social attitudes from taking shape in the new United States. The volume concludes with a series of three chapters that treat Franklin's reputation across time, whether among the nineteenth-century theorists about capitalism and the American Dream (Moses, Huang and Mulford) or among those who have found, across the centuries after his death, sustenance from repeated reading of his iconographic autobiography, the most frequently read of Franklin's extensive corpus of writings.

Notes

1. See Carla Mulford, "Franklin, Women, and American Cultural Myths," in *Benjamin Franklin and Women*, ed. Larry E. Tise (University Park: Pennsylvania State University Press, 2000), 104–28, 161–66, and for background on Franklin's interest in seeing women become more than men's pretty playthings (a common

view held about Franklin's attitudes about women), see "Benjamin Franklin, Traditions of Liberalism, and Women's Learning in Eighteenth-Century Philadelphia," in *Educating the Youth of Pennsylvania: Worlds of Learning in the Age of Franklin*, ed. John Pollack (Philadelphia: University of Pennsylvania Library, [2009]).

2. See Carla Mulford, "Figuring Benjamin Franklin in American Cultural Memory," *New England Quarterly* 71 (1999): 415–43, and "Benjamin Franklin and the Myths of Nationhood," in *Making America / Making American Literature: Franklin to Cooper*, ed. A. Robert Lee and W. M. Verhoeven (Amsterdam and Athens, GA: Rodopi, 1996), 15–58.

1

KEVIN J. HAYES

Benjamin Franklin's library

After Benjamin Franklin settled in Philadelphia and established himself as a printer, he returned to Boston to see his family, demonstrate his success to them, and retrieve his personal collection of books, which he had left behind upon first leaving Boston. The precise contents of Franklin's library at this time in his life is unknown. What is known is that his collection was substantial enough to impress the captain of the sloop that took him back to Philadelphia. When the sloop reached New York, the captain informed William Burnet, the colonial Governor of New York and New Jersey, about this bookish young man. The distinguished, scholarly governor asked to meet him. Franklin described their meeting in his autobiography: "The Governor treated me with great Civility, show'd me his Library, which was a very large one, and we had a good deal of Conversation about Books and Authors" (A, NCE 26).

Beyond what Franklin wrote in his autobiography, no additional comments survive to document their meeting, but the catalogue of Burnet's library provides a good indication of what he and Franklin talked about that day. The Governor was the son of Gilbert Burnet, Bishop of Salisbury. Among the handsomest volumes in his collection were finely bound editions of his father's works. He had an edition of Bishop Burnet's *Rights of Princes* (1682) bound in morocco, a large paper edition of his three-volume *History of the Reformation* (1679–1715) bound in red morocco with gilt edges, a large paper edition of his *History of His Own Time* (1724), and a copy of his *Exposition of the Thirty-Nine Articles* (1699) formerly in the possession of the Duke of Gloucester. Governor Burnet also had a good collection of *belles lettres*, science books, and travel writings. His library included a late sixteenth-century edition of Chaucer's *Works* (1687); an early sixteenth-century edition of Dante; the two-volume Bologna edition of Galileo's *Opere* (1656); Richard Hakluyt's *Voyages* (1599–1600); Samuel Purchas's compilation of voyages and travels, *Purchas His Pilgrimage* (1626), and Captain John Smith's *Generall Historie of Virginia* (1632).[1]

Containing 1,600 titles totaling around 3,000 volumes, Governor Burnet's library was one of the largest private libraries in colonial America at the time, approaching those of Cotton Mather and William Byrd. Franklin was obviously impressed with the collection. He would acquire for himself copies of several of the works Burnet owned. Perhaps the most important aspect of his encounter with Burnet is the deference the Governor paid to this young tradesman. Franklin's library let him surmount otherwise insurmountable class barriers. A substantial library had given this colonial printer and son of a chandler the opportunity to talk books with a colonial governor and son of a bishop. Knowledge of books, Franklin realized, offered an entry to society.

The Library Company of Philadelphia

After meeting Governor Burnet, Franklin longed for an even greater library than he had the means to assemble. Consequently, he devised a way to amass a large library without having to purchase all of the books himself. With several of his book-loving Philadelphia friends, he formed the Junto, a club designed for the mutual improvement of its members. At one meeting, he proposed that members club together their personal collections to form a library far exceeding what any of them could afford to assemble individually. Though the Junto agreed to the proposal, the plan to combine their own collections into one communal library failed. In this instance, Franklin recognized the utility of books but did not see their profound personal importance. Books are not merely repositories of ideas; they are objects that embody the personality of their owners, objects so personal that book owners are reluctant to let them out of their possession.

The failure of the Junto library did have an important effect on American library history: it led to the formation of the Library Company of Philadelphia in 1731. After realizing that a communal library would not work, Franklin and his friends decided to organize their library on different principles. Each man bought a share in the company, which provided the capital to purchase books that would form the core collection. Shareholders could borrow books from the collection and also help decide what books the company purchased. In Franklin's famous words, the Library Company of Philadelphia became "the Mother of all the North American Subscription Libraries" (A, NCE 57). Following Franklin's plan, similar library companies would be formed through the British colonies of North America.[2]

Franklin's personal input helped shape the holdings of the Library Company of Philadelphia; his personal collection of books also helped shape its contents. Shortly after its formation, Franklin donated a number of books, including his copy of John Locke's *Two Treatises of Government* (1728).[3] The establishment of the Library Company was one of Franklin's first major philanthropic endeavors. Donating important books from his own collection, he gave others the opportunity to read works that had helped shape his personal outlook. In the decades leading to American independence, few books were more influential than Locke's *Two Treatises on Government*. Many Americans read this book; some read the very copy Franklin had donated to the Library Company, whose membership included nine men who signed the Declaration of Independence.

The holdings of the Library Company also helped shape Franklin's personal library. Because he and his friends formed the Library Company as a cost-saving alternative to buying their own books, Franklin felt no compunction to duplicate its holdings in his own library. Many books typically found on the colonial gentleman's bookshelf are absent from the library of Benjamin Franklin mainly because he could borrow them from the Library Company. In some cases, however, Franklin did acquire books for his own library that he could have borrowed. For example, both his personal library and the holdings of the Library Company were rich in travel literature. The Library Company continues to thrive today as one of the finest research libraries in the United States. Many volumes from Franklin's personal library now form a part of its collections.

Bookman in London

Appointed agent of the Pennsylvania Assembly in charge of negotiating a dispute between the Assembly and the proprietors of Pennsylvania, Franklin returned to England in 1757. While in London, he took the opportunity to renew his friendship with James Ralph, whom he had not seen since the two had said good-bye over thirty years earlier. During the intervening decades, Ralph had had a varied, though not always profitable literary career culminating as an uncompromising political journalist and a diligent historian of England. Ralph was diagnosed with a terminal illness in 1761 and died the following January. When his library went up for sale in April, Franklin was present and eager to bid. His account books show that this was not the first auction he had attended while in London.[4] No additional information survives to document the other sales, but the record of Franklin's purchases at the Ralph sale constitute one of the most useful documents for understanding Franklin's library.

The books he acquired from Ralph's library reveal their shared interests. Ralph greatly enjoyed reading verse: Franklin obtained several volumes of poetry from his friend's library, including, most importantly, a 1669 edition of John Donne's *Poems*. Ralph's interest in the theater is reflected by multi-volume editions of the dramatic works of John Dryden and Philip Massinger, both of which Franklin purchased. Franklin also bid successfully for one of Ralph's own works, *Of the Use and Abuse of Parliaments* (1744), a historical survey of Parliament during the seventeenth and early decades of the eighteenth century. In terms of biographical significance, one volume Franklin acquired from Ralph's library stands out above the others, Samuel Keimer's *Caribbeana* (1741), a collection of essays, articles, and poetry describing events about a part of the New World that could prove instrumental to the political situation facing the colonies on the mainland.

Though Ralph's parliamentary history and Keimer's literary anthology each contained valuable information, both works also possessed a personal dimension for Franklin. James Ralph had passed away, but his strong political voice still spoke from the pages of his history. In his autobiography, Franklin would make Samuel Keimer, his former boss in Philadelphia, into an object of humorous derision. The presence of *Caribbeana* in his library, however, shows that Franklin was curious about what had happened to his old boss and that he recognized Keimer's most significant accomplishment. *Caribbeana*, after all, forms a major contribution to the literary history of the West Indies. Both men had been a part of Franklin's life; they now became a part of his library.

The American Philosophical Society

Franklin returned to Philadelphia in 1762, bringing his sizable library with him. He did not remain home for long. Again chosen as agent to represent Pennsylvania in London, he left Philadelphia the first week in November 1764. By now, Franklin was a formidable figure in Philadelphia literary and scientific circles, so much so that even in his absence he inspired further intellectual developments. Two decades earlier, Franklin had printed *A Proposal for Promoting Useful Knowledge among the British Plantations in America*, in which he proposed the American Philosophical Society, whose membership also included John Bartram and Thomas Bond. The society had stopped meeting by the mid-1740s. In 1750 another Philadelphia scientific society was established. The new organization went through several name changes but became known as the American Society by the mid-1760s. Its popularity led Bond to revive the Philosophical Society in 1767. The two groups clashed, because each was dominated by a different political faction: the American Society by the liberal Quakers, the American Philosophical Society by the Proprietary party. Scientific curiosity won out over political differences, and in 1768 the two societies set aside differences to concentrate on observing the forthcoming transit of Venus. At the end of that year, they united as the American Philosophical Society.[5]

In January 1769 the newly formed group met for the first time, electing Benjamin Franklin President and Thomas Bond Vice-President. With Franklin in England, Bond took the reins of leadership and assuaged any remaining antagonism. In June 1769, the Society's methodical observations of the Transit of Venus were successful. In 1771, the Society entered the world scientific community when it published the first volume of its *Transactions*. Franklin capitalized on the publication of the *Transactions* by arranging to have all European learned societies receive a copy. The European societies reciprocated by sending their own *Transactions* to the American Philosophical Society. The exchange greatly improved the society's stature as well as its library's holdings.[6] In the early nineteenth century, several books from Franklin's personal library would further enhance the Society's library.

Building a great personal library

In London, Franklin became deeply embroiled in the controversy over the Stamp Act and the subsequent efforts on the part of the British government to restrict American freedoms. His growing library reflects his mounting anger. He obtained copies of all the political pamphlets regarding the increasingly tenuous relations between Great Britain and North America. Surviving copies of some of these pamphlets contain many marginal comments in Franklin's hand. Marginalia provide a way to make a book more practical as well as more personal. Inscribing the margins of a book, Franklin was recording his thoughts and, in so doing, capturing the mood and the moment of first reading. The margin of a printed page is the place where author and reader meet. Once a book has been annotated, it stops being a one-sided authorial discourse. It becomes a dialogue.

One particular encounter in the early 1770s affirmed the value of marginalia to Franklin. A bookseller-friend who happened to acquire several volumes of annotated pamphlets offered the collection to him. Thinking that these heavily annotated volumes were formerly in the possession of his Uncle Benjamin Franklin, he bought the lot. His acquisition of these volumes seems motivated almost completely by personal reasons rather than practical ones. Though a few of the pamphlets hold ongoing literary or intellectual value – Increase Mather's *First Principles of New-England* (1675), John Milton's *Of True Religion* (1673) – most treat minor political or religious controversies of their day. The marginalia supposedly by his favorite uncle was what made them valuable to Franklin. To possess books his uncle had owned and read and annotated was irresistible.

Franklin expanded his library by purchasing books from individual book-sellers, but there were numerous other ways he obtained books during his time in London. He continued to attend auctions. A list of books he pur-chased from one auction, complete with lot numbers and prices fetched, reveals his passion for travel literature. At this sale, he acquired such works as Michel Adanson's *Voyage to Senegal* (1759) and Fredrik Hasselquist's *Voyages and Travels in the Levant* (1766). Adanson's primary interest was natural history, especially conchology, but his work contains much addi-tional information on the climate, economy, and manufactures of Senegal. Adanson's work is especially noticeable for his heartfelt appreciation of the Senegalese people. Hasselquist's work is respected for both the liveliness and the precision of his narrative. He, too, presents much information regarding the natural history of the Levant or what we today call the Middle East. He also takes an in-depth look at local customs.[7] Franklin subscribed to several books during his time in England, including Thomas Wildman's *Treatise on the Management of Bees* (1768), a work which remains a useful treatise on the subject.[8] Franklin's friendships with many of the leading scientists and literary figures of his day meant that he received numerous presentation copies, too.

Almost every presentation copy he received, it seems, has a personal story to tell. Take William Brownrigg's *Art of Making Common Salt* (1748), for example. Brownrigg inscribed the front flyleaf: "To Doctor Franklin From the Author." Franklin, in turn, supplied additional details regarding the occasion of the gift: "Received this valuable Book from the Author, when at his Seat near Keswick in Westtmoreland June 30. 1772. BF." Calling Brownrigg's *Art of Making Common Salt* a valuable book, Franklin was referring to its practical utility. The work discusses the process of making salt and the economics of salt manufacture. It strongly urges the British government to construct salt works and regulate salt quality. Franklin was already familiar with the book, which was originally published in 1748. He had had a copy in his possession as early as 1753, when he sent it to James Bowdoin, hoping Bowdoin would find it useful in the Massachusetts fisheries. Sending the book to Bowdoin, Franklin had encouraged him to share it with others in the same industry (P 5: 79). To a correspondent who had asked about how to pickle sturgeon, Franklin told him that "a great deal depends on the kind of salt to be used" and recommended that he consult Brownrigg's *Art of Making Common Salt*, which con-tained specific information about the salt the Dutch used to pickle herrings (P 11: 87).

Learning that Franklin would be traveling to Leeds with their mutual friend Sir John Pringle, Brownrigg wrote him during the second week of June

1772 to invite him to Ormathwaite, his villa near Keswick. Dr. Brownrigg, who had studied medicine at the University of Leiden under Hermann Boerhaave, had enjoyed a successful medical career but now had retired to devote himself to scientific pursuits. At Ormathwaite he built a laboratory, mineral museum, art collection, and library. Franklin accepted the offer, and his stay at Ormathwaite turned out to be a delightful one. With Mrs. Mary Brownrigg, Franklin discussed the making of Parmesan cheese and apparently supplied her with a recipe (P 20: 463). With her husband, Franklin took the opportunity of a storm to still the waves on Derwentwater by pouring oil on its surface. Together, he and Brownrigg published the results of their experiments in the *Philosophical Transactions of the Royal Society* and separately as a pamphlet, *Of the Stilling of Waves by Means of Oil* (1774). The story of Franklin's friendship with Brownrigg reveals that the presentation copy of Brownrigg's *Art of Making Common Salt* was more to Franklin than merely a book valuable for the information it contained. By the time he received this present, Franklin had already read and synthesized the information it contained. Now, it became a cherished possession. His inscription commemorates Franklin's visit to Ormathwaite and reinforces the inextricable link between memory and library.

Franklin's library expanded significantly throughout his time abroad. When his London landlady, Margaret Stevenson, moved to a new home on Craven Street in 1772, Franklin moved with her. Writing to his son William after moving, Franklin informed him,

> I am almost settled in my new Apartment; but Removing, and sorting my Papers and placing my Books and things has been a troublesome Jobb. I am amaz'd to see how Books have grown upon me since my Return to England. I brought none with me, and have now a Roomfull; many collected in Germany, Holland and France; and consisting chiefly of such as contain Knowledge that may hereafter be useful to America. (P 19: 361)

Franklin's description of the library's potential value suggests that he was starting to think about how he could put his personal library to use for the benefit of his countrymen.[9]

The library at Franklin Court

In terms of the development of his library, Franklin's time in France from 1776 to 1785 followed a similar pattern to his time in London. With the books he purchased, subscribed to, and received as presents, his library totaled over four thousand volumes by the time he returned to Philadelphia for good in 1785. Once home, he faced the daunting task of combining his Paris library with his Philadelphia collection and finding room for them all. He decided to build a large addition to his home, the second floor of which would constitute his library. "I hardly know how to justify building a Library at an Age that will so soon oblige me to quit it," he wrote his sister Jane Mecom, "but we are apt to forget that we are grown old, and Building is an Amusement." The library, 16 × 30½ feet, occupied the entire second floor of the new wing. He excluded a staircase, fearing it would take too much space away from his books. Instead, he accessed the library by going through a bed chamber or one of the closets in the old drawing room.[10] The library's lofty ceilings enhanced its majestic appearance. Visiting Franklin Court once the new wing had been completed, Manasseh Cutler described the library as "a very large chamber, and high studded. The walls were covered with book-shelves filled with books; besides, there are four large alcoves filled in the same manner. I presume this is the largest, and by far the best private library in America."[11]

To form his bookshelves, Franklin converted the cases he used to ship his books. He also had several additional cases made upon returning to Philadelphia. Each case formed a single shelf of books, and he managed to fill at least 117 of them. Filling the shelves was the easy part. Organizing the collection was more challenging. How should he arrange his books? What order would be best? Franklin asked himself such questions before he devised an ingenious solution.

Since Franklin's catalogue has disappeared, his own organizational scheme remains a mystery. The surviving evidence indicates that he decided against physically rearranging his books and instead found a way to catalogue his library that obviated the need for rearrangement. By numbering his bookcases, coding his books with case and shelf numbers, and creating a subject catalogue listing titles keyed to their identifying numbers, Franklin could easily locate any book. His copy of John Hill's *The Actor: A Treatise on the Art of Playing* (1750), for example, was the seventeenth volume in case forty-seven. Franklin therefore inscribed it "C47 N17." The system allowed him to access his books quickly by consulting the catalogue first.[12]

Franklin's cataloguing scheme is consistent with other clever devices he created in the late 1780s to facilitate the use of his library. He invented a chair that transformed into a stepladder for accessing the topmost shelves, which extended all the way to the ceiling. He also devised a kind of mechanical hand that could gently remove individual volumes from the upper shelves like a sticky-fingered giant. Even with the added convenience of his new inventions, Franklin was not doing the work of organizing the library himself. His grandsons Benjamin Franklin Bache and William Temple Franklin were helping him with the task. To be sure, they were the ones scrambling up and down their grandfather's ingenious stepladder.

Once he shelved all his books in the new wing of his Philadelphia home, they formed an impressive sight, not because of the external appearance of the books: Franklin did not put great stock in fine bookbindings. He did have Robert Aitken – the best bookbinder in Philadelphia – bind a few volumes for him in the 1780s, but for the most part his books were modestly bound. Franklin's library impressed visitors simply because it was Franklin's. That vast library was an outward sign of the great intellect that had collected and read the books it contained. Eventually confined to bed in his final illness, Franklin was separated from his library, but he still kept his grandsons busy, sending them back and forth from sick chamber to library to fetch books for him and having them continue the task of cataloguing the collection.

Polly Hewson, the daughter of Franklin's London landlady, had also settled in Philadelphia with her children. She stayed near her friend and mentor to comfort him in his final illness. Finding him confined to bed in great agony one day, she lingered by his side until the pain subsided, when she asked if he would like her to read to him. Of course he said yes, and she noticed a copy of Samuel Johnson's *Lives of the Poets* (1779) nearby. She opened the volume and read from the life of Isaac Watts. She had thought that the book might soothe him, but "instead of lulling him to sleep, it roused him to a display of the powers of his memory and his reason." Franklin repeated several poems from Watts's *Horae Lyricae* (1706) and "descanted upon their sublimity in a strain worthy of them and of their pious author."[13] Despite his discomfort, Franklin remained alert and happy to talk about books even on his deathbed.

The dispersal of Franklin's library

After his death, Franklin's library fell into obscurity. In retrospect, the decisions he made regarding his library seem strange. Though his 1772 letter to his son suggests that he was thinking about donating it to or transforming it into a public library, he neither donated it to an established institution nor established a new public facility for the purpose of housing his books. Decades earlier, James Logan – the finest classicist in colonial America – realized that his heirs were neither willing nor able to give his library the care it deserved, so he made provisions to establish the Loganian Library. As a result, Logan's library remained intact through Franklin's lifetime and survives today as part of the Library Company of Philadelphia.[14] Franklin had the foresight and vision to establish so many other lasting institutions beneficial to the public welfare that have survived, and thrived, but he did not make similar plans for his personal library.

There is some evidence to suggest that he considered leaving his books to the Library Company of Philadelphia. After returning from France, yet before his books arrived from there, he invited directors of the Library Company to his home. Arranging to meet with them, he intended to whet their bookish appetites and to nudge the Library Company out of the torpor into which it had fallen. The Director's Minutes show that Franklin "appeared to interest himself much in the Prosperity of the Library, and wished some steps could be taken to procure a convenient Lot to build on, and intimated that he had a valuable Number of Books which he intended for the Library whenever there should be a safe place to deposit them in, which he did not think was the case at present."[15]

These remarks suggest that Franklin wished to leave his personal library to posterity to such an extent that he wanted to assure it a safe and permanent home. Since the Library Company was still located in rented and increasingly overcrowded quarters in Carpenter's Hall, Franklin hesitated to let the Company have his books until it had an adequate facility to house them. By the time the Library Company had acquired a suitable lot on which to erect a new building, Franklin had already made other plans for the disposition of his library. His new will left most of his books to family members.

The will contained only one bequest to the Library Company, an eighteen-volume quarto edition of *Descriptions des Arts et Métiers* (1771–81) published by the Académie Royale des Sciences. The American Academy of Arts and Sciences received the more lavish thirty-two-volume folio edition of the same work. To the American Philosophical Society Franklin bequeathed *L'Histoire de l'Académie Royale des Sciences* (1704–84), a set of over eighty quarto volumes that constitute a record of important scientific discoveries spanning the eighteenth century.

In a way, it seems only natural that Temple should have inherited the library. Since birth, he had been a part of his grandfather's household, and he owed to him his education and his prestige. Living and working together in Paris for several years, the two had shelved their books together without distinguishing which books belonged to whom. Some of the surviving books listed in the inventories of Benjamin Franklin's library in France contain evidence of Temple Franklin's ownership. Giving his library primarily to his grandson Temple instead of making additional bequests to other deserving members of his extended family, Franklin sought to keep the lion's share of his collection together. The bequest is consistent with Franklin's behavior toward Temple in the last years of his life. After the two had returned from

France, Franklin had continued doing what he could for his grandson. He even managed to get Temple elected to the American Philosophical Society, a prestigious, and perhaps unwarranted, honor for a young man in his twenties who had yet to make any personal contributions to science. Arranging for membership to the Society, Franklin honored Temple but also sought to secure his grandson's place in the American intellectual world. As a member, Temple would be able to associate with some of the greatest minds in the nation, men who could impress upon him the responsibility that came with the generous bequest. Sadly, William Temple Franklin fell far short of his grandfather's hopes and expectations.

Despite Benjamin Franklin's best efforts to secure his grandson's future and to make him a leading member of the rising generation of Americans, Temple Franklin turned his back on the United States. Within months of his grandfather's death, he left Philadelphia for England, never to return. Temple went to England on behalf of Robert Morris, Jr., to dispose of over a million acres of Massachusetts land.[16] The precise status of his grandfather's bequest at this time remains uncertain. According to one account, Temple borrowed money from Morris, pledging the library as collateral. Other evidence suggests that Temple, though in England, retained ownership of the library until 1794, when he sold it to Morris outright.[17]

In either case, the library remained intact through mid-1794, when the British traveler and antiquary Henry Wansey passed through Philadelphia. As it turned out, Wansey was one of the last people to see the library as it appeared during Franklin's lifetime. Visiting his home at Franklin Court, Wansey took a tour through the home. Entering the room where Franklin kept his books proved to be a heady experience. Describing the visit in his *Journal of an Excursion to the United States of North America, in the Summer of 1794* (1796), he conveyed the awe he felt: "When I was shewn into this great man's library and study, my sensations almost overcame me . . . I felt a glow of enthusiasm grow in my mind, at visiting the late abode of this great man. I was now standing in his library, the scene of his vast labours."[18]

Soon after Wansey's visit, the library was removed from Franklin Court, and Robert Morris, Jr., took possession of Franklin's books. But he would not keep them for long. Robert Morris, Sr., faced serious financial difficulties over the next half dozen years, and the son's assets were inextricably intertwined with the father's. Their financial problems forced the sale of the library in 1801.[19] Morris chose Nicholas Gouin Dufief to sell the books. Around the same time Dufief undertook the sale of Franklin's books, his shop contained many other fine volumes, specifically those from the library of William Byrd.[20] According to one customer, Dufief moved his business to larger quarters on South Fourth Street – at the sign of Voltaire's Head – in order to accommodate Franklin's books.[21] The Franklin library, combined with the remains of the Byrd library, gave Dufief a collection of books that for a brief time excelled any other private library in the United States, with the possible exception of President Jefferson's. Franklin's library was sold piecemeal during the next few years. Over the course of the nineteenth century, it almost completely disappeared.

Notes

1. John Wilcox, *Bibliotheca Burnetiana: Being a Catalogue of the Intire Library of His Excellency William Burnet Esq; Deceased; Late Governor of New-England* (London: John Wilcox, [1730]).
2. Kevin J. Hayes, "Libraries and Learned Societies," in *Encyclopedia of the North American Colonies*, ed. Jacob Ernest Cooke, 3 vols. (New York: Charles Scribner's Sons, 1993), 3: 129–30.
3. Edwin Wolf 2nd and Kevin J. Hayes, *The Library of Benjamin Franklin* (Philadelphia: American Philosophical Society and the Library Company of Philadelphia, 2006), no. 2083. The remaining information about specific books in Franklin's library comes from this work and will not be cited separately.
4. George Simpson Eddy, ed., "Account Book of Benjamin Franklin Kept by Him During His First Mission to England as Provincial Agent, 1757–1762," *Pennsylvania Magazine of History and Biography* 55 (1931): 97–133.
5. Hayes, "Libraries and Learned Societies," 130–31.
6. *Ibid.*, 131.
7. John Aikin, "Hasselquist, Frederic," in *General Biography; or, Lives, Critical and Historical, of the Most Eminent Persons of All Ages, Countries, Conditions and Professions*, ed. John Aikin, Thomas Morgan, and William Johnston, 10 vols. (London: for J. Johnson, 1799–1815), 5: 76.
8. Bee Wilson, *The Hive: The Story of the Honeybee and Us* (New York: Thomas Dunne Books, 2004), 256.
9. James N. Green, "Thinking about Benjamin Franklin's Library," in *Finding Colonial Americas: Essays Honoring J. A. Leo Lemay*, ed. Carla Mulford and David S. Shields (Newark: University of Delaware Press, 2001), 343.
10. Carl Van Doren, ed., *The Letters of Benjamin Franklin and Jane Mecom* (Princeton: for the American Philosophical Society by Princeton University Press, 1950), 282, 295.
11. Manasseh Cutler, *Life, Journals and Correspondence of Rev. Manasseh Cutler, LL. D.*, ed. William Parker Cutler and Julia Perkins Cutler, 2 vols. (Cincinnati: R. Clarke, 1888), 1: 269.
12. For the discovery of Franklin's shelfmark, see Edwin Wolf 2nd, "A Key to the Identification of Franklin's Books," *Pennsylvania Magazine of History and Biography* 80 (1956): 407–09; Wolf, "The Reconstruction of Benjamin Franklin's Library: An Unorthodox Jigsaw Puzzle," *Papers of the Bibliographical Society* 56 (1962): 1–16.
13. Quoted in John Bigelow, ed., *The Works of Benjamin Franklin*, 12 vols. (New York: G. P. Putnam's, 1904), 12: 197.

14. Edwin Wolf 2nd, *The Library of James Logan of Philadelphia 1674–1751* (Philadelphia: The Library Company of Philadelphia, 1974), xlv–lvii.
15. Quoted in Green, "Thinking about Benjamin Franklin's Library," 344.
16. Thomas Jefferson to George Washington, March 27, 1791, in *The Papers of Thomas Jefferson*, ed. Julian P. Boyd, *et al.*, 32 vols. to date (Princeton University Press, 1950–), 19: 626.
17. [William Duane, Jr.,] "Dr. Franklin's Library," *Historical Magazine* 10 (1866): 123; George Simpson Eddy, "Dr. Benjamin Franklin's Library," *Proceedings of the American Antiquarian Society* 34 (1925): 206–26; Wolf, "Reconstruction," 4; Green, "Thinking about Benjamin Franklin's Library," 348.
18. David John Jeremy, ed., *Henry Wansey and His American Journal, 1794* (Philadelphia: American Philosophical Society, 1970), 113.
19. Wolf, "Reconstruction," 4; Green, "Thinking about Benjamin Franklin's Library," 348.
20. Kevin J. Hayes, *The Library of William Byrd of Westover* (Madison and Philadelphia: Madison House and the Library Company of Philadelphia, 1997), 102–03.
21. Duane, "Dr. Franklin's Library," 123. For the full story of the dispersal of Benjamin Franklin's library, see Kevin J. Hayes, "Introduction," *The Library of Benjamin Franklin*, 35–56.

2

DOUGLAS ANDERSON

The Art of Virtue

The title of this chapter is also the title of an unwritten treatise on the management of human character that Benjamin Franklin once thought of contributing to the world's extensive library of didactic literature. His friend Benjamin Vaughan looked forward to its publication. Along with Franklin's memoir, this manual of ethics (Vaughan thought) would help alleviate the anxiety and the pain that marred too much of earthly life. Even if its readers failed to follow Franklin's advice, Franklin's writing alone would delight the mind, and that prospect satisfied Benjamin Vaughan (A 140). But Franklin never got any farther than the title, and he never finished the autobiography to which Vaughan had attached many of his hopes for human reform. A prolific author of letters, pamphlets, proverbs, and newspaper columns of various kinds, Franklin was a disappointment when it came to the treatise, the monumental synthesis of intellectual life. And it is a good thing too. Virtue that required a barricade of books to fend off the assaults of appetite could scarcely hope to illuminate the surrounding moral darkness of the late eighteenth century. In any case, the provisional title that had aroused Benjamin Vaughan's expectations was misleading.

Virtue, as Benjamin Franklin understands it, is a means, not an end. Happiness is the end, the most desirable of life's good things. To achieve and to sustain it is a form of worship – in fact, the only form of worship capable of bringing delight to the Creator of the Universe, a mysterious entity, at once remote and intimate, to whom Franklin repeatedly directed a remarkably simple prayer of his own devising:

> O Powerful Goodness! bountiful Father! merciful Guide! Increase in me that Wisdom which discovers my truest Interests; Strengthen my Resolutions to perform what that Wisdom dictates. Accept my kind Offices to thy other Children, as the only Return in my Power for thy continual Favours to me. (A 153)

Compare these words to those of the Lord's Prayer, that liturgical mainstay of virtually every Protestant sect in the English-speaking world, and a clear picture of Franklin's ethical and spiritual aptitudes will begin to emerge. God's Heavenly Kingdom and man's daily bread, human trespass and divine forgiveness, worldly temptation and the snares of evil make no appearance in Franklin's prayer. No gothic shadows loom over his spiritual life similar to those that marked George Whitefield, for instance, or Jonathan Edwards, preachers whose revival sermons sometimes reduced their terrified congregants to howls of dismay. Franklin did, however, supplement his austere prayer with recitations of ceremonial dramatic verse that suggest his interest in a very different kind of religious and ethical theater.

He drew one of these from Joseph Addison's *Cato* (1713), a popular verse drama of the day. Franklin singles out a speech in which the play's stoic hero declares his conviction that God "must delight in Virtue, / And that which he delights in must be happy" (A 153). Another portion of his personal liturgy came from James Thomson, a poet whose elaborate Augustan meditation on *The Seasons* (1726–30) possessed the capacity to move Franklin to tears:

> Father of Light and Life, thou Good supreme,
> O teach me what is good, teach me thy self!
> Save me from Folly, Vanity and Vice,
> From every low Pursuit, and fill my Soul
> With Knowledge, conscious Peace, & Virtue pure,
> Sacred, substantial, neverfading Bliss!   (A 154)

Thomson's lines draw a little closer to Christ's traditional prayer, though human "bliss" or ecstatic delight remains the chief result of enrolling in Thomson's School of Good Supreme. Franklin's devotional tastes invariably point toward a blend of emotional and ethical destinations: at happiness, at kindness, at knowledge and "conscious Peace," not at the abject submission of human agency to divine will. He embraces a domestic, not a courtly or a feudal, model of the soul's home, an ethical posture that he is able to explain in a handful of pages concentrated in the second part of his most famous – indeed his only – book. How is it possible that this brief, beautiful, and ultimately liberating vision of moral life could be misunderstood?

"Bad commentators spoil the best of books," Poor Richard Saunders once explained in the pages of his popular almanac: "So God sends meat (they say) the Devil cooks." For nearly a century now, any number of malevolent or simply inattentive chefs have made a hash of Franklin's commitment to the pursuit of happiness through ethical self-discipline. His virtue (these skeptics argue) is little more than an artful pose. At worst, he is an apologist for imperialism or racism; at best, he is simply a complacent bookkeeper who tabulates his good and bad deeds the way a businessman keeps records of liabilities and assets. Even Franklin's admirers frequently concede the validity of this portrait and then struggle to redeem it on the grounds that Franklin is a realist, not a utopian: a practical man interested in practical deeds, not in the ineffable states of grace or the tortured realization of sin that revivalists sought to evoke, and certainly not in orthodox sectarian discipline.

Franklin kept his distance from both of the ideological extremes that characterized the professional clergy of his day. He befriended the great, open-air evangelist George Whitefield but resisted Whitefield's theological claims with little difficulty. Charitable religious appeals on behalf of widows and orphans might sometimes prompt Franklin to empty his pockets into the collection plate, but that was the extent of Whitefield's influence on Franklin's sentiments. The religious professionals in Philadelphia's established churches made even less impression on his spiritual life. They were (Franklin thought) doctrinal hacks. In his autobiography he makes no secret of his disgust at a representative contemporary sermon, but this criticism is comparatively mild when set against the fierce pamphlet war that Franklin conducted against Philadelphia's Presbyterian synod, in 1735, in defense of the heterodox Samuel Hemphill and his plagiarized sermons. "I rather approv'd his giving us good Sermons compos'd by others, than bad ones of his own Manufacture," Franklin recalled many years later (A 168). His residual bitterness is still evident in the cutting reference to manufactured preaching that the passage of over half a century has not made more palatable.

Franklin clearly anticipated the New Light movement in its fervent conviction that the institutionalized "church" badly needed regeneration, but beginning in 1728 his approach to the challenge is largely private. The "Articles of Belief and Acts of Religion" that he prepared in that year represent a personal experiment in reformed faith. They are the defining document of Franklin's early adulthood, the foundation of his fame, his influence, and the "constant Felicity" that he had been able to maintain through a long and tumultuous career. They are also the basis for one of the most misunderstood episodes in his highly episodic *Autobiography*.

At the urging of Benjamin Vaughan and Abel James, Franklin devotes much of the second part of his life story to a detailed description of a "bold and Arduous" self-improvement project: a program for adhering to thirteen primary virtues that Franklin had enumerated in his early twenties and positioned at the center of his ethical existence. After a brief recapitulation of his enduring religious beliefs, Franklin lists the virtues in what he takes to be a developmental sequence, building from Temperance and Silence at the beginning of the list toward Chastity and Humility at its conclusion in ascending order of difficulty. He reproduces in the *Autobiography* a sample page from the ivory tablets that he used to record his ethical failings, transcribes into its pages some of the inspirational language from the original "Articles of Belief," and outlines his ideal "Scheme of Employment" for the hours of the day.

The motto that Franklin drafted for the virtue of Order required him to be sure that "every Part of my Business should have its allotted Time," so, as part of his perfection experiment, he dutifully allots the hours for sleep, meals, prayer, self-examination, music, conversation, reading, and work. Franklin's definition of "Business," it quickly appears, is humanistically broad rather than strictly economic in its aims. His work day amounts to a tidy (and by contemporary standards revolutionary) eight hours, with a two-hour midday break, morning and evening intervals of "Study" or "Diversion," and a sobering "Evening Question" that seems modeled (at least implicitly) on a kind of microcosmic Last Judgment: "What good have I done to day?" The scope of these simple words suggests that Franklin's aim is not so much the efficiency of his schedule as the vindication of his life. He does not express any interest in reviewing the profitable deals he may have struck but in assessing his moral fitness on a much broader scale. If this understanding of human obligation reflects an accountant's bourgeois morality, then the modern world could use many more such moral accountants.

But Order, Franklin admits, the third of his thirteen virtues, gave him trouble. The schedule of a Master tradesman or a successful public figure was not always his own to control. An unusually good memory in his youth had compensated for unmethodical habits that grew more costly and more frustrating with Franklin's advancing age. He was, accordingly, tempted to give up the pursuit of Order altogether "and content my self with a faulty Character in that respect." By way of explaining his discouragement, Franklin abruptly offers a parable disguised as an anecdote that seems, at first, to undo all the careful behavioral tactics that his program of virtues and mottoes imposed. In introducing the theme of excuses, however, Franklin's story of the speckled ax captures a key feature of both his ethical imagination and the gradually unfolding design of his *Autobiography*.

The persistent difficulty that he encounters in his pursuit of Order, Franklin suggests, makes him appear:

> Like the man who in buying an Ax of a Smith my neighbour, desired to have the whole of its Surface as bright as the Edge; the Smith consented to grind it bright for him if he would turn the Wheel. He turn'd while the Smith press'd the broad Face of the Ax hard and heavily on the Stone, which made the Turning of it very fatiguing. The Man came every now and then from the Wheel to see how the Work went on; and at length would take his Ax as it was without farther Grinding. No, says the Smith, Turn on, turn on; we shall have it bright by and by; as yet 'tis only speckled. Yes, says the Man; but – *I think I like a speckled Ax best.* And I believe this may have been the Case with many who having for want of some such Means as I employ'd found the Difficulty of obtaining good, and breaking bad Habits, in other Points of Vice and Virtue, have given up the Struggle, and concluded that *a speckled Ax was best.* For something that pretended to be Reason was every now and then suggesting to me, that such extream Nicety as I exacted of my self might be a kind of Foppery in Morals, which if it were known would make me ridiculous; that a perfect Character might be attended with the Inconvenience of being envied and hated; and that a benevolent Man should allow a few Faults in himself, to keep his Friends in Countenance. (A 155–56)

This polished little story is much more than just a worldly joke. Franklin introduces it by explaining how one dimension of his nature repeatedly thwarts the organizational efforts of another: Want of Method undermining Memory, Faults eluding the vigilance of "painful Attention," Relapses neutralizing the "little Progress in Amendment" that Franklin is sometimes able to achieve. The encounter between the wily smith and his vain customer readily mirrors the pervasive friction between "my self" and my "Character" that is implicit in nearly all of the mottoes that Franklin writes for his virtues. It recasts, as well, the struggle between Principle and Inclination that he describes, in Part One of his book, as he debates the propriety of eating some nicely fried smelt (A 87–88). That earlier anecdote too mixes comic self-disclosure with a grim, emblematic truth: big fish invariably eat little fish, a vision of the universal cannibalism of life that Benjamin Vaughan had hoped Franklin's memoir might help redeem.

The speckled ax story incorporates a similar measure of emblematic richness disguised as triviality – a Bible hidden beneath a narrative joint stool, much like the family legend that Franklin retells in the memoir's opening pages. Why, after all, need an ax be equally bright on all its surfaces, unless one intends it strictly for display rather than use? Why does the smith abruptly propose his interesting and instructive bargain, rather than simply agree to perform an excessive service for an excessive fee? The events take shape with the alacrity of a fable, as if the forge and the stone were little more than camouflage for the smith's subtle, figurative identity. The impervious metal "Surface" of the ax oddly softens into its "broad Face" as the smith presses it as hard as he can against the abrasive wheel – an excruciating shift in terms that illuminates the foolish customer's interest in superficially flawless appearances. Franklin's words slyly anticipate the pained and prickly "Countenances" of friends who might be prone to take offense at conspicuous displays of benevolence.

To be sure, the anecdote offers to the rationalizing conscience a subtle texture of excuses. The smith originally seems content to provide a sharp ax on which only a tiny fraction of the metal head gleams with purpose, though he is not averse to the hard and heavy work that his customer's odd desire entails. The customer ultimately scales back his own unreasonable request, but not to the pragmatic level of the smith. "Something that pretended to be Reason" would almost certainly concur with the smith's initial willingness to settle for a keen edge alone. But something more complex than simply reason, or "extream Nicety," or worldly cunning prompts the self-deprecating (and Franklinian) words with which the weary customer concludes the tale: not "*I like a speckled Ax best*" but "*I think I like a speckled Ax best.*" This tentative concession to a hard truth, like the anecdote as a whole, is a finely hewn verbal tool, a dramatic embodiment of the ethical dialogue in Benjamin Franklin's conscience.

A careful reader of the *Autobiography* might readily detect in the words of the smith's chastened customer an echo of Franklin's own studied reticence, his wariness of declarative or dogmatic speech. The book repeats these strictures on "all positive Assertion" a few paragraphs after the ax anecdote to make sure the echo is audible. But the tactics of the ingenious blacksmith are also a version of Franklin's own methods of self-management, recast as an effective means of mortifying vanity without ridiculing human weakness. The ivory tablets in the small booklet where Franklin marks his faults are the first of two intriguingly flawed or "speckled" surfaces in this carefully orchestrated section of his book. The booklet is much more easily cleaned with a wet sponge than the rugged metal of the ax, perhaps, but its pages too are just as easily refilled with fresh evidence of the struggle against imperfection. Like the ax, the tablets are a mirror rather than a ledger: a contemplative medium more than a tool, much like the arduous dream of perfection that they purport to document.

Over the course of his life, Franklin proves to be a master of the deftly administered, and occasionally graceful, excuse. If there is an "art" to virtue, then a gift for formulating and appreciating excuses may be essential to its practice. The entire *Autobiography* unfolds beneath the umbrella of a formal apology for its inadequacies. These pages, Franklin suggests, are merely a long letter to his son, not the daunting legacy of a celebrated moralist. In any case, since his memoir is a written work rather than an oral reminiscence, it need not be "troublesome to others who thro' respect to Age might think themselves oblig'd to give me a Hearing" (A 44). Unlike a garrulous old relative, a book is easily set aside – a great advantage from the point of view of one's shiftless heirs but a disturbing truth for a writer. The "rambling" nature of his style, Franklin concedes, is a weakness. "But one does not dress for private Company as for a publick Ball" (A 57). The disorderly flow of memory is to be expected in the context of a casual chat; the gain in intimacy, however, more than compensates for the sacrifice of formal discipline. That gain, as well, is part of the human economy of excuses.

When Franklin resumes his story thirteen years after first beginning it, and a decade or more after putting it aside, he resumes as well the apologetic tactics with which the book began. Two letters from two old friends have, at length, led him to extend his memoir, Franklin announces, but he begins by pointing out that he is writing at a great disadvantage. His papers are in Philadelphia and he is in France. He has no copy of the first part of the narrative to which these new pages might be smoothly attached, and he has worn himself out in the "Affairs of the Revolution." Even after plunging back into an account of his early business success, Franklin finds occasion to continue his apologies. To his surprise and bemusement, a growing collection of valuable silver plate and china begins to fill the Franklin household as his printing enterprises thrive, but that change is really Deborah Franklin's fault (her husband sheepishly implies) and she is rather curtly inclined to defend her extravagance by asserting that "*her* Husband deserv'd a Silver Spoon and China Bowl as well as any of his Neighbours" (A 145). Franklin's capitalized adjectives underscore Deborah's symbolic intent and her stubborn loyalty, not her materialism, but they remain excuses, nonetheless.

Each of the mottoes that Franklin prepares for his thirteen cardinal virtues is subject to a similar play of contingency and excuse, dramatizing the inter-action between interior conviction and exterior performance on which the status of one's character turns: "Eat not to Dulness. Drink not to eleva-tion." "Resolve to perform what you ought. Perform without fail what you resolve." "Use no hurtful Deceit. Think innocently and justly; and, if you speak, speak accordingly." These precepts for three of the virtues on Franklin's list have interior and exterior dimensions that correspond to the complex ethical creature that they strive to govern. A temperate soul (Franklin notes) can be smothered by sensual excess or dissipated in social display, buried in food or diffused in drink. Resolutions begin in the privacy of the mind, but they cannot (or ought not) to remain merely private. Sincerity sometimes entails the protective concealment of benevolent deceit; it is not exclusively an attribute of one's public nature.

Being and doing exist in a subtle state of equilibrium that each of Franklin's precepts characterizes in some unique fashion, with "Chastity" offering perhaps the most surprising illustration of Franklin's ethical posture: "Rarely use Venery but for Health or Offspring," his precept advises, "Never to Dulness, Weakness, or the Injury of your own or another's Peace or Reputation." Very few readers get through this motto without feeling a measure of amusement at the "venereal" extremes it appears to entertain. The bawdy joke latent in the pun on "peace," however, quickly reverses its comic force once we appreciate the striking connection Franklin has drawn between the most selfish of human appetites and the most selfless of human feelings. The precept never openly invokes the idea of love, but love is the medium that unites our own well-being with "another's Peace." Charity and Chastity are implicitly fused in a precept that uses the sensual exterior as an avenue to interior transformation.

Franklin envisioned his incomplete *Art of Virtue* as an elaborate expansion of the precepts that he had prepared for his own use in the "Articles of Belief and Acts of Religion": a detailed "Comment" devoted to each of the thirteen attributes "in which I would have shown the Advantages of possessing it" and suggested "the *Means* and *Manner*" of obtaining it rather than simply offering yet another exhortation to be good. His model was the second chapter of the Epistle of James, supplemented by Franklin's long-standing conviction that it was "every one's Interest to be virtuous, who wish'd to be happy even in this World":

> But it so happened that my Intention of writing and publishing this Comment was never fulfilled. I did indeed, from time to time put down short Hints of the Sentiments, Reasonings, &c. to be made use of in it; some of which I have still by me: But the necessary close Attention to private Business in the earlier part of Life, and public Business since, have occasioned my postponing it. For it being connected in my Mind with *a great and extensive Project* that required the whole Man to execute, and which an unforeseen Succession of Employs prevented my attending to, it has hitherto remain'd unfinish'd.　　(A 58)

Here, perhaps, is the master excuse of all. The whole man is seldom free to concentrate all of life's energies on any single task, however great, extensive, or momentous it might be. Like the speckled ax, Franklin's book never achieves the high polish that he had intended. A collection of unpublished sentiments and "Reasonings" are all that remain to hint at the unfinished design.

But the terms of this excuse too may be more finished than they seem. In assembling hints and sentiments toward the making of a "Comment," Franklin is once again studiously avoiding arguments, prescriptions, exhortations, or treatises – all the apparatus of ethical authority that Benjamin Vaughan probably hoped to elicit from him. Unlike many of his admirers, Franklin is interested in starting moral conversations, not in pronouncing closure upon them. The operations of the conscience tend to be social rather than dictatorial, more like the interchange between the smith and his customer than like the sermons of Jedidiah Andrews, who managed to turn the carefully framed exhortation to ethical reflection in Philippians 4:8 into an utterly uninspired to-do list of five key chores for the conscientious Presbyterian. Andrews is the minister whose friendship Franklin enjoyed but whose preaching so disgusted him that he gave up his effort to rejoin "the public Assemblies": "My Conduct might be blameable," Franklin confesses, "but I leave it without attempting farther to excuse it, my present purpose being to relate Facts, and not to make Apologies for them" (A 148). If Philippians 4:8 could not arouse the ethical instincts of Jedediah Andrews, nothing would.

Franklin does not refer to the Bible very often in the *Autobiography*, and this is the only verse he bothers to transcribe at length. The language from Philippians is clearly important to him. He cites it in slightly excised form, as he describes his disappointment with Andrews's performance, and credits its language with inspiring him to return to his private form of worship: "Finally, Brethren, Whatsoever Things are true, honest, just, pure, lovely, or of good report, if there be any virtue, or any praise, think on these Things" (A 147). Like the precepts for his thirteen virtues, this passage presupposes a reciprocal relation between action and contemplation, between the outer and the inner ethical worlds. That is partly why its failure to promote a meaningful religious experience in "the public Assembly" struck Franklin as especially egregious.

His transcription stresses the Apostle's sequence of ethical modifiers by removing some cumbersome syntax from the King James translation, blending the true, the honest, the just, and the lovely into a seamless whole, much like the individual precepts appear so often to do in Franklin's list of virtues. Matters of "good report" emerge from the verse as inherently mixed phenomena: subtle compounds that contain elements of virtue and of praise in a shifting, and perhaps uncertain, relationship to one another. Every feature of the passage encourages its reader to address the equilibrium between being and doing, to contemplate the mutual influence they exercise on the conduct of life. Think on these things, the Bible appears to urge, as the indispensable complement to doing them. Franklin's 1728 "Articles of Belief and Acts of Religion" tries to exploit the same imaginative interrelationship as a means of shaping the development of his private character.

He had not left Boston or London very far behind when he drafted this extensive liturgical script, stretching his imagination (as he put it) to conceive of a "Chorus" of inhabited worlds, filling the Universe with an infinite variety of conscious beings and permanently extinguishing any sense of mankind's metaphysical uniqueness or importance. In the statement of "First Principles" with which the "Articles" begins, Franklin distinguishes between the "*Infinite Father*" of all created things and a range of subsidiary "created Gods" who mediate between finite life and its "*Supremely Perfect*" but inaccessible originator. Earth's subsidiary god, the "Author and Owner" of our solar system, strikes the young Franklin as a "*good Being*," one who "has in himself some of those Passions he has planted in us" and is "not above caring for us, being pleas'd with our Praise, and offended when we slight Him, or neglect his Glory":

> Next to the Praise due to his Wisdom, I believe he is pleased and delights in the Happiness of those he has created; and since without Virtue Man can have no Happiness in this World, I firmly believe he delights to see me Virtuous, because he is pleas'd when he sees me Happy.
>
> And since he has created many things which seem purely design'd for the Delight of Man, I believe he is not offended when he sees his Children solace themselves in any manner of pleasant Exercises and innocent Delights, and I think no Pleasure innocent that is to Man hurtful.
>
> I *love* him therefore for his Goodness and I *adore* him for his Wisdom.
>
> Let me then not fail to praise my God continually, for it is his Due, and it is all I can return for his many Favours and great Goodness to me; and let me resolve to be virtuous, that I may be happy, that I may please Him, who is delighted to see me happy. Amen. (P 1:103–04)

Franklin was not the first nor the last heterodox printer to invent his own divine ontology. Mark Twain indulges a very similar degree of conceptual freedom in the extraordinary ontological experiment of *The Mysterious Stranger* (1907), the late novel in which Twain lovingly revisits the press rooms of Keokuk, Cincinnati, or New York, where he had spent his pre-riverboat youth. But Twain's imaginary encounter with one of the created gods of the Universe is finally a much darker experience than Franklin's. The "Acts of Religion" that follow Franklin's statement of first principles, and his devotional recitations drawn from the poetry of Richard Blackmore or John Milton, portray an ethical collaboration between a creature who is only too aware of the irreducible disorder of his moral failings and a sympathetic (if vastly superior) colleague in the long struggle with imperfection that is created life.

Instead of the thirteen virtues and concise mottoes of the *Autobiography*, the "Acts of Religion" consist of fourteen "Supplications" for divine assistance in replacing an extensive array of weaknesses with strengths. Franklin declares his desire to avoid Atheism, Pride, Disrespect, Cruelty, Calumny, Avarice, and Craft, among many other destructive feelings or acts, and to cultivate an equally elaborate list of admirable qualities: loyalty, valor, humility, gratitude, charity and prudence:

> That I may possess Integrity and Evenness of Mind, Resolution in Difficulties, and Fortitude under Affliction; that I may be punctual in performing my Promises, peaceable and prudent in my Behavior,   Help me, O Father
>
> That I may have Tenderness for the Weak, and a reverent Respect for the Ancient; That I may be kind to my Neighbours, good-natured to my Companions, and hospitable to Strangers,   Help me, O Father
>
> That I may be averse to Craft and Overreaching, abhor Extortion, Perjury, and every kind of Wickedness,   Help me, O Father
>
> That I may be honest and Openhearted, gentle, merciful and Good, chearful in Spirit, rejoicing in the Good of Others,   Help me, O Father
>
> That I may have constant Regard to Honour and Probity; That I may possess a perfect Innocence and a good Conscience, and at length become Truly Virtuous and Magnanimous,   Help me, Good God,
>
>   Help me, O Father
>
>   (P 1: 108)

Unlike the Lord's Prayer or Franklin's own list of thirteen virtues, these supplications would pose a challenge even to a trained memory. Only the last five appear above. The entire group of fourteen – roughly one quarter of the "Articles of Belief" – is followed by four detailed acknowledgments of gratitude for various blessings (Knowledge, Literature, Air, Light, Corn, Wine, Water) that bring the first part of Franklin's liturgy to a close. The second part does not survive. The entire performance seems deliberately designed to thwart the mnemonic strategies that Franklin might have been tempted to use in order to reduce the recitation to an empty formula.

An accomplished actor, of course, might master the entire script and perform it flawlessly, as Franklin did with James Ralph's rendering of the Eighteenth Psalm. But in the process, the words would have much more opportunity to inhabit the performer, as the best dramatic utterance should, eliciting depths of feeling that ritualistic speech by itself seldom attains. The scope and wording of the "Articles of Belief and Acts of Religion" make evident Franklin's determination to act on the exhortation from Philippians: to make the inner and the outer moral "faces" mirror one another by transforming consciousness as well as behavior. His supplications repeatedly mix inward "possession" with outward "performance" in order to stress their inseparable nature and to acknowledge the extraordinary influence of the moral imagination over human conduct. The thirteen virtues and their mottoes in the *Autobiography* depict in concentrated form the same portrait of inner and outer reciprocity. "Imitate Jesus and Socrates," Franklin crisply reminded himself in the motto for Humility – advice intended not to fashion a nation of saintly martyrs but to expose, in the most challenging and painful way, the gap between intention and execution that is the mark of human life.

It is a convenient thing to be a reasonable creature, Franklin once wryly observed, since it enables us to manufacture "reasons" to cloak our desires, even from ourselves. The culprit, of course, is not "reason" but the same "something that pretended to be Reason" from the speckled ax story: imaginative ingenuity, the birthplace of creative excuses. The *Dissertation on Liberty and Necessity, Pleasure and Pain* that Franklin published in London three years before writing the "Articles of Belief" targeted these same powers of self-deceit. "Mankind naturally and generally love to be flatter'd," Franklin observed at the *Dissertation*'s conclusion, "Whatever soothes our Pride, and tends to exalt our Species above the rest of the Creation, we are pleas'd with and easily believe, when ungrateful Truths shall be with the utmost Indignation rejected" (P 1: 71). The ungrateful truth that he set out to disclose in the *Dissertation* – and in some measure throughout his life – was the radical equality of all creation, the utter emptiness of all human claims to a special place in the Universe. "My Printing this Pamphlet was another Erratum," Franklin regretfully observed in the *Autobiography*, but he is careful to apologize for his "printing" it, not his writing it.

The *Dissertation*, the "Articles of Belief," and Part Two of the *Autobiography* – Franklin's three key meditations on the Art of Virtue – all meet on this extraordinary open ground, a field of belief and action unencumbered by old narratives of creation and fall, sin and redemption, covenant and transgression, the elected and the rejected soul. "There is in all Men something like a natural Principle which enclines them to DEVOTION or the Worship of some unseen Power," Franklin wrote at the beginning of his Philadelphia career. We are moved "to pay Divine Regards to SOMETHING" (P 1: 102).

The name that he gave this superintending force in the prayer "prefix'd to my Tables of Examination," his booklet of thirteen virtues, was "Powerful Goodness." If the term sounds more and more like an oxymoron in our contemporary world, that fact may be an accurate measure of how much Benjamin Franklin still has to teach us.

3

PAUL E. KERRY

Franklin's satiric vein

Many of Franklin's multi-faceted contributions can be linked to specific phases of his career, but his satirical writing spans his entire life. From the Silence Dogood letters of his teenage years in Boston throughout his professional career and public service in Philadelphia and London, Franklin published satires. His satirical writing needs first to be located in the literary tradition of satire, for only then is it possible to see how his satires contribute to the eighteenth-century revival of the genre. Franklin's satirical writing gave shape to his outlook on society and politics, and it developed in ways that not only drew on but also improved on European techniques and themes. A representative sampling of Franklin's satires from different years in his life will highlight the ways in which his methods and aims changed over time, especially in the noticeable shift that took place in his concerns. It will also illustrate that Franklin remained committed to the principles of the Enlightenment. His earliest satires focused on social mores tied to local issues and parochial institutions. Franklin's satiric writings reveal that he became increasingly troubled by how imperial Britain treated its colonies. Finally, as his last satire makes clear, the issue of slavery troubled Franklin, so he launched an assault on the institution, which plagued the freshly founded United States of America.

Franklin's use of satiric strategies kept with but also broke from strict definitions of satire prevalent in his day. His satires, following the classical tradition, were designed to praise virtue and skewer vice. He dispensed with the traditional verse form and developed instead a narrative reportage style. In Franklin's early satirical critiques of local social issues, light humor was a trademark, but as his frustration with Great Britain grew, indignation would become the dominant mode. Samuel Johnson defined satire in his 1755 dictionary as a "poem in which wickedness or folly is censured," and he named Dryden, Swift, Pope, and Addison as exemplars of the genre. Similarly, the *Encyclopaedia Britannica* (1771) described *Satyr* or *Satire* as "a discourse or poem, exposing the vices and follies of mankind." Among the major satirists, the entry named Dryden and Pope as well as Horace, Juvenal, and Persius.[1]

Scholars today debate about the influence of classical models on modern satire. Yet, during the seventeenth and eighteenth centuries, Horace and Juvenal were considered pillars of the genre. Both writers attempted to define satire, but they differed about its method and purpose. Horatian satire commented on politics and society and sought to motivate constructive change, often through poking humor at the satiric targets. Juvenalian satire, rooted in *indignatio* or righteous anger, tended to be more acerbic in its attempt to provoke fervor against the issue or person targeted as the butt of the jest. Horace and Juvenal used satire to comment on societal ills and provide examples of injustice as well as to instigate improvement.[2]

In the British tradition, John Dryden (1631–1700) was the great rehabilitator of Roman satire.[3] He translated satires by Horace, Juvenal, and other writers, in effect redefining satire for the modern age. His *Discourses Concerning the Original and Progress of Satire* (1693) remained a standard work well into the eighteenth century. Dryden was partial to Juvenal over Horace and maintained that satirists were moral poets. He also rearticulated the classical purpose of satire, namely, to scourge vice, expose folly, and instruct in virtue.[4] Scattered quotations from Horace, Juvenal, Persius, and Dryden are found throughout Franklin's writings and attest that he admired the satirical tradition.

Over the course of the eighteenth century, satire would no longer be tied exclusively to verse. Jonathan Swift's prose pamphlet *A Modest Proposal* (1729) became the iconic English-language satire devoted to a social problem. Swift submitted that poverty and starvation in Ireland could be staved off were the Irish to sell their children to be eaten. Despite the mocking tone, his piece was largely misunderstood when it was first published, as readers' attention was riveted on the outrageous idea of cannibalism. Franklin also rejected verse in his satirical writings, and in many cases his satires were mistaken as actual reports.

Extracts in the *Pennsylvania Gazette* verify that Franklin imported and sold the satires of Juvenal and Persius as well as volumes of Addison and Steele's *The Spectator*, an English magazine that he read voraciously, as acknowledged in his *Autobiography* (P 2: 162 and 211). Franklin valued satire as a teaching tool. In 1751 he published his *Idea of an English School*, which includes a plan whereby major satirists from the classical tradition through to the eighteenth century are listed among readings for students (P 4: 107). In this significant document, Franklin proposed his vision of an educational curriculum, including, among other readings, *The Spectator*, Horace, Addison, Pope, and Swift, who is also quoted in *Poor Richard*

Improved (1750). Finally, Horace and the satires of Juvenal are listed among the books that Franklin owned (P 36: 338).⁵ He enjoyed reading satires and seemed, like his contemporaries, to have preferred the satirical models in the Roman tradition.

Franklin's earliest satires appeared without his name attached to them in James Franklin's (his brother's) Boston newspaper, *The New-England Courant*. The precocious sixteen-year-old apprentice to the newspaper employed a female pseudonym, a strategy he would repeat later, so that his brother did not know that the letters he received from the alleged Silence Dogood, a widow whose husband had been a country minister, were actually penned by his younger brother. The fourteen letters published between April and October of 1722 critique local subjects ranging from the idleness of students at Harvard to Massachusetts politics. The Silence Dogood letters strove for a naïve but thoughtful tone. Assuming the persona of a woman allowed Franklin to criticize men who denied their spouses access to learning in all areas, including writing, arithmetic, and wide reading (P 1: 10). The letters also impugned social injustice of any kind. "Dunces and Blockheads," those students who gained entrance to Harvard through their family's wealth, are pilloried. In the fifth letter, Franklin raised the subject of female education by creating an epistolary exchange between Silence Dogood and a man said to have written to ask her to target her "Satyrs" (satires) at "Female Idleness, Ignorance and Folly." Citing an unnamed authority (in actuality, Daniel Defoe), Silence Dogood contended that while it is women who are reproached, men deny women the "Advantages of Learning" and the "Advantages of Education." And she concluded that women, although accused of vice, are not any more susceptible to it than men (P 1: 15–16; 18–20).

Political corruption is heavily censured, particularly those cases when religion was used as a cloak over malfeasance. Silence Dogood's letter nine featured the epigram, *Corruptio optimi est pessima,* or corruption of the best person is the worst kind of corruption. Franklin used his satiric voice to castigate religious hypocrisy, where religion was used as a pretext to gain power or wield influence in public office. "Indignation not to be born" was how Silence Dogood described her feelings on the subject, thus placing the letter squarely in the satirical tradition. Franklin was apprehensive that a posture of piety would be used to justify political decisions that would allow an official "to cheat a whole country with his religion, and then destroy them under *Colour of Law*." His solution was simple and direct: one must take action not only for "religion" but also for "country" by "setting the Deceivers in a true Light, and undeceiving the Deceived" (P 1: 30–31). This is perhaps the most open expression of Franklin's political views in the Silence

Dogood letters, where he is in earnest and least in the medium of a fictional character.

The Silence Dogood letters are instructive on a number of levels. These epistolary observations from a rustic yet insightful single woman enabled Franklin to put forward views from the position of an outsider to Boston sophistication and politics. Thus, the letters bear a resemblance to Montesquieu's *Lettres persanes*, the "Persian Letters" published in 1721, only a year before Franklin's Silence Dogood series. Montesquieu did not attach his name to the publication. This is a collection of letters purported to be written by two Persian travelers in Bourbon, France, who ridicule French political, social, and cultural institutions. Oliver Goldsmith (*The Citizen of the World*, 1760) and others have been credited with adopting Montesquieu's method of satire. Strangely, Franklin is excluded from such an intellectual genealogy, yet he clearly was among the best eighteenth-century innovators of the genre.

Franklin's satiric voice is centered squarely in Enlightenment conceptions of truth, reliability, and community, conceptions founded on a critique of corruption, dishonesty, and religious factionalism. Refracted in Franklin's satires are key metaphors and processes of the Enlightenment – that is, throwing light on hypocrisy and undeceiving others. The culmination of Mozart's *Magic Flute* would articulate the point in precisely these terms in 1791: "The rays of the sun drive out the night, destroy the usurped power of hypocrites."[6] Moreover, Franklin's later satirical writing against Great Britain's treatment of its colonies as politically immature anticipates the definition of the Enlightenment that would be given its most potent form in Kant's classic essay, "Was ist Aufklärung?" ("What is Enlightenment?" 1784): "*Enlightenment is man's release from his self-incurred tutelage. Tutelage* is the inability to make use of one's own understanding without the guidance of another."[7]

Franklin's fictional personae are devised around a high regard for plain speaking and propriety. The mode he favors is honest, unpretentious, and responsible, giving readers the impression that the writer is normally averse to commenting on current affairs yet moved to speak out because aspects of society or government have become so corrupt as to require denunciation. Satire works only when there is a shared sense of community and morality. Franklin's great skill is evident in how he embodied the voice of the concerned citizen, allowing readers to feel that, by and large, their anxieties too were being represented.

The Silence Dogood letters foreshadow Franklin's tactics for getting controversial subjects published – that is, to assume a pseudonym and write as an interested party – and they intimate the themes that will engage

Franklin throughout his life: the status of women; education; religious zeal and hypocrisy; arbitrary government; encroachments on liberty. These considerations of his later life are not always recognized in his earliest work, but Franklin's parodies go beyond lambasting folly and inculcating virtue. They are calls to action designed, as Silence Dogood gently insisted, to "put in Practice" the recommendations (P 1: 36).

Franklin inveighed against religious zeal and hypocritical public religious displays. In 1730 *The Pennsylvania Gazette*, Franklin's own newspaper, published "A Witch Trial at Mount Holly."[8] When a man and woman were accused of witchcraft, the "evidence" brought against them was that they were said to have caused sheep to dance and pigs to speak. The examiner determined that the accused would be weighed against a Bible. If they were innocent, the Bible would outweigh them. Their second trial was a trial by water: if when placed in a river the accused sank, they would be considered innocent; however, if they floated, they would be considered guilty. The accused agreed to undergo the tests if two of their most vehement accusers would also undergo them. Franklin's satiric method created a situation in which the reader of this piece occupied the position of a well-informed traveler observing this spectacle with metropolitan aloofness and mirth. Yet, Franklin does not let the reader get away with merely observing the behavior of yokels, given the concern that the second trial might cause drowning (although no fatalities occur). Franklin combined deft humor and sober elements in his satires, at once disarming and yet alerting his readers to the dangers of overzealous judgments of others. In this case, the satire was taken to be a serious report in some European circles. Certainly it warned readers about the dangers of mob justice.

The satire has a further purpose other than to mock the credulity of witch trials. The talking hogs allude not only to the biblical Gadarene swine who had demons enter them, which itself resonates with the classical tradition of diverting evil onto another, but also to articulate biblical animals generally. Franklin's deeper question, even as the cosmopolitan, thinking spectator smirked at the preposterous notion of dancing sheep, relates to the question of biblical speaking serpents and talking donkeys and, by extension, to any kind of supernatural actions. The satire makes readers take stock of the rationality of their own beliefs. Although the main bolt of the satire is aimed at the absurdity of witch trials, the force of the bolt striking its mark reverberates through Franklin's strategic use of the word "Belief": how does one sustain belief of any kind in "Moses and all the Prophets and Apostles" when confronted with the weight of "Lumps of Mortality," in this case the supposed witches weighed against the Bible? The metaphorical question is this: how can the rich variety of human existence ever be measured against a narrow set of ancient unyielding rules?

Franklin's sensitivity to religion and arbitrary government in the Silence Dogood letters found expression in perhaps his best known and most carefully crafted satire, "The Speech of Miss Polly Baker" (1747).[9] Franklin's interest in local social matters, in this case the plight of a single mother of children by different men, is a keystone to his view of morality and the relationship between civil and ecclesiastical authority. This is a stylistically exceptional satire in that Franklin modeled on both classical and contemporary satire. The satire made a direct allusion to Swift's *A Modest Proposal*, as J. A. Leo Lemay has decisively proven.[10] Franklin's purposeful placement of "The Speech of Miss Polly Baker" in the tradition of English satire underscores how seriously he meant his subject to be taken.

Polly, an unpretentious woman who has accepted responsibility for her actions, challenges the civil court to which she has again been summoned. She defends herself, arguing that she has given her children the parenting they require. She critiques the double standard that exists in the application of punishments, that her punishment is greater whereas men are equal participants in the situation because they father illegitimate children. One man, she claims, is even a rising magistrate in the community, bringing to mind Franklin's particular venom against hypocrites in positions of political authority and his candid questioning of the unequal status of women in society. Polly's speech also probes the boundary between civic and religious authority. She has been barred from communion, suffered public humiliation, and fined for her moral transgressions. As an excommunicant already, she wonders what more punishment religious authorities can be allowed to impart. The satire continues this theme by taking up transatlantic ideas common to Enlightenment thinkers from Dublin and Edinburgh to Weimar: infanticide and abortion. Clearly and forcefully and yet no less eloquently than many of the eighteenth-century poets who had drawn attention to these hotly debated topics, Polly opines that infanticide and abortion are largely the result of society's puritanical views and policies. Franklin's satire is more gentle yet no less piercing than Voltaire's fusillades against religion. His solution foreshadows the separation of church and state in the United States: morality may be judged differently in the religious and civil spheres.

In 1751 Franklin's satiric mode, which had largely been directed at a range of intracolonial matters within Pennsylvania and its environs, took aim at major British policy, the transfer and sale of convicted criminals to the American colonies. In "Rattlesnakes for Felons," published anonymously under the pseudonym "Americanus" as a May 9 letter to the editor of *The Pennsylvania Gazette*, the writer drolly noted that Great Britain's reason for this policy was for the "IMPROVEMENT *and* WELL PEOPLING of the Colonies." Mocking a supposed "tender *parental* Concern in our *Mother Country* for the *Welfare* of her Children," Americanus proposed that "Rattlesnakes" should be sent to Great Britain as a sign of filial piety or at least as a sign of trade: serpents for "*Human Serpents*" (P 4: 131–33). Franklin denigrated eighteenth-century environmental anthropological speculations by reasoning that rattlesnakes should be sent to England in exchange for convicts since "they may possibly change their Natures, if they were to change the Climate" (P 4: 132). Franklin makes plain here that the colonies are fully capable of having a voice in decisions made against their interest and would in fact decry such decisions.

Significantly, the satire closed by referring to the parental position of Great Britain: "Our *Mother* knows what is best for us" (P 4: 133). This satire throws into relief key assumptions of Enlightenment thinking as they would develop in the second half of the eighteenth century, namely, that of becoming mature. British actions cast the colonies into a position of being mere children who are not of age to make their own decisions or know what is in their best interest. In 1776 Thomas Paine and Thomas Jefferson would frame the transatlantic conflict in paternal terms in *Common Sense* and the Declaration of Independence, respectively.

The practice of transferring prisoners to the colonies still grated on Franklin twenty years later, as evident in his satire, "A Conversation on Slavery," published in London's *Public Advertiser* in 1770. Here Franklin portrayed an American colonist venting his opinion to an Englishman on the subject: "We have made Laws in several Colonies to prevent their Importation: These have been immediately repealed here, as being contrary to an Act of Parliament. We do not thank you for forcing them upon us. We look upon it as an unexampled Barbarity in your Government to empty your Gaols into our Settlements; and we resent it as the highest of Insults" (P 17: 42). In 1766 Franklin had drafted "A Mock Petition to the House of Commons" taking up the issue of felons being transported to the American colonies. He again visited the theme in a 1787 satire, "On Sending Felons to America." Franklin displayed his antipodal awareness of Britain's burgeoning colonial system by cynically recommending felons be shipped to the "promising new Colony of Botany Bay" (Smyth 9: 630).

By the 1770s, Franklin's satirical punches were being thrown against Great Britain with increasing intensity. On September 11, 1773, "Rules by Which a Great Empire may be Reduced to a Small One" appeared anonymously in *The Public Advertiser*. A sardonic piece, its invective couched in twenty recommendations – in order to "*increase their Disaffection*" – the means by which Great Britain was oppressing the colonies (P 20: 397).

The sarcastic advice is given, for example, that Britain should invest its military with unconstitutional powers, levy taxes indiscriminately, dissolve local assemblies arbitrarily, redress grievances at leisure or not at all and so forth. Less than two weeks later, "An Edict by the King of Prussia" was published in the same paper on September 22, 1773. The mild humor of Franklin's earlier satires is nowhere to be found. Franklin does not assume the voice of an educated country widow nor a poor young woman dragged before the courts for moral laxity. He assumes the voice of power by donning the mask of King Frederick the Great of Prussia, whose military prowess and stern attempts to modernize Prussia were well known. Franklin's Frederick lays claim to England, because England was once settled by ancient Germans. Considered outrageous in Franklin's day, the satire projects a vision that, a century later, the English themselves would employ to construct a national identity rooted in an Anglo-Saxon heritage.

By having Frederick lay claim to England, Franklin essentially set up the colonial conditions needed to attack Britain. The Edict, couched in paternalistic language and paraphrasing actual Parliamentary statutes, announced a set of incredibly burdensome economic duties and impositions, such as requiring all trade vessels to stop and pay duties at the port of Danzig or legislating that no machinery could be used without a tax. The Edict was entirely biased toward Prussia so as to damage severely the development, even in areas of clear superiority, of its newly annexed colony, thus clarifying that the colony existed merely to be exploited. The prime example is the production of wool. Prussia, trumpets the Edict, would strengthen its wool industry by preventing its colony from producing any kind of wool whatsoever. The Edict reaches toward inanity when Frederick sharply restricts the making of hats. The tone of the piece is condescending, and Frederick insults the colonies with small gestures of supposed grace that serve in effect to reinforce the position of the colonies' weakness. The Edict asserts that disobedience will be considered "HIGH TREASON" and result in transport from the colony to Prussia (P 20: 413–18).

The conclusion of the Edict introduces a twist. The narrative voice that framed it at the start now inserts a note designed to shock readers. The devastating effect is achieved as the reporter observes that England had enforced precisely such impositions on her colonies and yet professed that these were reasonable, owing to a sense of love and duty. Indeed, the paternalistic relationship is used against Britain as the question is asked how a parent could treat a child in "a Manner so *arbitrary* and TYRANNICAL!" (P 20: 418). Ending a satire with a calculated jab was nothing new for Franklin, but to end "Edict by the King of Prussia" on the word "tyrannical" was a well-timed syntactical detonation designed to cause as much political damage as possible. The rhetorical explosion would have been sharply felt in London, where English identity was constructed to see itself as a protector of liberty, a land that stood for the kinds of Enlightenment ideals that shielded people precisely from such abuse. Similarly, the 1775 satire, "Dialogue between Britain, France, Spain, Holland, Saxony and America," is laced with harsh words and scoffs at Great Britain's self-posturing as a wise "Mother Country." The posture is a façade: America and Britain are on the brink of war (P 21: 600–04).

After the American Revolution and the establishment of the United States of America, Franklin was at the zenith of his popularity. When he stepped down from public office, he was pulled in many directions, for he would be a formidable ally on the new national stage. It is telling, therefore, that Franklin's final satire, written just a few weeks before his death, took aim at a grave problem facing the new nation: slavery. Franklin had already been focused on slavery once, in "A Conversation on Slavery," published in London's *Public Advertiser*, January 30, 1770. Here he had employed a Scot to chastise slavery in the colonies: "if you really had a true Sense of Liberty, about which you make such a Pother, you would . . . not endure such a Thing as Slavery among you" (P 17: 37–44). Although Franklin would be drawn into political service during the years of the American Revolution, he turned to the question of slavery once again as soon as he was freed from his role at the Constitutional Convention. It might well have been the Convention's political compromise on slavery that motivated him to take a vigorous public position against slavery in the last months of his life.

In 1789 Franklin wrote to Congress as President of the Pennsylvania Society for Promoting the Abolition of Slavery and then petitioned Congress against slavery and the slave trade in the same capacity in 1790. He had taken a calculated religious tack in a 1788 letter to John Langdon, who had been New Hampshire's delegate to the Constitutional Convention in 1787, when he stated that "slavery was repugnant to the political principles and form of government lately adopted by citizens of the United States." In a rare jeremiad, Franklin pronounced that slavery would delay "the enjoyment of the blessings of peace and liberty, by drawing down, the displeasure of the great and impartial Ruler of the Universe upon our country."[11] Attacking once more the anthropological environmental suppositions that he had disapproved in "Rattlesnakes for Felons," he wrote and signed his own name to "An Address to the Public" (1789), lambasting slavery as "an atrocious debasement of human nature" that broke the bodies and minds of its victims (Smyth 10: 67).

Each of these anti-slavery positions, and more, can be detected in his final satire, "On the Slave Trade," published in *The Federal Gazette* on March

25, 1790, and signed "Historicus." Perhaps Franklin meant to imply that "a historian," thus history itself, would stand in judgment of the young nation if it, against its own founding principles, continued the odious practice of trading in slaves. Certainly Franklin overtly used contemporary history. The satire, framed as a letter to the editor of *The Federal Gazette*, refers to a Georgia congressman's speech exhorting against "meddling with the Affair of Slavery, or attempting to mend the Condition of the Slaves" (Smyth 10: 87). Historicus then relays a fictitious speech given by an Algerian, Sidi Mehemet Ibrahim, ostensibly to apprise the Congressman of its existence. The speech actually draws attention to the absurd assumptions and cruelty at work in refusing to abolish slavery. The writer explains that in 1687 Ibrahim argued against the petition and prayers of Erika, a sect of Islamic purists, who sought to abolish the practice of holding Christians as slaves.

The speech becomes a fruitful anachronism. By placing it one hundred years earlier, in the seventeenth century, and in a foreign country with a non-Christian religion, Franklin is able to attack arguments supporting slavery in his own day. Ibrahim's spurious arguments are essentially the same as those being made in Franklin's day against freeing slaves: socio-economic, anthropological, and religious. Ibrahim raises the specter of an impending economic collapse that he declares would occur if slavery were to be abolished. He further implies the threat of raised taxes by asking who would indemnify the slave holders. Next, he fosters fear by predicting societal upheaval as he insinuates that manumitted Christian slaves wandering the streets would be ostracized and dangerous. The conclusion of Ibrahim's speech results in a resolution that enslaving Christians is "at best *problematical*; but that it is the Interest of this State to continue the Practice, is clear" (Smyth 10: 91). Franklin here condemns slavery and reveals that at bottom immoral economic interests were prevailing over the enlightened principles on which the new nation was founded.

Franklin cleverly turns racial stereotypes on their head as Ibrahim avers that Christians are by nature too lazy to "labour without Compulsion, as well as too ignorant to establish a good government" (Smyth 10: 89). Certainly Enlightenment thinkers were not immune to such pseudo-scientific anthropological theories,[12] but the satire leaves no space to consider this a valid argument, for the average reader would find himself or herself implicated in the subverted stereotype. Ibrahim accuses the reformers of overzealousness and of having misinterpreted the holy book, the "Alcoran." Here Franklin cleverly alludes to the New Testament: "*Masters, treat your Slaves with kindness; Slaves, serve your Masters with Cheerfulness and Fidelity*" (Smyth 10: 90).[13] The satire confronts ahistorical and distorted readings of the Bible that would use it to support American slavery. Ibrahim explains that Christian slaves are at least exposed to the truth of Islam and that to send them home would be to send them back to spiritual darkness and maltreatment. Franklin is not exploring Islam but rather undermining the ludicrous assumption that the institution of slavery was a Christianizing endeavor that benefited African slaves. To seal his point, Franklin has Ibrahim continue that if the Christians were returned, they might end up embroiled in one of the many religious wars in which their co-religionists engage. Thus, Franklin at the end of his life returned to one of his most cherished values: religious tolerance.

This final satire exhibits the range of Franklin's talents that had emerged in the previous three quarters of a century. During that time Franklin's concerns evolved, and he gave expression to them, from using the voice of a Massachusetts country widow to that of an African Muslim. His aims in the Silence Dogood letters and his other early satires were engaged with local affairs, social justice, religious rigidity and hypocrisy, society's view of women, educational opportunities, corruption in city politics, superstition and religious fanaticism in the provinces, and the relationship between civic and religious authority. In these satires Franklin's growing literary skill in the satirical tradition is evident. In Boston and Philadelphia he developed his satirical techniques, including the use of pseudonyms, the simple and direct voice that blended humor and sobriety, and a rhetorical strategy that enabled readers to be at first detached but then drawn in so as to recognize their own intolerance. His rhetorical mastery provided readers with a sense that they were being given a voice in these satires through which they could vent their indignation.

By mid-century Franklin's satires focused on the transatlantic problems of empire. He put his finger on a paradox of British identity: the liberal Britain which wanted to nurture mutually beneficial ties in trade and enlightened politics with the colonies and an imperial Britain that behaved autocratically and sought one-sided economic and political advantages. Franklin's satires during this period provide unusually clear lines along which to trace his growing impatience and wariness with imperial Britain.

The republic that Franklin helped to forge provided him with a new challenge. He used the genre of satire that had served him so well over so many decades to turn the nation's attention to the abolition of slavery. He saw in the United States a similar moral and political paradox developing that he had reproached in enlightened and yet tyrannical Great Britain. How could a young nation that claimed as one of its founding postulates "that all men are created equal" suffer the continuation of the inhumane institution of slavery, so openly defying this noble ideal of equality? Franklin had not departed from the Enlightenment principles that had informed all of his satires. He had many weapons at his disposal with which to attack slaveholding and in the last weeks of his life he deployed them all, but in none was he more systematic about dismantling the arguments used to support slavery than in "On the Slave Trade." Satire was Franklin's final political act on the new national stage.[14]

Notes

1. Samuel Johnson, *A Dictionary of the English Language* (London: Strahan, 1755). *Encyclopaedia Britannica; or, a Dictionary of Arts and Sciences, Compiled upon a New Plan* (Edinburgh: Bell and Macfarquhar, 1771).

2. See *The Cambridge Companion to Roman Satire*, ed. Kirk Freudenburg (Cambridge University Press, 2005); Claude Rawson, *Satire and Sentiment 1660–1830* (Cambridge University Press, 1994); *Teaching Satire: Dryden to Pope*, ed. Hermann Josef Real (Heidelberg: Carl Winter, 1992).

3. On British satire, see Gary Dyer, *British Satire and the Politics of Style 1789–1832* (Cambridge University Press, 1997) and Howard D. Weinbrot, *Eighteenth-Century Satire: Essays on Text and Context from Dryden to Peter Pindar* (Cambridge University Press, 1988).

4. *The Works of John Dryden*, 20 vols., ed. Edward Niles Hooker, H. T. Swedenberg, Jr., *et al.*, Vol. 4, *Poems 1693–1696* (Berkeley: University of California Press, 1974), 80.

5. For information about Franklin's books, see *The Library of Benjamin Franklin*, compiled by Edwin Wolf 2nd and Kevin J. Hayes (Philadelphia: American Philosophical Society and Library Company of Philadelphia, 2006).

6. "Die Strahlen der Sonne, vertreiben die Nacht, vernichten der Heuchler erschlichene Macht" (II, 30). Wolfgang Amadeus Mozart, *Die Zauberflöte. KV 620. Eine große Oper in zwei Aufzügen. Libretto von Emanuel Schikaneder*, ed. and 'Nachwort' by Hans-Albrecht Koch (Stuttgart: Reclam, 1991), 69. All translations mine.

7. "*Aufklärung ist der Ausgang des Menschen aus seiner selbstverschuldeten Unmündigkeit. Unmündigkeit ist das Unvermögen, sich seines Verstandes ohne Leitung eines anderen zu bedienen.*" Immanuel Kant, "Beantwortung der Frage: Was ist Aufklärung?" in *Was ist Aufklärung? Thesen und Definitionen*, ed. Ehrhard Bahr (Stuttgart: Reclam, 1989), 9–17, quotation at 9.

8. In 1731 the London *Gentleman's Magazine* published an edited version of Franklin's satirical report along with two other accounts, thus reinforcing the reality of the report.

9. It was published numerous times, in various versions. The first extant publication was in a London newspaper, *The General Advertiser*, April 1747. Later that year it was published in *The Maryland Gazette*. I follow J. A. Leo Lemay in preferring the *Maryland Gazette* version of August 11, 1747. See Lemay's "The Text, Rhetorical Strategies, and Themes of 'The Speech of Miss Polly Baker,'" in *The Oldest Revolutionary: Essays on Benjamin Franklin*, ed. J. A. Leo Lemay (Philadelphia: University of Pennsylvania Press, 1976), 91–120.

10. *Ibid.*, 99.

11. *Benjamin Franklin: Writings*, ed. J. A. Leo Lemay (New York: Library of America, 1987), 1170.
12. See Emmanuel Chukwudi Eze, "Introduction," in *Race and Enlightenment: A Reader*, ed. Emmanuel Chukwudi Eze (Oxford: Blackwell, 1997).
13. Master-and-servant relationships are outlined in Ephesians 6. Interestingly, the syntax and rhythm of Franklin's allusion applies more to Ephesians 5, in which marital relationships are outlined: "Wives submit yourselves to your own husbands, as unto the Lord" and "Husbands, love your wives, even as Christ also loved the Church" (22 and 25). Could it be that Franklin here is making a subtle double allusion and double criticism not only of biblical interpretations supporting slavery, but of those that derived biblical sanction to treat women as slaves?
14. See Bruce Granger, *Political Satire in the American Revolution, 1763–1783* (Ithaca: Cornell University Press, 1960) and *Benjamin Franklin, an American Man of Letters* (Ithaca: Cornell University Press, 1964); and Verner W. Crane, *Benjamin Franklin's Letters to the Press, 1758–1775* (Chapel Hill: University of North Carolina Press, 1950).

4

DAVID S. SHIELDS

Franklin in the republic of letters

In October 1778, the German physician Johann Adolf Behrends wrote Benjamin Franklin the eighteenth-century equivalent of a fan letter. In Latin, the language of Europe's literati, the doctor confessed to admiring Franklin as a human trinity: "founder of the fatherland, doctor of the human race on the matter of the bodies' electrical energy and illustrious member of the Republic of letters" (P 27: 656). Readers today know Franklin well in his roles as founder and scientist, but his literary personality has been explored differently – as a rhetorician, a humorist, and a print journalist.[1] Franklin's contemporary reputation as a member of the international community of thinkers and writers then known as the "republic of letters" has received less attention, even though his contemporaries hailed Franklin as an important citizen of this border-crossing "republic."[2] His work enabling the conversation of the artistic and learned and his labors securing the liberty of the international exchange of ideas clearly mattered to Franklin's contemporaries. What, precisely, was the republic of letters? How did Franklin come to loom so large in its affairs?

The name "republic of letters" came into being on the Continent and in England in the later 1600s to designate an imagined community made up of authors and readers who recognized neither national boundaries nor religious affiliations in their quest for the free exchange of ideas, beliefs, and convictions.[3] This community, a republic, not a kingdom, was organized by an implied social contract among equals. Not heritage, nor wealth, nor civil rank affected one's status in the community. The merit of one's work, as measured by that work's ability to withstand reasonable critique, solely determined one's status. Since its development among Renaissance humanists, the transactions of the republic of letters were conducted predominantly in manuscript, in letters exchanged by learned persons and philosophers in Europe and America. These private communiqués conveyed the latest discoveries of scientific investigation, philosophical speculation, and political theory.[4]

Governments and churches entertained suspicions about the free exchange of ideas, particularly when communications touched upon the prerogatives of rule or religious dogmas. To insulate thinking and writing from governmental and ecclesiastical interventions, groups organized such "republics," havens for conversations and sponsors for publications. Some republics were face-to-face venues of colloquy, such as the academies of northern Europe, the clubs and coffeehouses of the British Empire, the conventicles of Reformed Christianity, the collegia of Italy. Others, such as the Royal Society, the American Philosophical Society, and the Royal Society for the Encouragement of Arts, Manufactures, and Commerce, added to such face-to-face exchanges formal correspondence networks to communicate and receive findings from around the world. Still others comprised the networks of printers, booksellers, and readers of print.

The world of print did not coincide with the republic of letters in the eighteenth century. Much printed matter avoided the spirit of curiosity and creativity that characterized the communications of the republic of letters. Religious sectarian controversy, Grub Street humor, pornography and vulgar amusement, the vast literature of practical instruction, piety, and the equally ample body of official proclamations, laws, court findings, and decrees – all failed to express the interests of the republic of letters. And most news (the advertising, reports, public records, and commercial letters that filled gazette pages) was of little interest to those who communicated through the channels opened by their inclusion in the world of the republic of letters.

To understand how Franklin rose to eminence in the republic of letters, we must chart his work in America and Europe creating or participating in those domains upon which the republic's communications depended: libraries, clubs, learned societies, and associations. Franklin cultivated modes of communication and persuasion favored by the republic of letters – conversation, wit, and the familiar letter – in preference to the rhetorical and oratorical forms that dominated halls of government and the houses of religion. He increasingly directed the press to publicize the findings of the republic's free inquiries. Michael Warner's influential account of Franklin as a man of letters has shown how print saturated Franklin's literary sensibility.[5] This account will show how institutions besides the press shaped Franklin's sense of the republic of letters.

Franklin began his printing career apprenticed to a newspaper engaged in a Grub Street attack on scientific innovation. Whatever scientific world of letters existed in New England during the second decade of the eighteenth century circulated around Rev. Increase Mather (founder of the first American club devoted to scientific investigation) and his son Rev. Cotton

Mather (a member of the Royal Society and correspondent with many of the learned in Europe and America). *The New-England Courant*, edited by Franklin's older brother and pressmaster, James Franklin, lambasted inoculation, the progressive medical smallpox treatment that Cotton Mather championed in Boston. A cabal of pro-Anglican, anti-new charter, anti-science merchants and churchmen bankrolled James Franklin's paper.[6] The younger Franklin drank deeply of the *Courant*'s opposition politics and his older brother's whiggishness, but he did not imbibe the anti-experimental, anti-philosophical traditionalism of its early contributors.

If James Franklin's press office had any enduring influence upon Benjamin's intellectual formation, it came from the collection of books maintained there and the library of *The New-England Courant*'s contributor, merchant Matthew Adams, who permitted the younger Franklin free access to his books. Libraries shaped Franklin's sense of the literary world.[7] Adams's library, a collection largely of writings in English, contained "polite learning" (including Greek and Roman classics translated into English), useful knowledge, political theory, history, commercial treatises, *belles lettres*, and wit – all elements that Franklin found essential to his self-education. Adams's collection informed the young Franklin's ambition to gather a personal library.

Benjamin Franklin understood that his early reading would pave the way for his future success. For his club of acquaintances, the Junto in Philadelphia, a central element of their program of mutual betterment was sharing all books that members possessed. This clubbing of literary holdings became the genesis for North America's first subscription library, the Library Company of Philadelphia, chartered in 1731 by fifty young men contributing forty shillings each for books purchases. Other organizations arising from the Junto (the American Philosophical Society and the Academy of Philadelphia) would also have libraries. The development of Franklin's formidable personal library dated from his residency in England as agent for Pennsylvania and Britain's other middle seaboard colonies in the 1760s. Franklin haunted the booksellers' stalls in London and the library auctions of estates to build a collection that upon his return home would rank among the great individual libraries in North America.[8] Its contents reflected his own decidedly non-academic understanding of Enlightenment: the new literature of science abounded, as did works on travel, political history and theory, travel and geography, commerce, and *belles lettres*. Libraries in Franklin's view equipped the common people with the information and skills of thought and argument necessary for them to project their interests in the world. Late in life, he observed that the subscription libraries formed in imitation of the Library Company of Philadelphia "have improved the general Conversations of Americans, made the common Tradesmen and Farmers as intelligent as most Gentlemen from other Countries, and perhaps have contributed in some degree to the Stand so generally made throughout the Colonies in Defence of their Privileges" (A, NCE 57). Libraries enabled conversations.

For Franklin, knowledge optimally came about through communicative partnership and exchange. Conversation accomplished this, because interactive talk moved participants away from received opinions (as those offered in print) to a new, shared opinion. In an early essay, under the pseudonym Veridicus, Franklin wrote, "As a *pertinacious Obstinacy* in Opinion, and confident *Self-Sufficiency*, is possibly one of the greatest Vices, as well as Weaknesses, that the human Mind is capable of; so on the contrary a Readiness to give up a *loved Opinion*, upon due Conviction, is as great a Glory, as well as Happiness, as we are here capable of attaining."[9] For an opinion to become public opinion, or for it to become conviction, or for it to take on the integrity of knowledge or a communal value, it had to be adjusted to its most durable and impersonal form. Conversation, aiding in creating knowledge or forming values, enabled people to participate in this process of adjustment toward durability. The lecture, the sermon, and all forms of face-to-face hierarchical instruction seemed to Franklin to avoid enlisting people in the creation of mutual understanding and of new forms of knowledge. Such one-sided articulations forced people to accept established truisms, unexamined claims that served and preserved the old order.

While Franklin wholeheartedly embraced conversation as a means of improving one's intelligence, he regarded oratory more circumspectly, deeming it a useful human art that had the potential for harm. Conversation served communication among equals in the republic of letters; oratory and forensic rhetoric served authority in the unequal relations between church and state and the people they governed. Franklin schooled himself and his fellows in the art of oral persuasion, because as public men they would have to deal with authorities. Position papers enhanced the self-improvement agenda of the Junto, forcing members to organize thoughts and gain experience voicing their ideas among others. Franklin knew from reading history the influence of oratorical performance on public deliberations. He personally witnessed the power of the century's most potent religious orator, George Whitefield, and was fascinated not by Whitefield's calls for repentance and faith but by the expressive precision and force of Whitefield's speaking. Nevertheless, Franklin saw the problem that such eloquence created: demagogues might use it to gain power over people.

In his *Proposals Relating to the Education of Youth in Pensilvania* (1749), he recommended the teaching of History, because it would show "the wonderful Effects of ORATORY, in governing, turning and leading great Bodies of Mankind, Armies, Cities, Nations" (P 3: 412). Students would not learn history by listening to a professor expatiating rhetorically on the subject or parsing the most famous Latin and Greek orations. Rather, based on historical study, "Questions of Right and Wrong, Justice and Injustice, will naturally arise, and may be put to Youth, which they may debate in Conversation and in Writing" (P 3: 413). Franklin conceived oratory as a means to persuade people to action rather than to alter belief or understanding. Conversing and writing taught one the arts of thinking and communicating. What kind of writing? "Writing Letters to each other" (P 3: 408).

When we turn to Franklin's writings, we see little of the formal forensic rhetoric taught in schools. His memoirs document his abandonment of methods of forceful assertion and concerted argument in favor of an equivocal, Socratic method. His repeated employment of humor, analogy, and burlesque reveals that Franklin had absorbed a new theory of persuasion advanced by the third Earl of Shaftesbury in *Sensus Communis, an Essay on the Freedom of Wit and Humor* (1709), written as a letter to a friend.[10] Shaftesbury proposed that raillery was essential to forming public opinion, for it forced speakers to polish and restructure remarks to withstand mockery. Opinions that survived such scrutiny were strong enough to venture beyond the conversation of mocking friends to become a public idea. Spoken wit also created new communities, for spontaneous laughter revealed to a speaker the shared values among one's listeners, thus discovering "sensus communis."

Shaftesbury's picture of how to create new communities of opinion was an apt description of the intellectual function of the new world of clubs and private societies that had formed in the urban centers of Europe. In the privacy of club conversation, one obtained perfect liberty among friends. Only where liberty enjoyed protections could raillery perform its refining art on conversation in a clash of ideas and views. Benjamin Franklin's friendly club, the Junto, was "the best School of Philosophy, Morals and Politics that then existed in the Province" (A, NCE 48). Its requirement that members speak to a topic of common interest each session instilled in them "better habits of Conversation" (A, NCE 48). The Junto was a secret institution meeting in private homes, not public places. Its members created other secret clubs by which the sentiments of the Junto might be spread, increasing its influence.

Within the republic of letters, the great model for networking among secret fraternities was the Freemasons. Franklin joined the St. John's Lodge in Philadelphia sometime in the winter of 1730, reprinted *The Constitutions of the Free-Masons* in 1734, and was elected Grand Master of his lodge later that year. Participation in Freemasonry gave its members experience in operating in self-governing mini-republics, with constitutions, laws, elections, representatives, and civil ceremonies. This was particularly the case with the "modern" lodges such as Franklin's that operated outside the hierarchical framework of the "Antient" order more typical of European fraternities.[11] Freemasonry had a cultural mythology, an ethical program, and a projecting spirit to reform society at large through good works. It self-consciously cultivated both esoteric (secret among the brotherhood) and exoteric (public-oriented) activities. What was projected in secret would remake the public.

Like Freemasonry, the republic of letters had an ambiguous relationship to the public life of nation states. On one hand, it sought to be an insulated realm, inconspicuous to the surveillance and coercion of governments and churches. Yet it sought to scrutinize, criticize, and even renovate public life, whether the manners of the people, the practice of religion, or the policies of state administration. Quite literally, there was duplicity in the republic of letters regarding public relations: face-to-face exchanges took place in private societies protected by contractually maintained secrecy. Written exchanges and printed communications employed other protections.

The postal system operating throughout the imperial world from the mid-seventeenth century was notoriously porous.[12] Letters dispatched by sea captains, postal carriers, and coachmen were routinely opened and inspected for intelligence, sedition, or blasphemy. While the majority of postal traffic treated official matters or commerce, an increasing proportion of scientific and philosophical materials began circulating at the beginning of the eighteenth century. A new public, learned role emerged – the transactioneer, a provincial *savant* who sent letter-reports to the Royal Society, aiming to have the reports included in the volumes of the Society's *Transactions*. Franklin's friend and fellow Junto member, Joseph Brientnall, for instance, faithfully recorded his observations, even to the extent of communicating to London the experience of his own physical degradation and suicidal depression from a poisonous snake bite in 1746. Letters became a feature of cultural commerce among learned people.

Franklin was appointed Postmaster of Philadelphia in 1737. Under his leadership, Franklin sought to make the mails more secure and efficient. Franklin grasped that speed of communication was essential to the creation of a strong postal service. He improved the 1,600 miles of post roads, instituted round-the-clock relays of riders carrying regulation post lanterns, and established a weekly Philadelphia-to-Boston run of a mail coach.[13] Such efforts brought him the appointment as Deputy Postmaster General of the American colonies in 1753. As postmaster, Franklin possessed a franking privilege, so his own communications circulated the system gratis until the 1760s. This meant his newspaper, the newspapers for which he was a financial backer, his public pamphlets, his correspondence, and his magazines traveled free of postal charges.

Franklin was not above opening a letter, if it promised to be full of political matter, trade secrets, or privy intelligence on the arrivals of sellers and buyers. But he held a fundamental regard for the system that enabled the exchange of letters. From an early age, he had participated in a system of written conversation among inquiring persons. James Logan, the learned secretary of the Penn Proprietors, was his model correspondent. A bibliophile, classicist, and mathematician, Logan combined a genuine curiosity about the world he inhabited with an ambition to master politics, law, commerce, and mathematics. He corresponded with the young Franklin, and even entrusted his translation of Seneca's *Moral Distichs* to Franklin for printing – the first work of polite learning to issue from Franklin's press. Logan recommended books to the Library Company that the Junto had founded. And Logan introduced Franklin to men who became central correspondents in his scientific inquiries: Cadwallader Colden of New York, with whom Franklin speculated about how the rotational motion of the earth might influence maritime transits of shipping in the Atlantic; Rev. Jared Eliot, a New England agriculturalist who shared Franklin's interest in tracking hurricanes; Peter Collinson, London merchant and naturalist with whom Franklin shared mathematical magic squares and scientific information. Logan became an important access point to the republic of letters that Franklin was seeking to join, and Logan's friendships among the learned, especially the scientific community, would prove invaluable to his younger peer.

Franklin had a particular fascination with weather and attempted to theorize meteorological phenomena in terms of the physics of natural forces through the 1740s. Thunder storms turned Franklin's mind to that subject that would make him a world celebrity, a celebrity both within and beyond the republic of letters he was joining, in the early 1750s: electricity. Franklin became curious about electricity after seeing in Boston some exhibitions of the properties of static electricity in 1746. Peter Collinson, a patron of the Philadelphia Library Company, sent Franklin an electricity tube. Preoccupied with the tube, he reported his experiments and findings to Collinson, who read the letters before the Royal Society in London. When Collinson gathered the letters together, creating the first part of Franklin's *Experiments and Observations on Electricity* (1751), Franklin's views reached more public scrutiny. Translation of the work into French led to widespread testing of his suppositions on the Continent. As with all scientific novelties, the assertions gave rise to disputation, but trials supported Franklin's conclusions, and his book inaugurated consensus about the nature of electricity. The Royal Society awarded Franklin a Copley medal (1753) for the improvement of natural knowledge and elected him a fellow (1756). He would also be elected to membership in the Royal Academy of Sciences in Paris, the Royal Society in Göttingen, and the Batavian Society in Holland. And Franklin would become President of the American Philosophical Society.

While learned and scientific societies were cosmopolitan, accepting correspondents from throughout the western world, they grew increasingly exclusive in membership during Franklin's lifetime. In 1731, the Royal Society stipulated that candidates for membership be proposed in writing and endorsed by signatures of existing members. Connection with the established network of scientists became a practical requisite for someone's admission. Critical judgment was needed because the domain known as natural philosophy (i.e., scientific knowledge) was changing. The practice of natural philosophy had become popular among the genteel classes and among aspiring citizens, and volunteer savants sprouted in the big cities of North America and Europe, promoting questionable medicine, physics, and natural inquiry. As part of its Charter, the Royal Society had been granted permission to publish its findings. Before the end of the seventeenth century, the Society published its *Proceedings* and *Transactions*. Publication by a constituted scientific society became a certification of the worthiness of one's findings. While letter-writing among the networks of inquirers enabled the refinement and collaborative expansion of investigations, scientific work increasingly sought a summary articulation in print by a reputable press. When the American Philosophical Society reorganized itself in 1767 after a hiatus of twenty years, Franklin, its President, urged the gathering and printing of transactions. This commenced in 1771.

Critical colloquy was one of the hallmarks of the republic of letters. It presumed that the exchange and critique of a community of interested persons might improve thoughts, morals, expressions, and performances. Whether in philosophy, science, or *belles lettres*, the critical response sought truth by the application of standards, rules, and methods. While wit and raillery might give this process some sharpness and a touch of malice, the spirit of this critical conversation was ameliorative. Thus, it differed drastically from that spirit of malediction, factional zeal, and righteous assertion that typified the products of Grub Street.

In the cultural geography of the West at the beginning of the eighteenth century, Grub Street was that anarchic literary state against which the republic of letters defined itself. Named for the impoverished area of London called Moorfields, where clusters of poor scribblers congregated, Grub Street was known in Franklin's day as both the location in London and the kind of writing emanating from that location – hack writing that circulated on the margins of what was conceived as respectable literature. Historically, Grub Street had grown powerful because of the press, which burgeoned after the 1690s collapse of the licensing laws. Grub Street arose as a powerful entity, because when the Glorious Revolution dispossessed a generation of Tory college men from hopes of place and fortune, a handful of enterprising printers and booksellers reckoned a market could be made for books. Numerous college-trained writers found work, called "hack" work even then, writing for general readers.[14] These writers and booksellers had a radically experimental attitude about finding what sold, and they published anything from pornography to dictionaries designed to appeal to women. Anyone who made his or her living by the press in the first decades of the eighteenth century grasped the findings of Grub Street: stories about crime, natural prodigies, natural and induced disasters, royalty, wars, and fantastic colonial splendors in foreign lands generated sales.

Benjamin Franklin began his long career as published writer with two ballads in the Grub Street mode, "The Taking of Teach or Blackbeard the Pirate" and "The Light House Tragedy." Although he soon adopted the essays of Joseph Addison and Richard Steele's journal, *The Spectator* (1711–12, 1714), as his model for addressing common readers, embracing the literary ideal of politeness that both amused and instructed, Franklin always retained an ability to speak in Grub Street's lurid tones. His newspaper, *The Pennsylvania Gazette* (which Franklin and Hugh Meredith took over from Samuel Keimer in 1729), for all its interest as a repository of Franklin's essays and burlesques, was too local, too driven by occasion, too grubby, and too involved in the daily grind of common commerce to qualify fully as a vehicle for the republic of letters. This realization drove Franklin's various efforts to create magazines with Continental reference and readership and a cosmopolitan standard of literary accomplishment. *The General Magazine* (1740–41) in its name declared its ambition for a larger scope and broader readership. In print, the magazine became the regular face of the republic of letters.

Grub Street gave Franklin one important dimension of self-projection that he would tactically import into the republic of letters – a promiscuous sense of multiple characters, taken on as personae, when parading in print. From his first admonitions to Boston in the guise of Silence Dogood to his final impersonation as Islamic Prince Sidi Mehemet Ibrahim urging the enslavement of Christians in 1790, Franklin inhabited a stupefyingly various assortment of identities. The republic of letters tended to favor one's adopting an alter-ego, whether neoclassical or allegorical, in print or manuscript, and it also favored the presentation of one's own name if one wished to address the learned world. Richard Saunders was as close as Franklin got to an enduring alter-ego.

When Franklin went to England as agent of Pennsylvania and other colonies in 1757, he established his credentials in the polite world by connecting with the London clubs. He dined with the scientists of the Monday Club at the George and Vulture, and with the Club of Honest Whigs on Tuesday. He joined the Society of Arts, earned election to the Royal Society, and became a particularly useful member of a philanthropic organization, the Associates of Dr. Bray. He was known in his proper person, as a scientific celebrity and a politician. That region of the republic of letters that constituted the market for books during the course of the eighteenth century put an increasing premium on the celebrity of authors. John Tillotson, John Dryden, Alexander Pope, Isaac Watts, Joseph Addison, James Thomson, Bishop Berkeley, Jonathan Swift, Samuel Johnson – all were known as "authors." They emerged from behind the masks they had first worn in print. By mid-century, booksellers tended to feature named authors, leaving pseudonymous writers concentrated in the areas of political and religious controversy and of gallant verse and periodical politeness. Franklin's later works on electricity, his *Supplemental Observations* (1753) and *New Experiments and Observations* (1754), had both been published in London under his own name, as were their subsequent editions. Because they discussed the lightning rod as a practical means of protecting dwellings and controlling electrical discharges from heaven, these books inspired intense popular interest and generated a demand for multiple editions. When St. Andrews University awarded Franklin an honorary doctorate in 1759, his celebrity persona in Europe became "Dr. Franklin."

Yet Franklin found it necessary to retain a series of pseudonyms in his efforts to critique culture and politics, and his knowledge of Grub Street methods served him well in these years. The crisis over the Stamp Act, which was designed to tax any productions of or using paper, prompted Franklin to enter into print under various guises. Styling himself "Pacificus," "N. N.," "Americanus," "F. B.," "A Friend to Both Countries," "OLD ENGLAND in its senses," and with an eye to his audience, Franklin produced a series of fables, burlesques, reports, and serious essays for several London newspapers, including *The Public Advertiser*, *The London Chronicle*, and *The Gazetteer and New Daily Advertiser*. In the 1760s, the London papers had called into being readerships organized by political inclination. The papers made apparent their inclinations by the letters from correspondents they chose to publish. The "advertiser" papers such as *The Public Advertiser* and *The Gazetteer and New Daily Advertiser*, because they ran on proceeds from advertisements rather than on subscriptions or government subventions, were the most vocally independent of the Tory regime. They featured letters to the press expressing sympathy, such as the letters of *Junius*. These papers would become Franklin's favorite venues for coming before the English public. Moderate papers such as the *Morning Chronicle* featured communications on all sides of an issue. He avoided appearing in them. But he appeared repeatedly in the most open-minded of the Tory sheets. *The London Chronicle* had the greatest literary reputation of any of the metropolitan gazettes during the 1760s. Samuel Johnson had written the introduction of the first issue in January 1757. Published by J. Wilkie at the rear of the Chapter-House, the center of English print culture, where all the newspaper publishers drank and met in their informal club, the Wittengamot, the *Chronicle* combined extracts of governmental documents copied from the *The London Gazette*, original essays, several columns of foreign news, poetry, advertisements, and other notices. Eight pages, it issued three times a week, costing twopence halfpenny per paper. When Franklin wanted to address the mind of British officialdom he floated his pieces in *The London Chronicle*. In print, Franklin, the American agent, performed in a mode different from Dr. Franklin, the *savant*. A few of his British friends – David Hume, Joseph Priestley, but not Lord Kames – were possibly privy to the fact that he projected both identities in public papers.

In 1776 Benjamin Franklin was appointed Commissioner to France by the Revolutionary Congress of the United States. Retiring to the Parisian suburb of Passy, he secured a press, and gained entrée into the company of Madame Brillon de Jouy, the comtesse d'Houdetot, and Madame Helvétius. Having mastered all the other roles common in the republic of letters, Franklin in his seniority tackled the improbable persona of a *gallant*. In his "bagatelles" (the word refers to a "light composition," typically in music, but Franklin's were light pieces) addressed to Madame Brillon, Franklin simultaneously played philosopher, wit, and flirt, approximating the sophisticated and mercurial repartee of polite French drawing rooms.

In some ways, the French salon epitomized the republic of letters in the eighteenth-century Atlantic world, bringing together in exquisite tension men and women, print and conversation, sense and wit, philosophy and amusement. By the 1770s the salons had become so invested in Rousseau's doctrines of simplicity and common humanity that the assembly was no longer comprised of the nobility and gentility alone. Franklin could play at being a Quaker, a natural philosopher, a tradesman turned citizen of the world. In this world, Franklin was a celebrity of the first magnitude, adept at the range of performances that made him appear important in every register of conversation. Some, including John Adams, rankled at Franklin's fame and his variety of performances and self-projections. Adams, however, could never get beyond the more traditional ideal, common in British North American culture, wherein individual character was best expressed in one's offering to the world a stable and consistent set of virtues. Franklin's long immersion in an increasingly complicated transatlantic republic of letters had taught him to play at being "Franklin," to put aside character for personality (or perhaps more precisely, personalities).

Madame Helvétius performed another benefit to Franklin besides serving as his muse. She introduced him to the company of the Freemasonic Lodge, the so-called "lodge of the nine sisters" (the muses) – Les Neuf Sœurs – an international assembly of scientists, philosophers, and literati.[15] One had to have published a work of learning or created a masterwork in the arts as a precondition of membership. This lodge attempted to constitute "Solomon's House," a universal gathering of the learned and the creative. Enrolled in 1778, Franklin was elevated to the directorship of the Lodge's educational arm, La Musée de Paris, a public institution. He initiated a publishing group, the Société Apollonienne, in this athenaeum, printing lectures and tracts delivered in the series of public readings. Presiding over the Musée for three years, Franklin sponsored Thomas Jefferson's admission. In Paris, Franklin, as a member of Les Neuf Sœurs, stood at the center – the Solomon of Solomon's House – of the republic of letters, where conversation and print, science, art, and religious speculation flourished, in the company of the world's savants.

Too often the republic of letters has been construed as a realm constituted in and by print. But the republic, in Franklin's day, was something more. Too emphatically scholars have bound Franklin to his own and his partners' printing presses up and down the Atlantic seaboard. Franklin had other affiliations and roles. Master of the posts, brilliant correspondent, drawing-room wit, clubman, political committeeman, scientific transactioneer, projector, philosopher, and yes, the most effective political satirist publishing in the English-speaking world during the Revolutionary era, Franklin did not, as some have claimed, make the republic of letters. It existed before he came of age and prospered in places that he never visited or influenced as printer or bookseller. Franklin did, however, create certain of its domains in America, and no American in the eighteenth century inhabited the republic of letters more extensively.

Notes

1. James Green and Peter Stallybrass, *Benjamin Franklin, Writer and Printer* (Newcastle, DE: Oak Knoll Press, 2006).
2. Ezra Stiles, President of Yale College, spoke of Franklin as a member of the republic of letters, as did Rev. Abiel Holmes, who solicited Franklin's opinions

regarding the creation of a library. See their unpublished letters: Stiles, December 4, 1786, and Holmes, February 16, 1789: Papers of Benjamin Franklin and Packard Humanities Institute, "republic of letters," at http://franklinpapers.org/franklin/framedVolumes.jsp.

3. Dena Goodman, *The Republic of Letters: A Cultural History of the French Enlightenment* (Cornell University Press, 1996), 15–23.

4. H. J. M. Nellen, "In Strict Confidence: Grotius' Correspondence with his Socinian Friends," in *Self-Presentation and Social Identification: The Rhetoric and Pragmatics of Letter Writing in Early Modern Times*, ed. Toon van Houdt, *et al.* (Leuven and Brussels: Leuven University Press, 2002), 290–304.

5. Michael Warner, *The Letters of the Republic: Publication and the Public Sphere in Eighteenth-Century America* (1990; Cambridge, MA: Harvard University Press, 2006), 73–96.

6. Carolyn Garrett Cline, "The Hell-Fire Club: A Study of the Men Who Founded the *New-England Courant* and the Inoculation Dispute They Fathered" (MA Thesis, Indiana University, 1976). On the controversy, see Carla Mulford, "Pox and 'Hell-Fire': Boston's Smallpox Controversy, the New Science, and Early Modern Liberalism," in *Periodical Literature in Eighteenth-Century America*, ed. Mark L. Kamrath and Sharon M. Harris (Knoxville: University of Tennessee Press, 2005), 7–27.

7. Margaret Barton Korty, *Benjamin Franklin and Eighteenth-Century American Libraries* (Philadelphia, PA: American Philosophical Society, 1965), 5–15.

8. See Edwin Wolf 2nd and Kevin J. Hayes, *The Library of Benjamin Franklin* (Philadelphia: American Philosophical Society and Library Company of Philadelphia, 2006).

9. Veridicus [Benjamin Franklin], *Pennsylvania Gazette* (March 27, 1735). In *Franklin: Writings*, ed. J. A. Leo Lemay (New York: Library of America, 1987), 253.

10. See David S. Shields, *Civil Tongues and Polite Letters in British America* (Chapel Hill: North Carolina University Press, 1997), 23–44.

11. Stephen C. Bullock, *Revolutionary Brotherhood: Freemasonry and the Transformation of the American Social Order, 1730–1840* (Chapel Hill: University of North Carolina Press for the Omohundro Institute of Early American History and Culture, 1998), 52–76.

12. Alex L. ter Braake, *The Posted Letter in Colonial and Revolutionary America* (State College, PA: American Philatelic Research Library, 1975), B1–47.

13. William Smith, "The Colonial Post Office," *American Historical Review* 21 (1916): 258–75.

14. Philip Pinkus, *Grub St. Stripped Bare: The Scandalous Lives and Pornographic Works of the Original Grub Street Writers* (London: Constable, 1968), 23–41.

15. Nicholas Hans, "UNESCO of the Eighteenth Century: La Loge de Neuf Sœurs and Its Venerable Master, Benjamin Franklin," *Proceedings of the American Philosophical Society* 97, v (October 1953): 516–21.

5

JOYCE E. CHAPLIN

Benjamin Franklin's natural philosophy

Seven years before he died, Franklin confided a regret to his friend and fellow naturalist Joseph Banks. "I begin to be almost sorry I was born so soon," the elderly American wrote, "since I cannot have the happiness of knowing what will be known 100 years hence" (Smyth 9: 74–75). Would knowledge of the future have made Franklin happy? The hundred years that followed Franklin's 1783 letter to Banks would to a large extent render obsolete Franklin's reputation as a natural philosopher. Franklin seems to prefigure modern scientists, meaning people who (unlike him) make a living by working within a specialized branch of science. In his own time, however, he was a philosopher, a person who did not support himself through his work in science and whose wisdom crossed multiple social, intellectual, and political borders. As a natural philosopher, Franklin had authority in all matters, including political ones. That was crucial to his personal fame and to the authority he would bring to the American War for Independence from Great Britain. Yet even during his life, Franklin witnessed transformations in natural philosophy that would, after his death, make it into the professionalized and specialized fields of modern science.

At the start of Franklin's life, natural philosophy belonged to a unified field of philosophy covering all topics; by the end of his life, most of those who studied the sciences no longer thought of themselves as contributing to a field of knowledge that included theology, moral philosophy, and natural philosophy. Franklin himself aided the shift by working in experimental science, which was fast becoming a central component of modern science. He would be celebrated as a philosopher in the old sense, yet admired as an innovator in the new science of experimentation. Only someone who was active in the sciences when he was, at mid-century, could have won compliments for both. Timing was everything.

Becoming a philosopher

For someone who would eventually be celebrated as a natural philosopher, Franklin's approach to the sciences was remarkably elliptical and sketchy. Franklin would have only two years of formal schooling, which ceased when he was ten (A 52–53). Not for him the learned and Latinate culture that still inflected natural philosophy and that he might have learned at Harvard College, to which his father had once aspired to send him. He was instead largely self-taught and remained keenly aware that he was so. As an adult, he would be both careful not to give offense by becoming too argumentative yet also defiantly iconoclastic, unwilling to conform to certain conventions about the role of the natural philosopher.[1]

It is clear that Franklin had, in his Boston youth, read everything he could get his hands on, from popular periodicals to self-help literature. He had learned arithmetic during his brief time at school and used books on navigation to teach himself some geometry (A 63–64). But he had no grounding in higher mathematics, a significant mark of his distance from university-trained natural philosophers.[2]

Nor did Franklin initially accept the received pieties of natural philosophy. Most men of science insisted on their religious orthodoxy and even proclaimed that their study of nature revered the divine Creation. Troubled by what he perceived as the growing irreligion of his day, chemical experimenter (and Christian evangelizer) Robert Boyle had endowed a series of London lectures to assure listeners of God's creative force over nature. Franklin read some of the published lectures, around age fifteen, but they failed to convince him. "It happened that they wrought an Effect on me quite contrary to what was intended," he later confessed. Rather than dissuade him from a Deism that queried the truth of divine revelation, the lectures made him into "a thorough Deist" (A 114–15).

Franklin later regretted his irreligion (he became a great proponent of the idea that the physical creation was important evidence of a Prime Mover) and began to take natural philosophy more seriously. As a young printer in London in the 1720s, he was so dazzled by Isaac Newton's fame that he hoped to be introduced to him by an acquaintance. And while in London, Franklin met and tried to impress Hans Sloane, a man of science who later became president of the Royal Society of London. Somehow, Franklin had already discovered that learned societies, including the Royal Society, had been established as alternatives to universities and welcomed information from ordinary people, including American colonists and the self-taught.[3]

By this time, Franklin had the confidence to try his hand at natural history. While not perfectly distinct from natural philosophy, which sought to explain the causes of things, natural history tended to be descriptive rather than analytic, and it tended to focus on living nature rather than inanimate matter. Franklin's first extant writings on the natural world were parts of a journal he kept at sea, when returning to America from England in 1726 (P 1: 72–99). A set of close observations of the Atlantic Ocean and its forms of life, the journal broke no new ground yet showed Franklin's keen eye for the details of the natural world and his lively manner of writing up those details.[4]

After he had returned to America and was settled in Philadelphia from 1726 onward, Franklin read his way further into the sciences. He helped to form a reading group for young working men, the Junto, which was the foundation for the Library Company of Philadelphia (A 116–18, 130). Both the Junto and the Library Company had books on natural philosophy, though Franklin discovered an even better trove in the private library of James Logan, a wealthy and learned Philadelphian. It is likely that Logan's books, and Logan's conversation, offered Franklin his first opportunities to explore serious work in science. The two men shared an interest in optics, for example, and Franklin was one of a very few to whom Logan showed drafts of his work in the sciences, some of it eventually published in London and Leiden.[5]

The first thing that Franklin did with his reading was to recommend it to others. He was an important promulgator of science, not least because he was always looking for material to round out his newspaper, *The Pennsylvania Gazette,* and his almanac, *Poor Richard* (after 1748, *Poor Richard Improved,* expanded by twelve pages). Franklin used the paper mostly to publish items relating to health, including some of his early work on political arithmetic, the science of human population, what we would now call demography and epidemiology. And he was careful in his newspaper and other publications never to offend any individual person or political group, knowing that his success as a printer depended on appealing to all. His ruthless self-discipline in this regard would eventually affect the way in which he framed his claims in natural philosophy.[6]

If Franklin's newspaper hinted at his eventual scientific style, his almanacs indicated his assumptions about what science was. Above all, he assured his readers (and himself) that advances in natural philosophy were the glories of the modern age. He reprinted verses in *Poor Richard Improved* for 1756 (P 6: 327) that said as much:

> How long did Ptolomy's dark Riddle spread
> With Doubts deep puzzling each scholastic Head,
> Till, like the Theban wise in Story fam'd,
> Copernicus that Sphynxian Monster sham'd.

Franklin here embraced and celebrated the idea that the ancient philosophers, including Ptolemy, who had once supplied the foundation for natural philosophy, had been routed. The sixteenth-century Polish astronomer
Copernicus had challenged the Ptolemaic worldview, insisting that the earth
revolved around the sun, not vice versa.

The verses were a shorthand way to designate progress and they endorsed
a more general shift away from the Aristotelian natural philosophy that had
reigned in the middle ages, particularly at the schools or universities. The
"scholastic Heads," as *Poor Richard* described them, had sought, above
all, to comprehend the causes and essences of things. They did so through
reason, particularly logical deduction, which proceeded through syllogisms
from an observed phenomenon to a statement about the essential causes
that underlay the phenomenon. Fields such as mathematics and astronomy
were regarded as lesser skills, because they dealt only with the external and
quantifiable characteristics of material things, not their essences.

Scholastic natural philosophy was never a stable or undisputed tradition, but it underwent new criticism during the sixteenth and seventeenth
centuries, as Franklin recognized when he told his readers that Copernicus
had shamed Ptolemy's "Sphynxian Monster." Franklin admired the British
philosophers who had ridiculed Scholasticism, including Francis Bacon,
"The great deliverer he! Who from the gloom / Of cloister'd monks, and
jargon-teaching schools, / Led forth the true Philosophy" (P 3: 339). These
verses, reproduced in *Poor Richard Improved* for 1749, give the standard
criticism that universities (which grew out of monasteries) were sites of
murky dispute to which the new learned societies (like the Royal Society
of London) were alternatives. The poetry also expresses the suspicion that
the old natural philosophy, by pondering hidden forces that shaped matter,
could not establish anything remotely true.[7]

Although many critics of Scholasticism actually retained some elements
of the Aristotelian tradition, they nonetheless sought theories of nature that
required no occult forces. Without denying the existence of extra-material
entities, such as the human soul, natural philosophers assumed that matter
itself was inert. For that reason, René Descartes had made his famous distinction between mind and matter. Like the Schoolmen, however, Descartes proceeded rationally, through logical deductions. Like them, as well, he assumed
that natural philosophy was part of a larger philosophical endeavor. The
title of his masterwork, *Principia Philosophiae* (1644), indicated as much.
Many of Descartes's contemporaries, including Gottfried Wilhelm Leibniz,
made similar assumptions.[8]

Isaac Newton sought to separate natural philosophy from the rest of philosophy, a radical act that explains why the young Franklin had been keen,

in London, to meet the revolutionary figure in science. Newton agreed with Descartes, and others, that matter and motion were the central topics of natural philosophy, but he rejected the rational deduction that continued to characterize that philosophy. He instead championed mathematics as the key to nature's order, holding that the calculus, particularly, could analyze physical pattern (especially astronomical motion). His science relied on observation and calculation, not reason. In order to emphasize his break with the past and his disagreement with his contemporaries, Newton named his great work, *Principia Mathematica Naturalis Philosophiae* (1687), in deliberate contrast to that of Descartes. Yet that work, because published initially in Latin and replete with higher mathematics, remained part of the learned culture of a minority.[9]

Newton by no means limited his ambitions to his methods. He was known at least equally for his conclusions, as with his theory of gravitation. How did material entities move, especially in relation to each other? Newton hypothesized that a physical object exerted force in proportion to its mass; if two heavenly bodies had unequal mass, for instance, one would orbit the other. Such gravitational forces could be measured and the motion of bodies predicted. Newton's conclusions had implications not only for large objects in the skies, but for all of matter. The theory of gravitation – bodies acting upon each other in proportion to their masses – could be applied to the invisible particles that composed matter, which could presumably attract or repel each other, thus causing the characteristic forms of matter as well as their alterations in form or position.

That explanation did not satisfy Cartesians, or indeed many others. Debates over gravitation and over the nature of matter proceeded in parallel. Why should bodies behave in the fashion that Newton had defined? Did gravity have no mechanical cause? Newton never specified such a cause, which implied that it was somehow inherent in the material entities themselves. He assumed that, while matter itself was inert, it had properties added to it by an external force, presumably God. Other theorists like Descartes proposed, in contrast, that matter's invisible particles had specific configurations that would explain phenomena such as motion.

Franklin was typical of the many people who were Newtonian without having any interest in the fine points of Newton's theories or in the disputes they elicited. He instead read popularized explanations of Newton's *Principia*. Vernacular prose, poetry, iconography, and public lectures and sermons all extolled the clarity, truth, and usefulness of Newton's work. The most widespread quasi-Newtonian idea was the concept of a mechanical universe, a clockwork cosmos created by God and then set to run, providentially, without God's everyday intervention. Popular notions of Newtonian gravitation also encouraged a widespread assumption that balance, meaning equilibrium among opposing forces, governed the universe. Franklin helped promote Newtonian philosophy, as when his 1748 almanac described Newton as "the prince of astronomers and philosophers" and reproduced verses that marveled how he had "*Trac'd the boundless works of God, from laws sublimely simple*" (P 3: 250).[10]

At first, Franklin gave no indication that he aspired to do natural philosophy himself, although his almanacs showed his continuing interest in natural history. He needed to predict the weather for his almanac, which required astronomical observations (to calculate the changes of season and general meteorological conditions) and description of the conditions around him. In letters to fellow American naturalists, Franklin began to consider the weather beyond the mid-Atlantic region, even to the point of speculating about weather patterns over the entire North Atlantic Ocean. While this aspect of Franklin's work has received little attention, it was significant. He was entering a new tradition of the explorer–naturalist, someone who voyaged (or read accounts of voyages) in order to discover broader patterns of natural phenomena over the earth. Thus had the mariner–naturalist William Dampier investigated the winds and currents over the Atlantic and Indian oceans. Thus too had astronomer Edmund Halley traced magnetic variation over the Atlantic. Franklin read both Dampier's and Halley's works, as well as those of many other explorer–naturalists.[11]

Finally, Franklin used his almanac to encourage others to observe nature. He published a long description of microscopes in *Poor Richard Improved* for 1751 (P 4: 90–94). And he encouraged his neighbors to get up at five o'clock on a spring morning in 1753, don spectacles (presumably dimmed with protective lampblack), and observe a Transit of Mercury over the sun (P 4: 406–08). All in all, Franklin made sure that his almanac would be interesting and up to date for each "Dear Reader" who perused it for information about astronomy or any of the sciences (P 3: 3–4).

Doing experimental natural philosophy

By the 1740s, Franklin was not just reporting science, but doing it. He was typical of an upsurge in interest, on both sides of the Atlantic, in experimental science. If Newton's mathematics did not invite widespread participation in science, experiments did. By the second quarter of the eighteenth century, science lectures – dramatic demonstrations of magnetism, chemical reactions, air-pumps, optical effects, and electricity – were extremely popular in Europe. Some demonstrations were little more than loud and flashy entertainments; others lectured audiences about the meaning of experiments and the value of natural philosophy; still others promoted specific theories. Instrument makers, authors, and printers all began to produce items that consumers could use to bring experimentation home with them. Instruments such as barometers, microscopes, and even air-pumps were eventually stylish household accoutrements, as were pamphlets and books that described their utility.[12]

Many of these instruments and printed guides were expensive. Franklin's first exposure to them probably came in the learned society he had helped to create. By the late 1730s, the Library Company of Philadelphia used collective funds to acquire scientific instruments and as early as 1740 it sponsored lectures on science that were public, meaning open to members and their guests. As in Europe, these were sociable events that implicitly instructed men, and their female guests, in polite behavior, which by this point included the ability to converse knowledgeably on topics in natural science.[13]

Franklin was also busy training himself to do experiments. He seems to have relied on two works for his eventual expertise. The first was Isaac Newton's *Opticks* (1704), a book that, in contrast to the earlier *Principia*, Newton published in English and wrote to encourage readers to follow his example by doing their own simple experiments. Much more widely read than the *Principia*, the *Opticks* would help to make experimentation an acknowledged form of inquiry into nature. Franklin also read Jean Theophilus Desaguliers, *A Course of Experimental Philosophy* (1734–44), an illustrated work that showed the use of different instruments.[14]

In 1744, Franklin published his first contribution to theories of nature, an *Account of the New Invented Pennsylvanian Fire-Places...* (1744). The pamphlet promoted his first known invention, an early prototype of the so-called Franklin stove. He collaborated with a local ironworker to produce and sell the metal components with which a person could construct a Pennsylvania fireplace. That device was designed to use convection to circulate heated air more abundantly through a room. The heat it emitted was one source of warmth; the pressure that the warm air exerted on cold drafts that entered the room was another (P 2: 419–45).

However practical Franklin's invention may have been, the pamphlet in which he promoted it also hinted at the prodigious and ambitious reading that he had been doing. Its footnotes included Desaguliers's *Course of Experimental Philosophy* as well as several experimental accounts of heat. His discussion of heat, moreover, made it clear that Franklin had absorbed several widely received hypotheses about material phenomena: that matter was composed of tiny particles, that elastic fluids (including air) were forms of matter in which the particles were widely spaced and could move rapidly, and that heat caused expansion of an elastic fluid by making its component particles move even further apart. Franklin had cleverly published a work that had multiple levels of appeal: it was a descriptive and useful pamphlet for some readers and a philosophic investigation of heat and air for others.[15]

On a visit to Boston in 1743, Franklin saw his first real demonstrations of science. Archibald Spencer, an itinerant lecturer, ran through several of-the-moment topics, including "Sir Isaac Newton's Theory of Light and Colours" (presumably from the *Opticks*) and how "Fire is Diffus'd through all Space," meaning a demonstration of electricity. Impressed, Franklin arranged for Spencer to give his lectures to the Library Company, publicizing them both in his *Pennsylvania Gazette* and in a separate advertisement. Shortly thereafter, Franklin and three other members of the Library Company used a recent gift of equipment that generated electricity to do their own experiments. His colleagues were Philip Syng, a silversmith, Thomas Hopkinson, a lawyer, and Ebenezer Kinnersley, a former Baptist minister who had found a second career in itinerant demonstrations of electricity. Franklin quickly established himself as the lead experimenter of the four, so it was he who reported their findings to the London donor, Peter Collinson, who had sent the equipment. Franklin then had those and other of his letters on science published in London as his *Experiments and Observations on Electricity* (1751).[16]

In those essays, Franklin made points that would, breathtakingly, take electricity from the realm of mysterious phenomenon to observable fact of science. He described electricity as a distinct form of matter, not as an epiphenomenal attribute of different material substances. (The word "electricity" comes from the Greek word for amber, once thought to create the phenomenon.) Other theorists had been describing electricity as a material thing, but they tended to think of it as two forms of fluid substance, one with an attractive capacity and one with a repulsive one. Franklin countered such arguments by theorizing that electricity was one subtle fluid or elastic substance (not unlike air or heat) composed of particles. Objects did not generate different kinds of electricity. Instead, they either had an equilibrium of positively and negatively charged particles, or they were charged below this balance (negatively) or above it (positively). The charge was never actually created *de novo* nor entirely lost. It merely changed its configuration, a property that later scientists would refer to as the law of charge conservation, and one that showed Franklin's debt to Newtonian concepts of balance. With striking confidence, Franklin introduced new definitions and terms – battery, positive and negative, plus and minus – that physicists and engineers have continued to employ.[17]

As importantly, Franklin's 1751 essays on electricity made key points about experiments and about physical experience generally. He and the other Library Company experimenters were concerned about their credibility to European savants, so they made their procedures as clear and simple as possible. Other than the electrical device sent from London, they used relatively ordinary materials: cork spheres, metal bodkins or pins, silk thread, and so on. With these simple materials, four fairly ordinary colonials redefined a form of matter that had mystified the European experts. Above all, Franklin's emphasis on sensation, how electricity felt and how physical perception was central to experimentation, validated the post-Newtonian shift away from rational deductions that were divorced from actual experience in the physical world.[18]

The brilliance and elegance of Franklin's physical investigation of the world were further evident in his kite experiment. In this, he elevated a metal point high into thunderclouds; the metal conductor sent a charge down the kite-string to a metal key. Thus, Franklin conjectured a way to prove the identity of lightning with electricity, a proof first done in France. He capped that achievement with a practical invention: the lightning rod. Raised above a house or other building, the metal rod then ran down into the earth, literally grounding the structure. Franklin's lightning rod helped to vindicate Francis Bacon's prediction that science would have multiplying useful applications.[19]

Franklin was now a famous natural philosopher. Appreciation of his work noted its contribution to definitions of matter, no small question, and its use of the experimental philosophy. In a typical summary, Yale clergyman and professor Ezra Stiles wrote a Latin oration that called Franklin (who had just received an honorary Yale degree) "Philosophorum Princeps," first among philosophers (P 5: 500). Even more impressive, the Royal Society gave its coveted Copley medal to Franklin in 1756, "on Account of his curious Experiments and Observations on Electricity."[20]

Franklin adored the acclaim but was strategically absent from debates over different theories of natural philosophy. He had benefited greatly from a quarrel between French Newtonians and Cartesians. By claiming that Franklin had vindicated Newton's theories, the former group gave Franklin free and unexpected publicity, including the translation of his *Experiments and Observations* into French. Indeed, many of Franklin's assumptions about matter, including its particulate nature and its propensity toward balanced states, betrayed a debt to Newton. But Franklin was careful not to side openly with his French champions or lord it over their anti-Newtonian opponents. He wrote a letter to one of his French critics, the Abbé Nollet, but never sent it.[21]

Nor is it clear that Franklin embraced a distinct school of natural philosophy. To be sure, he thought of himself as modern, even as an heir of Bacon,

Newton, and the rest. In 1767, for example, Franklin had Benjamin Martin paint him with a bust of Newton. But Franklin also fashioned himself as a self-educated experimenter, someone who, in contrast to the learned and mathematical investigators of nature, came to the truth all the more easily for his indifference to philosophical arcana. Good evidence of his indifference appeared in his comic essay on farting, in which Franklin dismissed both of the important philosophic schools of the day. "What Comfort can the Vortices of Descartes give to a Man who has Whirlwinds in his Bowels! The Knowledge of Newton's mutual *Attraction* of the particles of Matter, can it afford Ease to him who is rack'd by their mutual *Repulsion,* and the cruel distensions it occasions?" (In all of Franklin's surviving papers, this is his only reference to Descartes.) The essay handily combined two of Franklin's goals: his early determination, from his start as a printer, to avoid taking sides in arguments, and his subsequent delight, as an autodidact, in flouting convention, as in this remarkably offensive (if hilarious) bagatelle (P 32: 399–400).

Franklin's diplomatic caution served him well. His reputation for dispassionate wisdom made him a coveted spokesman on a variety of topics, including political ones; he served several political positions in Pennsylvania and later acted as a London-based agent for that and other colonies. His public roles would culminate in his triumphant diplomacy in France during the American Revolution, during which Franklin guaranteed French recognition of and assistance to the breakaway republic.

Once he was a public figure, and a very busy one, Franklin lamented his inability to give his full attention to philosophy. His responsibilities may have kept him from elaborating or promoting his theories, but they remained touchstones of debate in natural philosophy. German mathematician Franz Maria Ulrich Theodor Hoch Aepinus, for example, hypothesized that Franklin's theory of electricity as an elastic fluid that contained mutually repulsive (positive and negative) particles could be used to explain magnetism and might perhaps be used to explain still other forms of matter. While Franklin was preoccupied with American affairs in France, associates defended his electrical theories against critics – they managed to do so even in London during the War for Independence![22]

Despite the press of business, Franklin managed to keep inserting essays on new topics into his ever expanding *Experiments and Observations,* five English editions of which appeared during his life, along with a major French version of 1773. And he published several free-standing works on hydrography, the science of bodies of water, an ancestor of oceanography. Preeminent among these were his and his cousin's 1768 chart of the Gulf Stream, the first ever done. Franklin helped execute two later Gulf Stream charts. The third and last appeared in his long essay, published in the *Transactions* of the American Philosophical Society for 1786 and traditionally called "Maritime Observations." That essay offered an analysis of circulation in the Atlantic Ocean and was the culmination of Franklin's long interest in weather, climate, and the atmosphere. It was a significant contribution to the emerging tradition of explorer-naturalism that had begun with Dampier and Halley and would flower with the later work of Alexander von Humboldt.[23]

Franklin continued to be regarded as a scientific authority and patron. Just before he left Paris, he served on one of the French commissions that investigated and denounced the German healer Franz Anton Mesmer, who had brought his theory of animal magnetism to Paris, along with his therapies, which involved exposing patients to magnetized material. (It also involved Mesmer's erotic stroking of his female patients.) Franklin also witnessed early attempts at ballooning and sent descriptions of balloons to correspondents. And he brought much-needed support to the early republic's two fledgling learned societies, the American Philosophical Society (which he had helped found) and the American Academy of Arts and Sciences. All in all, he tried to keep his hand in.[24]

The world was nevertheless changing around him. Franklin knew that the sciences were focusing on much more specialized questions. Electrical experiments required a complicated array of devices, many of them early attempts to measure the force of electric charge. And new fields required entirely novel equipment, vocabulary, and concepts. Chemical experimentation was a case in point. Franklin knew two of the main protagonists, and rivals, of early chemistry. Both the Reverend Joseph Priestley and Antoine Laurent Lavoisier worked with "air," which they helped to redefine as a substance that held several parts, the most significant of which would subsequently be named oxygen. Franklin followed his friends' work but recognized that their experiments were developing a much more specialized line of inquiry than was the case with his electrical experiments, with their cork balls and commonsensical language.[25]

Meanwhile, his status as a philosopher became, of all things, a political liability. During the US Constitutional Convention, a Georgia delegate assessed Franklin (a Pennsylvania delegate) in a way that summarized the shift. "Dr. Franklin is well known to be the greatest philosopher of the present age," the man from Georgia allowed – "the very heavens obey him." Yet he also remarked, "But what claim he has to be a politician, posterity must determine." The guarded compliment made clear that natural philosophy had been separated from other forms of human knowledge, including politics.[26]

And so it would go on, until the sciences became professional special-
ties whose different practitioners rarely ventured into each other's fields.
Still less do scientists proclaim themselves philosophers. Only after Albert
Einstein stated that physics might one day define a unified theory – of matter, the universe, and everything – would some scientists again consider
themselves to be interpreters of cosmic meanings, whose theories of being
and time are suitably philosophic. But that development occurred long after
Franklin's death. After him, the United States would have many gifted leaders but, for better or worse, none of them would be philosophers in the
sense that Benjamin Franklin had been, meaning someone whose contributions to natural philosophy gave him authority over human as well as natural
realms.[27]

Notes

1. For overviews of Franklin's life, see Carl Van Doren, *Benjamin Franklin* (New
   York: Viking Press, 1938); J. A. Leo Lemay, *The Life of Benjamin Franklin*,
   2 vols. to date (Philadelphia: University of Pennsylvania Press, 2005–).
2. Paul C. Pasles, "The Lost Circles of Dr. Franklin: Ben Franklin's Missing Squares
   and the Secret of the Magic Circle," *American Mathematical Monthly* 108
   (2001): 489–511.
3. Joyce E. Chaplin, *The First Scientific American: Benjamin Franklin and the
   Pursuit of Genius* (New York: Basic Books, 2006), 31–33.
4. *Ibid.*, 34–38.
5. Edwin Wolf 2nd, *The Library of James Logan of Philadelphia, 1674–1751*
   (Philadelphia: Library Company of Philadelphia, 1974), xvii–li.
6. Chaplin, *The First Scientific American*, 45, 46–47.
7. Steven Shapin, *The Scientific Revolution* (University of Chicago Press, 1996).
8. Stephen Gaukroger, *Descartes: An Intellectual Biography* (Oxford: Clarendon
   Press, 1995).
9. Richard S. Westfall, *Never at Rest: A Biography of Isaac Newton* (Cambridge
   University Press, 1980).
10. Margaret Jacob, *The Newtonians and the English Revolution, 1689–1720*
    (Ithaca, NY: Cornell University Press, 1976); Otto Mayr, *Authority, Liberty, and
    Automatic Machinery in Early Modern Europe* (Baltimore, MD: Johns Hopkins
    University Press, 1989); Simon Schaffer, "Newtonianism," in *Companion to the
    History of Modern Science*, ed. Robert C. Olby, *et al.* (New York: Routledge,
    1990), 610–26; Larry Stewart, *The Rise of Public Science: Rhetoric, Technology,
    and Natural Philosophy in Newtonian Britain, 1660–1750* (Cambridge Univer-
    sity Press, 1992); Mordechai Feingold, *The Newtonian Moment: Isaac Newton
    and the Making of Modern Culture* (New York: Oxford University Press for the
    New York Public Library, 2004).
11. Chaplin, *The First Scientific American*, 117–23, 145–53; Anna Neill, "Buccaneer
    Ethnography: Nature, Culture, and Nation in the Journals of William Dampier,"
    Eighteenth-Century Studies 33 (2000): 165–80; Alan Cook, *Edmond Halley:
    Charting the Heavens and the Seas* (Oxford: Clarendon Press, 1998).

12. Simon Schaffer, "Natural Philosophy and Public Spectacle in the Eighteenth Century," *History of Science* 21 (1983): 1–43; Jan Golinski, *Science as Public Culture: Chemistry and Enlightenment in Britain, 1760–1820* (Cambridge University Press, 1992); Geoffrey V. Sutton, *Science for a Polite Society: Gender, Culture, and the Demonstration of Enlightenment* (Boulder, CO: Westview, 1995); Alice N. Walters, "Conversation Pieces: Science and Politeness in Eighteenth-Century England," *History of Science* 35 (1997): 121–54.

13. Chaplin, *The First Scientific American*, 59–63; Edwin Wolf 2nd, *"At the Instance of Benjamin Franklin": A Brief History of the Library Company of Philadelphia, 1731–1976* (Philadelphia: Library Company of Philadelphia, 1976); James Delbourgo, *A Most Amazing Scene of Wonders: Electricity and Enlightenment in Early America* (Cambridge, MA: Harvard University Press, 2006).

14. I. Bernard Cohen, *Franklin and Newton: An Inquiry into Speculative Newtonian Experimental Science and Franklin's Work in Electricity as an Example Thereof* (Philadelphia: American Philosophical Society, 1956), 151–284; John Heilbron, "Experimental Natural Philosophy," in *The Ferment of Knowledge: Studies in the Historiography of Eighteenth-Century Science*, ed. G. S. Rousseau and Roy Porter (Cambridge University Press, 1980).

15. Cohen, *Franklin and Newton*, 214–66; Chaplin, *The First Scientific American*, 84–88.

16. I. Bernard Cohen, "The Mysterious 'Dr. Spence,'" in Cohen, *Benjamin Franklin's Science* (Cambridge, MA: Harvard University Press, 1990), 40–60; J. A. Leo Lemay, *Ebenezer Kinnersley: Franklin's Friend* (Philadelphia: University of Pennsylvania Press, 1964); Cohen, *Benjamin Franklin's Experiments: A New Edition of Franklin's Experiments and Observations on Electricity* (Cambridge, MA: Harvard University Press, 1941), 47–77.

17. Cohen, *Franklin and Newton*, 365–480; J. L. Heilbron, *Electricity in the 17th and 18th Centuries: A Study of Early Modern Physics* (Berkeley: University of California Press, 1979), part 4.

18. Simon Schaffer, "Self Evidence," *Critical Inquiry* 13 (1992): 327–62; Jessica Riskin, *Science in the Age of Sensibility: The Sentimental Empiricists of the French Enlightenment* (University of Chicago Press, 2002), chapter 3.

19. Cohen, "The Kite, the Sentry Box, and the Lightning Rod," in *Benjamin Franklin's Science*, 66–109.

20. Raymond Phineas Stearns, *Science in the British Colonies of America* (Urbana, IL: University of Illinois Press, 1970), 625–26.

21. Cohen, *Franklin and Newton*, 481–514; Sutton, *Science for a Polite Society*, chapter 3.

22. Cohen, *Franklin and Newton*, 515–73; Chaplin, *The First Scientific American*, 265–66, 276–78.

23. Lloyd A. Brown, "The River in the Ocean," in *Essays Honoring Lawrence C. Wroth*, ed. Fredrich R. Goff (Portland, ME: Anthoensen Press, 1951), 69–84; Philip Richardson, "Benjamin Franklin and Timothy Folger's First Printed Chart of the Gulf Stream," *Science* 207 (1980): 643–45; Ellen Cohn, "Benjamin Franklin, Georges-Louis Le Rouge and the Franklin/Folger Chart of the Gulf Stream," *Imago Mundi* 52 (2000): 130–32; Chaplin, *The First Scientific American*, 195–200, 317–24; Nicolaas Rupke, *Alexander von Humboldt: A Metabiography* (Frankfurt am Main: Peter Lang, 2005).

24. Brooke Hindle, *The Pursuit of Science in Revolutionary America, 1735–1789* (Chapel Hill: University of North Carolina Press for the Institute of Early American History and Culture, 1956), 263–71, 271–72; Chaplin, *The First Scientific American*, 293–325.

25. Heilbron, *Electricity in the 17th and 18th Centuries*, 78; Henry Guerlac, *Lavoisier, the Crucial Year: The Background and Origin of his First Experiments on Combustion in 1772* (Ithaca, NY: Cornell University Press, 1961).

26. Max Farrand, ed., *The Records of the Federal Convention of 1787*, 4 vols. (New Haven: Yale University Press, 1911), 3: 91.

27. The author thanks David Armitage and James Delbourgo for their comments on an earlier draft of this essay.

6

FRANK KELLETER

Franklin and the Enlightenment

I

Franklin and his contemporaries may never have seen themselves as members of a unified intellectual movement, but they did believe that their world was historically distinct in a number of ways. The term *reason*, contested as it was in the eighteenth century, widely served to signify this sense of distance from earlier periods. The same is true for the name, *Benjamin Franklin*, which came to stand for all sorts of things but almost always symbolized the promise or threat of a new age of human autonomy. "Had Franklin drawn lightning from the clouds [three hundred years ago]," Thomas Paine noted in *The Age of Reason* (1794), "it would have been at the hazard of expiring for it in the flames."[1] Paine implied that in the Middle Ages, Franklin's scientific discoveries – his disenchantment of nature – would have challenged the authority of the Catholic church, and he might have been burned at the stake. Yet in his own enlightened times, Franklin was seen as a representative man of his age, and his discoveries and inventions symbolized social and political revolutions of the highest magnitude, as in Turgot's popular witticism, "[Franklin] seized the lightning from the sky, and the sceptre from tyrants."[2]

Modern readers are duly suspicious of such utopian pronouncements. In hindsight, they recognize that the Enlightenment never existed as a homogenous set of ideas or as a coherent ideological program. Instead, opposing understandings of enlightened thought and action coexisted, not always peacefully. Different schools and creeds formed rigid antagonisms, surprising coalitions, new mixtures. The Enlightenment was obviously not the sum total of its constituent parts – empiricism, deism, moral-sense philosophy, economic liberalism, republicanism, revolutionary utopianism, and so forth – because these parts don't add up. Nevertheless, we can speak of the Enlightenment once we recognize that under this heading, disparate forces interacted in a common attempt to redefine the meaning of human reason.

The Enlightenment, in other words, did not exist as a set of shared beliefs and convictions, but it produced shared ways of arguing a point as rational.

Thus, whatever ideological stance it took, enlightened reason always regarded itself as a *critical*, *democratic*, and *constructive* faculty. Reason was considered a *critical* faculty because it attempted to free human understanding from *dóxa* or *opinion*. That is, reason freed human understanding from "that Assent, which we give to any Proposition as true, of whose Truth yet we have no certain Knowledge" (John Locke).[3] Hence, to exercise one's reason in an enlightened manner did not simply mean to speak the truth; it meant to eliminate a falsely established belief. Even more: to exercise one's reason meant to speak and act against all authorities that had an interest in perpetuating falsehood. To exercise one's reason meant to distrust the official pronouncements of ruling powers and elites. Along these lines, to read Greek or to be a good rhetorician did not make a person more reasonable but more powerful. Consequently, when Franklin proposed the solution to a specific problem in physics (in a letter to John Perkins), he concluded: "If my Hypothesis is not the Truth itself, it is least as naked: For I have not...disguis'd my Nonsense in Greek, cloth'd it in Algebra, or adorn'd it with Fluxions" (P 4: 442).

Enlightened knowledge, Franklin implies, exists independently of the "schools," independently, that is, of scholastic learning and, in this case, mathematical training. In Franklin's times, to be reasonable did not mean to be more intelligent or more learned than the next man, but it meant to free oneself from dogmatic beliefs. Thus, the exercise of one's reason was not simply an act of confirmation. On the contrary, people like Franklin almost habitually suspected that official censure is always directed against truth. Looking back on his youthful conversion to deism (that is, to a post-Christian brand of enlightened religion), he noted in *The Autobiography* that he took this step because "[s]ome Books *against* Deism fell into my Hands...It happened that they wrought an Effect on me quite contrary to what was intended by them" (A 113–14, emphasis added). Not just the veracity but the ill repute of deism convinced him to become "a thorough Deist."

Enlightened reason was not based on wisdom, tradition, or authoritative institutionalization. It is in this sense that enlightened reason was considered not only a critical but also a *democratic* faculty – even though that was not the term used by Franklin and his contemporaries. Indeed, the word *democracy* for most of them had a pejorative meaning, connoting demagoguery and mob-rule. Instead, they spoke of democratic reason as *common sense*, a sense of reason common to all people, regardless of social status and educational background.

Common-sense philosophy combined the democratic and the critical aspects of enlightened reason. It argued that truth is always plain. People require no superior intellect to understand what is true. Nevertheless, it was held that most people are actually unable to discern plain truth, because they have never learned to trust their own senses. Instead, they unthinkingly subscribe to established opinions (what contemporaries called "prejudices") or to the doctrines canonized by powerful institutions. Franklin reacted to this dilemma in the same manner as did John Locke and Immanuel Kant: he maintained that all received knowledge could and must be tested *empirically*. Knowledge needed to be examined by one's own senses and reason and not accepted as what other people tell us or what we can read in books, even if those books were written by great philosophers. So instead of simply *believing* that lightning is an articulation of God's wrath (as eminent theologians asserted) we need to *examine* lightning with our own eyes – and we will come to different conclusions. Transferred to the political realm, this "courage to think for oneself," as Kant called it, had far-reaching consequences.[4] Suddenly, no power on earth was exempt from critical scrutiny.

Franklin symbolized this democratic aspect of enlightened reason in more than one way. When he claimed that it is more important to know what a man can do than where he comes from, he was essentially talking about himself, both as a self-made man and as an American. Franklin's popularity among European (especially French) intellectuals in the eighteenth century had everything to do with his marginal status as a colonial. After all, there was something inherently provincial in the Enlightenment's conviction that truth is a matter of common sense and free public deliberation, and not a matter of divine inspiration, social standing, or scholastic training. Franklin shrewdly exploited this topos when he went to Versailles dressed as a backwoodsman. In this manner, Dr. Franklin, the beaver-hatted member of the Royal Medical Society in Paris, came to embody the worldwide commonality of enlightened reason: an American, a wilderness philosopher, solves some of the most difficult problems of European science – what better proof for the universality of human reason!

Far from being a merely affirmative or contemplative faculty, enlightened reason saw and presented itself as a force that actively shapes and improves human living conditions. Enlightened reason is thus a *constructive* faculty. In this view, to understand nature ultimately means to domesticate nature. And to domesticate nature – to seize the lightning from the sky – means to construct new possibilities and environments for human life in the service of communal, perhaps even universal, well-being. Enlightened ideologies may fight over the actual features of these rational environments and over the ways to get there, but they share a fundamental optimism concerning the malleability of human society (though not concerning the goodness of human nature). In this sense, there is an inherent connection between Franklin's lightning rods and his establishment of lending libraries (making education accessible to all people, not just to a small coterie of learned men), between his experiments in electricity and his various political projects, from his vision of a Greater Britain in the 1750s to his advocacy of American independence in the 1770s and on to the federalist constitutionalism of his final years. In all these cases, human thought and action are supposed to do more than understand and praise an existing, divinely ordained order of things. Human thought and action now exhibit their divine origins – as most enlightened thinkers believed – by devising projects of self-improvement. More than any other American founder, Franklin has come to represent this enlightened paradigm, in which reason no longer moves from Platonic astonishment to pious trust but actively distrusts the necessity of things as they are. This kind of reason confidently works to construct new worlds for human happiness.

II

We could stop here and come away with a heroic image of Franklin and the Enlightenment. However, Franklin was not born a paragon of the American Enlightenment but had to be *made* one, in a long process of interpretation and appropriation. Thus, if we want to understand Franklin in his own times, we should be wary of overtly homogenizing readings of his life and works. To a certain degree, even the contemporaries had their doubts. John Adams – no unprejudiced observer of Franklin's career, to be sure – wrote to Benjamin Rush on April 4, 1790: "The History of our Revolution will be one continued Lye from one end to the other. The essence of the whole will be that Dr. Franklin's electrical Rod smote the Earth and out sprang General Washington."[5]

Adams's sarcasm draws our attention to the fundamentally *historical* character of the American Enlightenment and Franklin's involvement in it. Franklin's biography and the history of the early republic are revealingly similar in this regard, because in both cases the process of self-making was far more diversified and far more contingent than popular versions suggest. Franklin's enlightenment can be described as a dynamic process rather than an unwavering commitment to a specific political ideology. This does not mean, however, that his philosophy was erratic, nor that it was historically idiosyncratic. Behind all positions he took and behind all successive roles he played in his day, we can trace a fairly consistent set of intellectual dispositions. Concerning these dispositions, it is difficult to argue against the dominance of *utilitarian* thought in Franklin's version of the Enlightenment. *Useful* is a key term in his writings. "What signifies Philosophy that does not apply to some Use?" he asked in a 1760 letter to Mary Stevenson (P 9: 251). Even natural catastrophes were functional in this manner. Writing three years after the disastrous earthquake of Lisbon, Franklin reflected that such catastrophes arc ultimately beneficial to human knowledge and human happiness:

> [A] great number of strata of different kinds are brought up to day, and a great variety of useful materials put into our power, which would otherwise have remained eternally concealed from us. So that what has been usually looked upon as a *ruin* suffered by this part of the universe, was, in reality, only a preparation, or means of rendering the earth more fit for use, more capable of being to mankind a convenient and comfortable habitation.　　(P 7: 357)

Franklin's optimism should not blind us to the fact that almost all enlightened philosophies were troubled by the problem of *usefulness*, because the rational utility of cataclysmic changes, both natural and intellectual, is not easily established or defended. If human reason is at core a critical faculty, one that engages in questioning traditional commitments and obligations, what prevents reason from becoming a purely destructive force, doing away with time-tested checks on human depravity and eliminating necessary consolations? This was the question famously asked by Edmund Burke in *Reflections on the Revolution in France* (1790). When Burke published his book, numerous competing answers were already in circulation. Among the most popular was the moral-sense philosophy of the Scottish Enlightenment. Francis Hutcheson, for example, had realigned enlightened reason with traditional notions of moral legitimacy in *Inquiry Concerning Moral Good and Evil* (1725). To Hutcheson, human beings have an inner sense – an unerring feeling – of what is proper and true. Thus, according to Hutcheson, our own emotions, if freed from authoritarian influences and social affectations, are the surest way of determining whether a proposition or an action is reasonable or not. If unadulterated, such intuitions provide *self-evident* truths, truths that all feeling creatures must agree on, no matter what their brainpower, social status, or education.

In an argumentative pattern typical of most Enlightenment debates, Adam Smith refined this idea by criticizing it. In *Theory of Moral Sentiments* (1759), Smith objected to Hutcheson's conviction that a given action is self-evidently moral if it is accompanied by genuinely delightful sensations. Smith rejected this idea not only because people can feel honestly good when doing bad things (taking revenge, for example), but also because a single individual is never capable of surveying all possible results of his or her actions. What is reasonable to the best of my knowledge – and what my emotions honestly approve of – may still have dire consequences for my environment or for myself. Nevertheless, Smith wanted to hold fast to the concept of a self-evident, non-elitist rationality. Therefore he concluded that an individual can act reasonably by disregarding his own immediate interests and thus by putting himself in the position of what he called an "impartial spectator." In other words, the enlightened individual, as envisioned by Smith, transcends subjectivity to assess the causal effects of his or her chosen conduct. Smith's *Theory of Moral Sentiments* regarded the social consequentiality of an action as the prime indicator of its morality (without having to resort to institutionalized ethics and without leaving the question of morality to capricious emotions). In Smith's view, the meta-subjective *public good* became the measurement of rational practice and the limit of individual well-being.

When Smith called on enlightened individuals to aspire to the meta-subjective perspective of an impartial spectator, he prepared for various later developments in enlightened thought. Thus, his critique of popular moral-sense philosophy came full circle in Jeremy Bentham's *Introduction to the Principles of Morals and Legislation* (1789), where Bentham defined the principle of *utility* as a form of self-observation that qualifies subjective needs and actions by weighing them against collective needs and actions. Bentham advised enlightened statesmen to reorganize society so as to achieve "the greatest happiness of the greatest number," a formula he adapted from Hutcheson's *An Inquiry into the Original of Our Ideas of Beauty and Virtue* (1725).

It is helpful to view Franklin's concern with *utility* in light of these other theorists and philosophers. Like Smith and Bentham, he thought that Hutcheson's understanding of reason as an intuitive and emotional faculty provided a solution far too simple. Even so, Franklin shared Hutcheson's commitment to a self-evident, non-elitist, indeed democratic rationality. Refusing to believe in the popular eighteenth-century dream of transparent emotions, he nevertheless upheld the idea that reason is common to *all* people and that the task of enlightened politics therefore is to ensure "the greatest happiness of the greatest number." In revolutionary America and the early republic, this utilitarian ideal proved particularly attractive, because its calculus was pragmatic rather than idealistic: it didn't claim to produce universal happiness and equality but only to construct the most favorable conditions for pursuing both. Thus, utilitarianism was able to accommodate conflicting interests in a heterogeneous society. Most importantly, it was able to criticize established institutions of church and state without denying their social efficacy. This double attitude of radical criticism and pragmatic affirmation was most obvious in Franklin's concept of religion.

The basic stance of Franklin's theology can be summarized as follows: he questioned the epistemological validity of revealed religion but affirmed its political necessity. At times, this attitude came close to claiming that the major good of religious faith is to keep the ignorant masses from sloth and insurrection.[6] But such Voltairean resentment of the *canaille* was not a central feature of Franklin's view of religion. True, his ideas of human nature were frequently closer to Hobbes than to Locke: "If Men are so wicked as we now see them *with Religion* what would they be if *without it?*" he asked in an anonymous letter from 1757 (P 7: 749).[7] Nevertheless, like most enlightened writers, Franklin tended to stress the constructive aspects of faith over its prohibitive functions. Like Locke in *The Reasonableness of Christianity* (1695), Franklin praised traditional forms of religious worship because they provided a widely accepted foundation for social morality. The same, he thought, could not be said about some of the more innovative and radical forms (scientific or natural) of enlightened religion. Accordingly, in *The Autobiography* he recounted how his conduct toward friends and family deteriorated after his conversion to deism. In turn, fellow deists wronged him without showing signs of bad conscience. In *The Autobiography* he concluded, "I began to suspect that this Doctrine [of deism] tho' it might be true, was not very useful" (A 114).

It is tempting to read this sentence as a victory of utilitarian (constructive) reason over deist (critical) reason. Yet despite his realization that deism was morally deficient, Franklin refused to reconvert to any of the socially more useful forms of Protestant Christianity. Instead, he designed an entirely *new* theology, which he thought would do justice to both his critical and his social-utilitarian interests. His early attempts at biblical iconoclasm can be read in this way, as when he devised new and more enlightened versions of the Lord's Prayer (P 1: 99, 101ff.) or of the first chapter of the Book of Job (Smyth 7: 432). Even more outspoken are his religious proposals in *The Autobiography*, where he offered a multi-denominational catalogue of principles said to contain "the Essentials of every known Religion," while being "free of everything that might shock the Professors of any Religion" (A 162). Ultimately, this basic version of human belief was closer to deism than to traditional Christian forms of worship, but it attempted to make critical reason socially useful.

On the whole, what Franklin presented was a natural religion with the additional assumption that God created human beings not only as rational but as moral beings. Thus, similar to earlier enlightened notions of a non-institutionalized, popular *ur-form* of Christianity, such as in Locke's

Reasonableness of Christianity, Franklin's universal religion claimed to be comprehensible to all people without specialized training or authoritative exegesis. It was a self-evident faith. More importantly, it was a democratic faith, and this not only because the people at large could believe in it, but because the anti-schismatic character of this faith made possible the close cohabitation of widely different kinds of people. In this sense, Franklin's enlightened theology aimed not at establishing an unrivaled dogmatic truth but at organizing a peacefully inhabitable social environment in the face of religious diversity.

It is no coincidence that this idea took center stage in the writings of an American colonial. Like most American founders, Franklin was deeply concerned with problems posed and solutions suggested by a cultural environment unlike any in eighteenth-century Europe. In fact, to say that a certain idea might be true, but not very useful, takes on a special meaning and urgency in a diversified frontier and settlement culture. Franklin explicitly searched for religious and political institutions that were suitable and necessary for the highly improbable formation of a post-classical, post-European republic in faraway provinces. That he did not want to have this search confused with traditional forms of worship and government is evident in the name he proposed for his new sect (which was to be organized as a secret society): "the Society of the *Free and Easy*" (A 163).

Franklin's proposed Society of the Free and Easy cannot be written off as simply a case of secularization, substituting the old clergy with the new bourgeois priests of worldly reason. His friendship with the most celebrated evangelist of his time is a case in point. Apparently, what Franklin found congenial in George Whitefield was not the doctrine of immediate grace but the performative brilliance with which Whitefield advocated this idea. The orthodox colonial clergy objected to Whitefield's evangelism, because they regarded it as a shrewd stage effect, a matter of commercial self-promotion.[8] Franklin, however, was intrigued exactly by this point. Having a professional interest in social engineering, as most American founders had, he concerned himself less with Whitefield's message than with the methodical stringency with which the itinerant preacher transformed his body and voice into perfect instruments of mass persuasion:

> He had a loud and clear Voice, and articulated his Words and Sentences so perfectly that he might be heard and understood at a great Distance... His Delivery... was so improv'd by frequent Repetitions, that every Accent, every Emphasis, every Modulation of Voice, was so perfectly well turn'd and well plac'd, that without being interested in the Subject, one could not help being pleas'd with the Discourse.   (A 179–80)

Franklin went on to calculate that Whitefield's voice could be heard by 30,000 people simultaneously, if each person in his audience took up two square feet. The author of *Poor Richard's Almanack* – himself a master of modern mass-communication – apparently recognized his own kind here. While Franklin might have found little truth in Whitefield's doctrine, he was so impressed by the preacher's *savoir faire* that he immediately responded to the sermon's appeal and donated money to Whitefield's orphanage in Georgia – not, however, without securing for himself the printing rights for the sermons of George Whitefield, with whom he now entered into a "civil Friendship" beyond religious differences (A 178).

This episode points to a central dilemma in Franklin's utilitarian view of reason: such reason is useful *for what* – and for *whom*? Whitefield and Franklin, the first transatlantic media celebrities, are similar, because their careers, as well as their spiritual or rational charisma, were based on the purposeful application of ever more efficient techniques of self-promotion. So if Franklin recognized something revolutionary, possibly even something American, in Whitefield's igniting of what came to be called the Great Awakening, this was because Whitefield was particularly attuned to the communicative needs of a heterogeneous, latently democratic society. Similarly, Franklin's own social pragmatism best made sense in a diversified and highly mobile provincial environment. With this, some vital questions concerning the limits and consequences of enlightened reason in the eighteenth century arise.

III

Human reason is a critical and constructive faculty, so the employment of this faculty, according to the enlightened paradigm, is always a collective and communicative act. In this sense, Benjamin Franklin's fondness for clubs, societies, epistolary networks, and other formalized means of intellectual exchange is typical of the Enlightenment at large. Such forums for debate, concerned as they are with discursive rules and regulations, pay tribute to the enlightened conviction that there can be no such thing as private, inspired, or genius-like knowledge. On the contrary, the Enlightenment holds that all human understanding is mortal understanding, requiring the joint construction, by mortal subjects, of meta-subjective methods of rational argument. As a result, enlightened thought has always been highly self-reflective concerning its own linguistic conditions of possibility. Franklin, too, was intensely interested in optimizing mortal, subjective reason by contriving ideal linguistic and social conditions for its employment. His Junto, for example, a philosophical debating circle similar to numerous others in the eighteenth century, was meant to institutionalize, as consistently as possible, meta-subjective forms of communication. *The Autobiography* comments on the communicative guidelines of this club:.

> Our Debates were...to be conducted in the sincere Spirit of Enquiry after Truth, without Fondness for Dispute, or Desire of Victory; and to prevent Warmth, all Expressions of Positiveness in Opinion, or of direct Contradiction, were after some time made contraband and prohibited under small pecuniary Penalties. (A 117)

There is an irony here: Franklin's communicative reason appears almost like a parlor game, which, like all forms of competition, has winners and losers. Once more, we need to ask: *cui bono?* Who profits from this kind of reason? Franklin provided an answer in *The Autobiography*, when he slyly praised the "Socratic Method," defined as a way of debating that avoids opinionated or antagonistic expressions, only to add that this method helped him to obtain "Victories that neither my self nor my Cause always deserved" (A 65). But what type of reason brings undeserved, or unreasonable, victories? There are various occasions in Franklin's writings when this question becomes pertinent, as when the narrator of *The Autobiography* tells us how he relaxed his rational (i.e., vegetarian) diet after he smelled fried codfish in Rhode Island:

> Hitherto I had stuck to my Resolution of not eating animal Food; and on this Occasion, I consider'd...the taking every Fish as a kind of unprovok'd Murder, since none of them had or ever could do us any Injury that might justify the Slaughter. All this seem'd very reasonable. But I had formerly been a great Lover of Fish, and when this came hot out of the Frying Pan, it smelt admirably well. I balanc'd some time between Principle & Inclination: till I recollected, that when the Fish were opened, I saw smaller Fish taken out of their Stomachs: Then, thought I, if you eat one another, I don't see why we mayn't eat you. So I din'd upon Cod very heartily and continu'd to eat with other People, returning only now and than [sic] occasionally to a vegetable Diet. So convenient a thing it is to be a *reasonable Creature*, since it enables one to find or make a Reason for everything one has a mind to do. (A 87–88)

This seems to take enlightened utilitarianism to the extreme: a self-serving reasoning legitimizing whatever appears advantageous to the individual. Similarly, Franklin's perfectly enlightened treatise on *A Modest Enquiry into the Nature and Necessity of a Paper-Currency* (1729) looks a bit less enlightened – or its enlightenment takes on a new meaning – when we read about the results of this treatise: "My Friends...who conceiv'd I had been of some Service, thought fit to reward me, by employing me in printing the Money, a very profitable Jobb, and a great Help to me"

(A 124). Exactly this kind of pragmatic easiness and freedom led Franklin to praise industry not as a virtue in itself, but as something that helped him to construct a controlled self-image with which he could impress his neighbors. Thus, in *The Autobiography* he describes how he "took care not only to be in *Reality* Industrious and frugal, but to avoid all *Appearances* of the Contrary" (Λ 125). Not even narcissism seems to motivate this search for moral perfection, but a will to dominance and profit: "Thus being esteem'd an industrious thriving young Man, and paying duly for what I bought, the Merchants who imported Stationary solicited my Custom, others propos'd supplying me with Books, and I went on swimmingly" (A 126).

It is easy to see why sociologist Max Weber, one of the first modern analysts of the capitalist work ethic, chose Benjamin Franklin to illustrate what he meant by the word "rationalization": a "psycho-physical habitus" that subdues even the most private strivings to the requirements of material success.[9] This is a very widespread criticism of Franklin and of the American Enlightenment, if not of American society, at large: freedom from external authorities enables the enlightened individual "to find or make a Reason for everything one has a mind to do," especially for getting rich at another's – and one's own – expense.

Indeed, there is no denying that the Lockean tenet of individual self-creation enables the human subject to treat itself like an object. One possible result is "internal colonization": emancipated from external authorities – above all providence and chance – the enlightened individual turns into its own master and monitor, so that individual happiness quickly becomes an imperative.[10] Not only financial success or social reputation but also spiritual fulfillment, aesthetic receptivity, and sexual well-being can now be pursued with economic precision and methodical rigor. Such rigor marks Franklin's model for the "bold and arduous Project of arriving at moral Perfection" (A 148). Franklin's model equips the moral subject with a catalogue of thirteen easy-to-follow rules, whose conscientious observance promises nothing less than absolute self-identity. As an autonomous being, Franklin implies, you can be happy – in fact, you *have* to be happy, because if you're not, you're a self-produced failure.

According to modern critics of the Enlightenment, such happiness demands a price higher than self-mastery: it requires that all moral, aesthetic, dietetic, and sexual needs be systematically subordinated to the laws of utility. This "dialectic of Enlightenment," as Max Horkheimer and Theodor W. Adorno called it, threatens to turn the enlightened promise of emancipation against itself. Indeed, Franklin tells us that in practicing his thirteen character-building measures, he had to refrain not only from openly amoral actions but also from jokes and puns. A statement like this seems to suggest that enlightened reason makes short work of the imagination and of other sensual pleasures. Ever since Romanticism, this has been a staple argument in critiques of the Enlightenment.

Again, however, it is useful to place Franklin and his contemporaries in their historical contexts. True, the enlightened skepticism toward received opinions contained a critique of *poiesis* – of human image-making – itself. But Locke himself did not criticize the sensuality of imaginative art but rather art's role in ascribing a supernatural aura to political and clerical power. The Enlightenment's campaign was not against imagination and fantasy but against endowing worldly institutions with an imaginary and fantastical nimbus.

On the whole, almost all enlightened philosophies agreed that affections and passions are essential parts of human reason, not its binary opposites. The utilitarian search for "the greatest happiness of the greatest number" may have been fraught with all sorts of practical and mathematical problems, but it adopted a firmly anti-ascetic position, as did Franklin when he ate codfish.[11] Similarly, the oft-discussed pursuit of happiness, as envisioned by Locke and later Thomas Jefferson, was explicitly not about the target-oriented hunt for one specific object whose possession promises final well-being.[12] Echoing Locke's *Essay Concerning Human Understanding* (1689/1700), Adam Smith explained in *The Wealth of Nations* (1776) that "the desire of bettering our condition" is "a desire which . . . comes with us from the womb, and never leaves us till we go into the grave."[13] Pleasure means searching and activity, not ownership and rest. According to this logic, Adam Ferguson concluded in *An Essay on the History of Civil Society* (1767): "Happiness arises more from the pursuit, than from the attainment of any end whatsoever."[14]

Not surprisingly, enlightened literature tended to sensualize reason itself, frequently using sexual metaphors to describe acts of thinking and deliberation. More surprisingly for modern readers, these rational pleasures were often personified in none other than Benjamin Franklin, whom many have conceived as a prophet of bourgeois self-discipline and capitalist profit-hunting. Thomas Paine, for one, found fault with people who seek happiness only in the enjoyment or production of material goods – "[t]he mere man of pleasure . . . and the mere drudge" – contrasting their doomed lives with the example of those who will be truly happy in old age because their interest in philosophy and science provides them with "a continual source of tranquil pleasure." Romantics may consider the concept of "tranquil pleasure" a contradiction in terms, but it is striking to note that Paine selected Franklin, of all people, to represent this sensual rationality: "[H]is mind was ever young; his temper ever serene. Science, that never grows grey, was always his mistress. He was never without an object."[15]

So if we decide to follow Weber in seeing Franklin as the embodiment of "innerworldly asceticism," we at least need to explain what (or whom) Paine was referring to – and what it could possibly mean when Franklin's *Autobiography* defined itself against "the lives of . . . absurd monastic self-tormentors" (A 138). Attempting such explanations, we will probably find that what looks like a dark dialectic of self-mastery and self-denial was frequently motivated by the American Enlightenment's pragmatic tendency to negotiate between competing rational claims on human happiness. Thus, it may be more than just a sign of self-discipline when people go to the gym or keep doctor's appointments for regular check-ups. Nothing less than love of life may be at the bottom of such rational measures employed by people who are, as Franklin was, intensely aware of their dependence on a mortal mind and body. What we are in need of, then, is a reading of Franklin's Enlightenment that can account for the (aesthetic) pleasures of his writings – for his humorous styles and sly ironies, even self-mockeries – without denying their utilitarian basis, but also without reducing them to generic examples of purely didactic wit. By allowing Franklin to be interpreted in the context of his own time, we would gain a fuller understanding about having a sense of humor, and a mindset, different from our own.[16]

Notes

1. Thomas Paine, *Collected Writings*, ed. Eric Foner (New York: Library of America, 1995), 699.
2. Quoted in Adrienne Koch, ed., *The American Enlightenment: The Shaping of the American Experiment and a Free Society* (New York: George Braziller, 1965), 53.
3. John Locke, *An Essay Concerning Human Understanding*, ed. Peter H. Nidditch (Oxford: Clarendon Press, 1975), 44.
4. Immanuel Kant, *Werkausgabe*, 12 vols., ed. Wilhelm Weischedel (Frankfurt am Main: Suhrkamp, 1968), 5: 283.
5. Quoted in: Joseph J. Ellis, "Habits of Mind and an American Enlightenment," *American Quarterly* 28 (1976): 150–64, quotation at 150. The heterogeneity of Franklin's career and reputation is described in Gordon Wood, *The Americanization of Benjamin Franklin* (Harmondsworth: Penguin, 2004). According to Wood, Franklin took on many successive roles in his lifetime: gentleman, British imperialist, patriot, diplomat, American.
6. Compare Franklin's Letter to ——, December 13, 1757 (P 7: 294).
7. For a more open affirmation of Hobbes, see Franklin's 1737 letter to James Logan (P 2: 184) and his 1782 letter to Joseph Priestley (P 37: 444).
8. Compare Frank Kelleter, *Amerikanische Aufklärung: Sprachen der Rationalität im Zeitalter der Revolution* (Paderborn: Schöningh, 2002), 295–310.

9. Max Weber, *Gesammelte Aufsätze zur Religionssoziologie I* (Tübingen: Mohr, 1988), 518.

10. For "internal colonization," see Jürgen Habermas, *Theorie des kommunikativen Handelns*, 2 vols. (Frankfurt am Main: Suhrkamp, 1995), 2: 489.

11. On enlightened sensualism, compare Kelleter, *Amerikanische Aufklärung*, 37–40.

12. See Locke, *Essay Concerning Human Understanding*, 251–57.

13. Adam Smith, *An Inquiry into the Nature and Causes of the Wealth of Nations*, ed. R. H. Campbell, *et al.* (Oxford University Press, 1976), 341.

14. Quoted in: Peter Gay, *The Enlightenment: Vol. 2: The Science of Freedom* (New York: Norton, 1996), 339.

15. Paine, *Collected Writings*, 771.

16. I wish to thank Christy Hosefelder, Alexander Starre, and Daniel Stein for assistance and critique.

7

KERRY WALTERS

Franklin and the question of religion

Throughout much of his life, Franklin was ambivalent and on at least one occasion downright agonized about his own religious beliefs. This tension is honestly reflected in his private letters and memoranda, although not so much in his carefully crafted public essays, lectures, and autobiography. A good deal of his ambivalence can be attributed to the fact that he, like so many of his contemporaries, was caught in a worldview clash that muddied religious belief by encouraging competing loyalties.

Born, as he tells us, to strict Calvinist parents, reared "piously in the Dissenting Way" and "religiously educated as a Presbyterian" (A 113), Franklin, as a precocious teenager, quickly became an ardent champion of the so-called New Learning exemplified by the empiricism and materialism of thinkers such as Francis Bacon, John Locke, and Isaac Newton. Franklin's enthusiasm for the Enlightenment ethos remained a constant thread throughout the rest of his life, although time and maturity took the edge off its youthful zeal. But he also retained elements of the Calvinism, most notably an interest in the "Conduct of Life," and perhaps a belief in divine providence, into which he was born and which he thought he had shaken off. Intellectually and emotionally, Franklin was comfortable with the Enlightenment worldview that challenged the earlier Calvinist one. But the influence of his Calvinist tradition never completely disappeared, and to the end of his days he occasionally defended certain positions that sound relatively orthodox.[1]

To his credit, Franklin himself usually recognized the patchwork complexity of his religious beliefs, and this recognition gave him the freedom to acknowledge their provisionality and show remarkable tolerance for the religious beliefs of others. Franklin expresses this humility in several places, but perhaps its most succinct statement comes from two 1738 letters intended to assuage his parents' anxiety over reports of his apostasy. "You both seem concern'd," he wrote, "lest I have imbib'd some erroneous Opinions." And, he admits, "doubtless I have my Share." But,

> I imagine a Man must have a good deal of Vanity who believes, and a good deal of Boldness who affirms, that all the doctrines he holds, are true, and all he rejects, are false...If I am in the wrong, I should not be displeas'd that another is in the right. If I am in the Right, 'tis my Happiness; and I should rather pity than blame him who is unfortunately in the Wrong. (P 2: 203)[2]

The tension in Franklin's religious thought is very real indeed, and it serves no purpose to deny just how complicated and sometimes inconsistent it can be by attempting to pigeonhole Franklin in one simple religious category or the other. This chapter will highlight some of the most significant moments in Franklin's religious development and attempt to sketch its general flow from Franklin's early years to his final ones. But I make no claim of "answering" the question of Franklin's religion. Doing so risks buying into the charming pretense of simplicity that Franklin worked so hard to cultivate.

"Our *Geese* are but *Geese*"

In his *Autobiography*, Franklin writes that he was converted to Enlightenment deism at the age of fifteen. He had already begun to lose faith in the religion of his parents, and he confesses to "evading as much as I could the common Attendance on publick Worship, which my Father used to exact of me" (A 113). His reading of a handful of anti-deistic tracts that he had picked up in the hopes of bolstering his failing Calvinist allegiance soon clinched his change of allegiance. "It happened that [these tracts] wrought an effect on me quite contrary to what was intended by them; for the arguments of the Deists, which were quoted to be refuted, appeared to me much stronger than the refutation; in short, I soon became a thorough Deist" (A 113–14). Before long, the young Franklin was immersing himself in the writings of British thinkers such as Lord Shaftesbury, Anthony Collins, and John Toland, each of whom defended the "natural" or "rational" religion of deism.

Eighteenth-century deists accepted the existence of an impersonal deity who created a universe defined by uniform natural laws, but who in no way subsequently interfered in the operations of the natural order. Miraculous interventions were rejected by deists as contrary to both the divine intention and the natural order. Moreover, the deity who created a universe governed by predictable and orderly natural laws also created rational humans capable of understanding and manipulating them. Thus, humans needed no "sacred" text to comprehend God or reality. A rational investigation of the natural order was sufficient. Finally, deists insisted that the ritualistic worship was both unnecessary and conducive to superstition. For them, the most appropriate way to honor the deity was through the exercise of reason and the practice of virtue.[3]

Like many religious converts, Franklin was anxious to proselytize his newfound deism. One way in which he proclaimed it was by gleefully sniping at Boston's Calvinist establishment in his pseudonymous "Dogood Letters" that appeared in 1722 in his brother James's paper, the *New-England Courant*. But he also took on anyone wishing to debate him on religious matters and quickly established himself as a thorn in the side of Boston's religious establishment. "My indiscrete Disputations about Religion," he remembered years afterwards, "began to make me pointed at with Horror by good people, as an Infidel or Atheist" (A 71).

Anyone horrified by the comparatively tame "Dogood Letters" would have positively recoiled three years later, when Franklin wrote and published a pamphlet with the ponderous title *A Dissertation on Liberty and Necessity, Pleasure and Pain* (1725). Composed while Franklin served as journeyman in a London printing house, the *Dissertation* was his first sustained attempt to push to its logical conclusion the New Learning's critique of Christianity. It was also in many respects the most philosophically sophisticated of all his writings on religion.

The immediate impetus for the *Dissertation* was William Wollaston's defense of liberal Christianity in his influential *The Religion of Nature Delineated* (1722). In this treatise, Wollaston tried to show that there was no necessary conflict between deism's claim that the divine First Cause ordained a "just and geometrical arrangement of things" – an arrangement in accord with the mechanistic model defended by Newtonians – with Christian beliefs in free will, moral responsibility, and punishment or reward in an afterlife. Wollaston's attempt to marry Christianity and natural religion was clumsy, but it appealed to many readers who, like Wollaston and the young Franklin, found themselves bewildered and unsettled by the clash in worldviews between Christianity and the Enlightenment.

Franklin's point of attack was Wollaston's very deistic interpretation of the created order as a "just and geometrical arrangement of things." This claim, Franklin insisted, is incompatible with free will and responsibility. If the First Cause has indeed created a geometrical universe, then whatever happens is necessary, absolutely determined by antecedent sequences of causes and effects. Because natural laws apply uniformly to all aspects of reality, human behavior, including what passes for human acts of the will, is likewise determined. Ultimately, then, nothing occurs but what has been willed by God's initial act of creation: the notion of free agency on the part of humans is illusory. As Franklin puts it, "if the Creature is thus limited in his Actions, being able to do only such Things as God would have him to do, and not being able to refuse doing what God would have done; then he can have no such Thing as Liberty, Free Will or Power to do or refrain from an Action" (P 1: 62).

Moreover, if human activities are the direct or indirect consequences of divine will and if (as Wollaston claimed) God wills only the good, then it follows that "Evil doth not exist," for "there can be neither Merit or Demerit in Creatures," and any talk of reward or punishment in an afterlife is beside the point (P 1: 59). Humans believe that evil is real only because they confuse the frustration of desires with normative evil and the satisfaction of desires with normative good. But Franklin insisted that the pain of frustration and the satisfaction of pleasure are experiences that carry no normative weight whatsoever.

Franklin was fully aware of just how startling his thesis would be to readers, especially readers who, like Wollaston, were trying to navigate a way between traditional Christianity and the New Learning. Indeed, he seemed to relish the consternation he anticipated provoking in them. In a note at the *Dissertation*'s end, he addresses those who might find offensive his defense of thoroughgoing materialism:

> Mankind naturally and generally love to be flatter'd: Whatever sooths our Pride, and tends to exalt our Species above the rest of the Creation, we are pleas'd with and easily believe, when ungrateful Truths shall be with the utmost Indignation rejected. "What! bring ourselves down to an Equality with Beasts of the Field! with the *meanest* part of the Creation! 'Tis insufferable!" But, (to use a Piece of *common* Sense) our *Geese* are but *Geese* tho' we may think 'em *Swans*; and Truth will be Truth tho' it sometimes prove mortifying and distasteful. (P 1: 71)

Franklin's *Dissertation* was the high water mark of his allegiance to the minimalist religion of reason inspired by the New Learning. The treatise shows that Franklin was much more consistent in his embrace of materialism than many other deists of the eighteenth century. He clearly saw that the standard deistic insistence on uniform and deterministic natural law dealt a mortal blow to the possibility of free will and moral responsibility.

"I have made to myself a God"

But consistency isn't everything. Franklin's pamphlet had scarcely been printed when he began to have second thoughts about his savaging of morality. Over the next three years, he rethought his position, ultimately coming to the conclusion that publishing the *Dissertation* was a great error. In later life, he tried to find and destroy as many copies of it as he could.[4]

Why did Franklin so quickly repudiate the *Dissertation*? There are probably several factors that influenced the decision, and most of them came from the hard school of experience. One was Franklin's meeting with a number of people whose lives seemed to challenge his clever argument that a deterministic universe renders morality illusory. In his *Autobiography*, he tells us that several personal encounters around this time with a series of rogues as well as saints convinced him that some people just seemed more decent than others, thereby calling into question the *Dissertation*'s repudiation of moral distinctions (e.g., A 102–03). Moreover, Franklin began to worry that the determinism defended in the *Dissertation* provided no incentives for either individuals or communities to strive for excellence, for personal improvement, or social reform. This sort of philosophical apathy, Franklin feared, could easily roll over into anarchy, a fear remaining with him to the end of his life.

Finally, the youthful Franklin's easy acceptance of materialism came up against a frightening encounter with his own mortality. Toward the end of his sojourn in London, Franklin was befriended by a Quaker merchant, Thomas Denham. Denham took the young man under his wing, paid for his passage back to Philadelphia, and in general seems to have become a second father to Franklin. On their return to the colonies, Denham and Franklin both fell ill. Franklin came close to dying, and Denham did. This tragedy profoundly affected Franklin, propelling him into an existential crisis that convinced him that humans need more, both psychologically and spiritually, than a distant and aloof First Cause deity. Humans crave religion, not metaphysics, and the grieving Franklin realized he was no exception to this general rule.[5] In the months following Denham's death, Franklin seemed to have drifted, seeking to reconcile his existential need for deep meaning with his philosophical fidelity to the New Learning. Whether he realized it or not, he was facing the same problem William Wollaston had.

Franklin's breakthrough came in 1728, and is recorded in a private memorandum he entitled "Articles of Belief and Acts of Religion." This document, which contains both a creed and a litany, summarizes Franklin's hard-won religious alternative to both supernaturalist Calvinism and mechanistic deism. It records the great religious insight of his life. The litany of the "Articles and Acts" is eclectic, combining deistic hymns to reason with fervent and vaguely Christian-sounding petitions for divine guidance. There's really nothing extraordinary about it. But the creedal half of the document is quite different, and worth quoting at some length:

> I BELIEVE there is one Supreme most perfect Being, Author and Father of the Gods themselves.

For I believe that Man is not the most perfect Being but One, rather that as there are many Degrees of Beings his Inferiors, so there are many Degrees of Beings superior to him.

Also, when I stretch my Imagination thro' and beyond our System of Planets, beyond the visible fix'd Stars themselves, into that Space that is every Way infinite, and conceive it fill'd with Suns like ours, each with a Chorus of Worlds for ever moving round him, then this little Ball on which we move, seems, even in my narrow Imagination, to be almost Nothing, and my self less than nothing, and of no sort of Consequence.

When I think thus, I imagine it great Vanity in me to suppose, that the *Supremely Perfect*, does in the least regard such an inconsiderable Nothing as Man. More especially, since it is impossible for me to have any positive clear Idea of that which is infinite and incomprehensible, I cannot conceive otherwise, than that He, *the Infinite Father*, expects or requires no Worship or Praise from us, but...is INFINITELY ABOVE IT...

But since there is in all Men something like a natural Principle which enclines them to DEVOTION or the Worship of some unseen Power;

And since Men are endued with Reason superior to all other Animals that we are in our World acquainted with;

Therefore I think it seems required of me, and my Duty, as a Man, to pay Divine Regards to SOMETHING.

I CONCEIVE then, that the INFINITE has created many Beings or Gods, vastly Superior to Man, who can better conceive his Perfections than we, and return him a more rational and glorious Praise...

It may be that these created Gods, are immortal, or it may be that after many Ages, they are changed, and Others supply their Places.   (P 1: 102–08)

What are we to make of this intriguing document? There are two standard interpretations. One is that it is patent nonsense, a theological spoof scribbled by a young man already notorious for his iconoclastic grandstanding.[6] The other is that it is a sincere statement of belief in the literal existence of multiple deities, with an over-God, whose being is absolutely inaccessible to humans, mediated through a second level of lesser but more accessible deities.[7]

But both readings are problematic. There's simply no evidence that Franklin intended his "Articles and Acts" as spoof. The entire document exudes a sense of deep conviction and heartfelt seriousness not apparent, for example, in the earlier, obviously satiric "Dogood Letters." Franklin's intellectual repudiation of the *Dissertation*, as well as the personal soul-searching that preceded the "Articles and Acts," only underscores the likelihood that they are not satiric. Neither is there any reason to think that Franklin espoused a literal polytheism in the "Articles and Acts." He was, after all, a man who had imbibed both Christianity's rejection of "pagan" polytheism as well as the Enlightenment's rejection of "superstition." It makes no sense to conclude that Franklin, a man who could not bring himself to take seriously the Christian doctrine of the Trinity, would find polytheism rationally acceptable or emotionally satisfying.

So we must search for a different interpretation, one that takes the "Articles and Acts" seriously without taking them literally, acknowledges that Franklin's religious perspective is intricately latticed with both deistic and Christian strands that sometimes fit awkwardly with one another, and recognizes that his emotional need to relate to something greater than himself was in continuous tension with his rational suspicion that the need could not be met in any conventionally religious way. The genius of Franklin's "Articles and Acts" is his recognition that his religious beliefs were deeply layered and not always compatible, along with his willingness to embrace rather than artificially resolve the incompatibilities. Franklin saw them as all somehow gesturing at the reality of God. Instead of approaching them with an *either–or* razor, he sought to hold them in a creative *both–and* tension.

On the one hand, Franklin was convinced that the universe must have a divine First Cause: only a divine power is forceful enough to create reality itself. But Franklin, unlike conventional deists, no longer believed that reason could reveal anything about this divine First Cause other than that it must exist for anything else to exist. "[I]t is impossible," he says, "to have any positive clear idea of that which is infinite and incomprehensible." For someone once steeped in deism, this acknowledgment of the limits of human reason was a very big step indeed.

On the other hand, Franklin felt a pressing personal need for contact with a wise, benevolent, good, and loving deity. Moreover, he believed that all humans feel the same need: "there is in all Men something like a natural Principle which enclines them to DEVOTION," he says. So in order to meet this fundamental need, humanity, quite without any conscious awareness of what it does, invents intermediary, "created Gods" that provide the emotional support persons crave but cannot receive from the unknowable, unapproachable First Cause. These "created Gods," venerated by the faithful of all the major world religions, are fictions, not independent beings. They are artifacts born from the human longing for God. They are projections which, while assuaging a universal human need, nonetheless inevitably reflect in their specifics the historical place and time from which they arise. This would explain why Franklin wrote that the "created Gods" come and go, changing identity and character to fit shifting times.

But these gods, regardless of the forms they take, have very real psychological and social value. Belief in and worship of them give humans a sense of direction and purpose in life and provide a foundation for normative direction and social stability. Their existence, fictional though it might be, is an antidote to the spiritual and moral apathy that leads to the anarchy Franklin feared his *Dissertation* might encourage. The great *both–and* of Franklin's "Articles and Acts" is to value the benefits that "worship" of the "created Gods" brings, while at the same time acknowledging that the gods are only perspectives, relativistic attempts to put names and faces on the First Cause, which remains forever hidden from us. Most people at most times, of course, are unaware of this *both–and*. They imagine their gods to be objectively, independently existent. This misconception is generally a happy one, so far as Franklin is concerned, because of his conviction that the conventionalities of traditional religion serve as socially necessary checks on human behavior. Thus, religious faith, he writes elsewhere, "will [always] be a Powerful Regulator of our Actions, give us Peace and Tranquility within our Minds, and render us Benevolent, Useful and Beneficial to others" (P 1: 269). Were the common crowd to discover the *both–and* truth about their gods, the consequences could be catastrophic.

But for someone like Franklin, who has recognized the "created Gods" for the artifacts they are and yet who needs an intimate relationship with the cosmos just as much as any other person, a simple, traditional faith is no longer an option. What is needed in order to live with the knowledge that our "gods" are really just artifactual attempts to somehow make contact with the unfathomable First Cause is what the philosopher Richard Rorty, in a different context, refers to as "ironic commitment," that is, the ability to commit wholeheartedly to a belief that one knows can never be anything but provisional.[8] Ironic commitment, in the context of Franklin's "Articles and Acts," is the ability simultaneously to confess that the gods one worships are fictions but nonetheless to dedicate oneself to them as if they were actual. Ironic commitment, in other words, is the ultimate embrace of the *both–and* tension. It is the capacity, as Franklin says in a later document, for the worshiper honestly to acknowledge, "I have made to myself a God," while sincerely confessing that this god "abideth alway[s] in mine House, and provideth me with all Things" (P 6: 123).

"GOD governs in the Affairs of Men"

Although Franklin never again wrote as fully on the "created Gods" as he did in his 1728 "Articles of Belief and Acts of Religion," there are several references to them throughout his later writings. Most notable is a liturgy Franklin helped draft in the early 1770s, when he resided in England and was a member of the Thirteen, a club of savants that included the likes of Josiah Wedgwood, the dissenting minister David Williams, and James "Athenian"

Stuart. Unable to concur with conventional Christianity but desirous of some outlet for religious expression, these men drafted "A Liturgy on the Universal Principles of Religion and Morality," which, in language reminiscent of the "Articles and Acts," refers to "local Gods" to which the "theologists" of "various Nations, Sects and Parties" have "imputed" anthropocentric characteristics.[9]

At other points in his life, however, Franklin either forgot that he had "made to himself a god," instead writing as a literal instead of an ironic believer, or he referred to God in such a way as to deliberately reveal that he was speaking only of a socially and morally useful fiction. The ambiguity can sometimes be settled by looking at context, but in other places Franklin's meaning is unresolvable. Nowhere is this ambiguity more resistant than in his writings on providence.

Shortly after writing the "Articles and Acts," for example, Franklin penned a private memorandum sketching the contents of a "Doct[rine]. To be Prea[che]d" (1731) in which he defends the conventional religious claim that God "loves such of his Creatures as love and do good to others: and will reward them either in this World or hereafter." This passage suggests a very undeistic acceptance of "special providence" (i.e., the interference of God in the world – in this case, the rewarding "in this World" of those who are good). But whether Franklin really believed in divine providence, as a residual belief from his Calvinist background, or whether the vocabulary here is geared toward a general audience Franklin thought not ready for his "created Gods" thesis, remains unclear.[10]

Franklin returned to special providence the very next year in a manuscript entitled "On the Providence of God in the Government of the World," a draft of a speech created for his Philadelphia Junto. In it, Franklin defended the thesis that God "sometimes interferes by his particular Providence and sets aside the Effects which would otherwise have been produced by [natural] Causes." Again, interpretation is difficult. But a later passage in the same manuscript suggests that Franklin might have defended special providence here because of what he took to be the social and moral utility of the belief. "If God does not sometimes interfere by his Providence," wrote Franklin,

tis either because he cannot, or because he will not; which of these Positions will you chuse? There is a righteous Nation grievously oppress'd by a cruel Tyrant, they earnestly intreat God to deliver them; If you say he cannot, you deny his infinite Power...; if you say he will not, you must directly deny his infinite Goodness. You are then of necessity oblig'd to allow, that 'tis highly reasonable to believe a Providence because tis highly absurd to believe otherwise. (P 1: 269)

References to divine providence will reappear occasionally in Franklin's subsequent writings, often with similar ambiguity. In June 1787, while serving as a delegate to the Constitutional Convention, Franklin proposed that sessions be opened with prayer. His justification was that God's "superintending Providence," which carefully watches over creatures as insignificant as sparrows, surely needed to be invoked in a course of action so momentous as the creation of a new nation. "Have we... forgotten that powerful Friend?" Franklin asked his fellow delegates. "[D]o we imagine we no longer need [his] assistance?" But whether Franklin literally believed that the providential aid of the divine "powerful Friend" could be called down, or whether he was trying to appeal to the better nature of bitterly deadlocked delegates, just isn't clear (Smyth 9: 601).

Similarly, in an often-quoted letter written to Yale President Ezra Stiles, Franklin sets forth his "Creed," which includes the belief that God "governs [the universe] by his Providence."[11] Does "providence" here mean the uniform pattern of natural law, a claim with which a deist could concur? Does it mean supernatural intervention by God, a claim that would appeal to Franklin's piously dissenting parents? Is Franklin voicing one of those morally and socially useful fictions that the "created Gods" underwrite? Or is Franklin, an old and tired man when he (one month before he died) wrote the letter, simply preserving his waning energies by scribbling down a platitude that he knows will please Stiles and satisfy posterity?

"...What would they be if *without it*?"

Although it is unclear exactly what Franklin meant when he wrote about providence, his insistence that religion is essential to personal and social morality is not at all ambiguous. Except for the period shortly before and after the 1725 composition of the *Dissertation*, Franklin remained convinced that proper "Conduct of Life" is supremely important and that religious belief at its best promotes it. This conviction was inspired by three not entirely compatible sources: his Calvinist background, deism, and his low estimation of human nature.

As a young man, Franklin read and was highly impressed by Cotton Mather's *Bonifacius: An Essay upon the Good* (1710). This book urged readers to devote their lives to helping their fellow humans through individual deeds as well as by cooperating in the creation of philanthropic societies devoted to civic improvement. Mather insisted that a necessary condition for performing such good works was an honest, ongoing, and typically Calvinist program of internal discovery, evaluation, confession, and repentance of one's own moral weaknesses. Only when the corruption within has been ferreted out by brutal self-examination can an individual hope to do good. Franklin's reading of *Bonifacius* gave him "a Turn of Thinking that had an Influence on some of the principal future Events of my Life" (A 58).[12] Although he rejected Mather's belief in a stern and judgmental God, he was deeply influenced by his emphasis on moral living.

The self-improvement scheme for the day-by-day cultivation of thirteen virtues that Franklin famously describes in his *Autobiography* has its roots in Mather. Franklin's subsequent reading of the deists exposed him to a religious alternative to Calvinism. But he was struck that both deism and the Christianity of his youth shared a high regard for morality. The exercise of virtue was considered by the deists to be the purest, most rational, least superstitious mode of paying homage to the Supreme Being. Genuine worship consisted in improving one's personal character and society, not congregating in darkened churches chanting unintelligible creeds.

So both of the worldviews between which Franklin and his contemporaries were caught agreed on the importance of morality, and this agreement was not lost on Franklin. From his own worldly experiences and, perhaps, from a held-over conviction from his Calvinist background about the sinfulness of human nature, Franklin had little confidence that humans were rational enough to cultivate virtue without the carrot-and-stick incentives offered by conventional religion. In a 1780 letter to Joseph Priestley, for example, Franklin sadly compared humans to wolves and plaintively hoped "that human Beings would at length learn what they now improperly call Humanity!" (P 31: 455). Original sin, Franklin wrote elsewhere, is a "Bugbear set up by Priests," but this doesn't prevent him from concluding that humans have something fundamentally broken within them when it comes to moral capacity. "Men I find to be a Sort of Beings very badly constructed, as they are generally more easily provok'd than reconcil'd, more disposed to do Mischief to each other than to make Reparation" (P 2: 114; Smyth, 9: 452).[13]

This lupine brokenness is so resistant to the claims of reason, worried Franklin, that it can only be checked by encouraging the mass of humanity to believe that God punishes and rewards vice and virtue, both now and in the afterlife. As a proponent of "created Gods" in his "Articles and Acts," Franklin had no idea whether this claim was objectively true. But as someone vitally alert since his repudiation of the *Dissertation* to the social dangers of free thought, Franklin was convinced that it made no difference whether the belief was actually true or false. What mattered was that it helped people be a bit less wicked than they otherwise would be. In a 1786 letter to an unknown correspondent (perhaps Thomas Paine), Franklin worried that "a great Proportion of Mankind consists of weak and ignorant Men and

Women, and of inexperienc'd and inconsiderate Youth of both Sexes, who have need of the Motives of Religion to restrain them from Vice, to support their Virtue, and retain them in the Practice of it till it becomes *habitual*." Telling the truth about religion would be great folly, he concluded, for "if Men are so wicked as we now see them *with Religion* what would they be if *without it?*" (P 7: 294, 295).

Conclusion

My chapter opened with the claim that there is no "answer" to the question of Franklin's religion, if by "answer" one means a one-dimensional, easily classifiable label. As is true of many of us, Franklin's religious thought, while containing several identifiable and resilient strands, is a sometimes bewildering intersection of a number of threads that are sometimes at cross purposes. Judged harshly, Franklin might be seen as either hopelessly muddled in his religious beliefs or hypocritically reluctant to admit publicly to skepticism. But a far fairer evaluation of Franklin's religious sensibilities would be to see them as the struggles of a man caught in the sometimes frightening and sometimes exhilarating enterprise of trying to birth a religious perspective that would satisfy his heart as well as his head. In the process, he stumbled across a position that I have compared to Richard Rorty's ironic commitment, a position that was undoubtedly difficult at times for him to sustain. The difficulty accounts for the ambiguity in his religious writings. Such ambiguity bothers those scholars and others who prefer things neater than this. Franklin, who attempted for the greater part of his life to embrace the tension of *both–and* when it came to things religious, would not have been overly concerned by such consternation. Indeed, it probably would have amused him.

Notes

1. For more on the worldview clash between Calvinism and the New Learning, see my *Benjamin Franklin and His Gods* (Urbana and Chicago: University of Illinois Press, 1999), 17–42, and *Rational Infidels: The American Deists* (Durango, CO: Longwood Academic, 1992), 44–83.
2. For an extended discussion of Franklin's religious tolerance, see *Benjamin Franklin and His Gods*, 130–51.
3. For more on deism in Franklin's day, see my *The American Deists: Voices of Reason and Dissent in the Early Republic* (Lawrence: University Press of Kansas, 1992), 1–50, and *Rational Infidels*, 3–43.
4. Parts of this section have been adapted from my John Templeton Foundation Lecture, "Franklin and His Gods," March 22, 2006, Christ Church, Philadelphia, Pennsylvania, as part of the Benjamin Franklin Tercentenary Celebration.

5. As Franklin later asked, "Are there twenty Men in Europe at this Day, the happier, or even the easier, for any Knowledge they have pick'd out of Aristotle?" His answer to this question was obvious. See "To the Royal Academy of Brussels," in *Franklin's Wit and Folly: The Bagatelles*, ed. Richard E. Amacher (New Brunswick, NJ: Rutgers University Press, 1953), 68–69.
6. See, for example, Elizabeth E. Dunn, "From a Bold Youth to a Reflective Sage: A Reevaluation of Benjamin Franklin's Religion," *Pennsylvania Magazine of History and Biography* 111 (October 1987): 501–24.
7. The preeminent defender of the polytheism interpretation is Alfred Owen Aldridge, in *Benjamin Franklin and Nature's God* (Durham, NC: Duke University Press, 1967).
8. Richard Rorty discusses ironic commitment in *Contingency, Irony, and Solidarity* (Cambridge University Press, 1989).
9. David Williams, "More Light on Franklin's Religious Ideas," *American Historical Review* 43 (1938): 803–13. See also Nicolas A. Hans, "Franklin, Jefferson, and the English Radicals," *Proceedings of the American Philosophical Society* 98 (1954): 406–26, and E.V. Lucas, *David Williams: Founder of the Royal Literary Fund* (London: John Murray, 1920).
10. For more on Franklin's views concerning divine providence, see *Benjamin Franklin and His Gods*, 96–112, and *Rational Infidels*, 68–71.
11. Letter to Ezra Stiles, March 9, 1790, in *The Works of Benjamin Franklin*, 10 vols., ed. and intro. Jared Sparks (Boston: Charles Tappan, 1844), 10: 423.
12. For an analysis of Calvinist influence on Franklin's moral thought, see William Pencak, "Benjamin Franklin's Autobiography, Cotton Mather, and a Puritan God," *Pennsylvania History* 53 (January 1986): 1–25.
13. For more on Franklin's dark view of human nature, see Ronald A. Bosco's brilliant "'He that best understands the World, least likes it': The Dark Side of Benjamin Franklin," *Pennsylvania Magazine of History and Biography* 111 (October 1987): 525–54.

8

JAMES CAMPBELL

The pragmatist in Franklin

In an afterword to a volume celebrating the tricentennial of Franklin's birth, Edmund S. Morgan writes: "*Pragmatism* is the word most commonly used to describe Franklin's way of dealing with the world. We don't mean by it an adherence to the philosophy of Charles Sanders Peirce or William James... We mean, I think, simply a willingness to compromise in pursuit of some goal, a willingness not to insist on some abstract principle in transactions with other people, a willingness to make concessions." As an example of this willingness, Morgan points to the Great Compromise at the Constitutional Convention in 1787 that broke the deadlock over representation between the large and the small states.[1] I find in Morgan's passage a pair of suggestions: an interpretation of the meaning of Franklin's life and work, and an interpretation of the meaning of "philosophical" pragmatism. While I find Morgan's interpretation of Franklin quite sensible, his interpretation of philosophical pragmatism I find less so. He is correct to indicate that few see much of a connection between the pragmatism of Franklin and the pragmatism of Peirce and James (and Dewey). I believe, however, that we should.

This chapter will explore two themes: the range of Franklin's pragmatism and his place in the pragmatic tradition. First, it presents a view of Franklin's pragmatism that is, explicitly at least, broader than Morgan's, indicating that Franklin's religious and moral and scientific thinking is just as pragmatic as his political thinking. Then it suggests that Franklin's overall approach should be seen as being largely parallel with the later academic and social movement that we call philosophical pragmatism. When Poor Richard reminds us in his *Almanack* for 1749 that "*Words* may shew a man's Wit, but *Actions* his Meaning" (P 3: 336), his emphasis upon actions rather than words is a broadly pragmatic stance that bridges any attempt to separate Franklin from philosophical pragmatism, or philosophical pragmatism from him. Similarly, in 1784, when Franklin remarks in *Information to Those Who Would Remove to America* that in America, "people do not inquire concerning a Stranger, *What is he?* but, *What can he do?*" (Smyth 8: 606), his interest is the pragmatic primacy of individual achievement over ascription. Social status is not something that can be inherited in Franklin's America; it must be earned by an individual's performance of the tasks of social living. Actions and consequences that contribute to human betterment are what matter to our lives; theorizing, speculation, and bogus notions of superior status remain unimportant.

The range of Franklin's pragmatism

Regarding Franklin's pragmatism in politics, our first consideration, other commentators preceded Morgan in pointing to the generally pragmatic inclination in Franklin's political thinking. For some, the pragmatism of Franklin's political thinking lies in its emphasis upon the futility of political thinking about abstractions like "the state" or "justice" when such speculations yield only verbal solutions. For others, Franklin's pragmatic emphasis is more positive, upon the resolution of problems as they are encountered in our ongoing social lives.[2] In addition to his example of the Great Compromise, Morgan points to numerous other instances of Franklin's political pragmatism, beginning locally. "Franklin learned his pragmatism in Philadelphia," Morgan notes,[3] with the creation of various institutions of civic improvement, like the Junto, the Library Company, the American Philosophical Society, the Pennsylvania Hospital, and the Philadelphia Academy. A very brief survey of Franklin's pragmatic political writings, in addition to those that were related to the just named institutions, would include: *Plain Truth* (1747), *Observations Concerning the Increase of Mankind* (1754), *Causes of the American Discontents before 1768* (1768), "An Edict by the King of Prussia" (1773), and his 1790 essay on Sidi Mehemet Ibrahim and the slave trade.[4]

Franklin's political efforts were always related to his understanding of our social existence and often to the establishment of the institutional machinery necessary to make our common lives more successful. He worked both to create a series of unifying structures to advance the public good and to emphasize cooperative procedures like dialogue and education to foster greater democracy. His political goal was always pragmatic: creating a working system in the social realm rather than a pretty system of ideal truths. His focus was upon advocating policies, not producing treatises detailing how things ought to be. While Franklin's pragmatic spirit is often disparaged in contemporary politics (and ethics) as being devoid of "principle," surely acting to advance human well-being, and fostering lives of virtue and service to make this advance possible, demonstrate principles of some importance.

We must recognize, of course, that Franklin failed to overcome many of the customary prejudices of his social situation in the areas of gender and race and class. Still, his efforts across a remarkable range of issues force us to recognize as well the importance of his focus on action. If we concern ourselves with addressing specific political problems, as Franklin did, rather than with theorizing about more abstract topics, and if we continue our attempts at cooperative inquiry and experimentation to address these problems, as Franklin did, we should be able to create better social lives. This aspect of Franklin's thought and work is pragmatic.

Franklin's religious life began in Boston, where he reacted against its late Puritan strictures by swerving into free thought. In *A Dissertation on Liberty and Necessity*, written in London in 1725, he rejects freedom and declares responsibility irrelevant. Soon after, however, in his essay "On the Providence of God in the Government of the World," he supports the opposite position of the reality of freedom. Eventually Franklin concluded that the issue of freedom, like many other issues of a broadly religious nature, did not lend itself to easy resolution. Consequently, he decided that this sort of metaphysical inquiry itself should be abandoned and that we should pursue "*Truth, Sincerity and Integrity* in Dealings between Man and Man" (A 114). This pragmatic emphasis upon responsibility – upon action over words – directed the rest of his life. Franklin turned from the futility of doctrinal disputations to a focusing upon the advancement of human well-being through service.

A brief survey of Franklin's religious thought would include, in addition to the pieces just mentioned, his defenses of Samuel Hemphill in 1735, "A Parable against Persecution" (1755), and many statements of his religious beliefs: his recognition of general providence, his expectation of some form of immortality, the primacy of reason over revelation, and the need to focus upon advancing good conduct rather than orthodoxy – making "good Citizens" rather than conventional "Presbyterians" (A 147). We might also include here his preference for building lighthouses rather than memorial chapels in gratitude for deliverance from the dangers of the sea.[5] In considering these, and related, religious themes, Franklin emphasized two points. The first is that some form of religion seems necessary. To be *virtuous* required that individuals be *religious*, at least in a broad sense in which a belief in a benevolent and watchful God provided a foundation for the education of youth and offered ongoing support for the morally unsteady. Think, he writes, "how great a Proportion of Mankind consists of weak and ignorant Men and Women, and of inexperienc'd and inconsiderate Youth of both Sexes, who have need of the Motives of Religion to restrain them from Vice, to support their Virtue, and retain them in the Practice of it till it becomes *habitual*, which is the great Point for its Security." While admitting that such restraints are not fool-proof, Franklin asks: "If Men are so wicked as we now see them *with Religion* what would they be if *without it?*" (P 7:294–95). His response to the tendency of religions to overemphasize orthodoxy is to foster the practical service role of religion in social training. This approach would help young people to develop a more community-oriented stance and adults to maintain it. Franklin's second religious theme is that we should not take doctrinal issues too seriously. He urges us to deal pragmatically with indeterminate doctrines – like Christ's Divinity – by suggesting that, while we will never find out before death whether they are true or false, as long as they seem to produce positive results such doctrines of institutional religion may be taught. He is thus attempting to maintain the social value of the institutions without having to decide, one way or the other, about their particular doctrines.

Too often, Franklin notes, religion is unpragmatic: "seemingly *pious Discourses*" take the place of "*Humane Benevolent Actions*," and "*Good Works*" are devalued while "*Good Words* [are] admired in their Stead" (P 8: 155). As Poor Richard phrases this point in 1753, "Serving God is Doing Good to Man, but Praying is thought an easier Service, and therefore more generally chosen" (P 4: 406). The religious stance that Franklin eventually adopted, deism, offered only a minimal theological apparatus. In a universe created by a loving but distant God, we find ourselves charged to use reason to solve the mysteries of nature through cooperative and rational means so that we may live more comfortable lives. With this basic theological scaffolding in place, Franklin himself rejected the more complex systems presented by mainstream religions. One reason was that maintaining these religious systems absorbs valuable time and deflects limited energy from service into insoluble debates. Worse still, Franklin believed that these more complex religious systems often follow their failures to convert others by debate with attempts to enforce their orthodoxies against the "heretical" claims of conflicting systems. Throughout Franklin's pragmatic religious thought runs the central importance of naturalized religion for directing our concerns to human well-being.

Franklin's ethical thinking can be found in many places beyond his plan for "moral Perfection" in the *Autobiography* (A 148) and the economic aphorisms of *Poor Richard's Almanack* that he later gathered into *The Way to Wealth* (1758). Examples of Franklin's ethical thinking include such pieces as the Socratic dialogue, "A Man of Sense" (1735), "The Speech of Miss Polly Baker" (1747), and even his sketch of a "*Moral* or *Prudential Algebra*" from 1772.[6] Considered as a whole, Franklin's moral thinking contains a rejection of religious morality; and, in its place, he offers a rich philosophical defense of individual service to advance the common good. He began, of course, with a focus upon an individual moral regimen designed to develop personal virtues like temperance and order and justice. His moral vision was not exclusively personal, however, and he also considered the worth of social customs through an evaluation of their results. Throughout, his emphasis was upon the development of a morality that aimed at expanding human happiness.

Only in a pragmatic context of seeking to advance human well-being is it possible to understand adequately Franklin's emphases upon the development of virtues like industry and frugality and upon the curtailment of religious interference in people's lives. His is thus a natural morality, one that emphasizes the importance of human consequences over theological groundings or socially sanctioned precedents. For Franklin, our moral task is improving the well-being of our fellow citizens. "At the Day of Judgment," he writes, "we shall not be asked, what Proficiency we have made in Languages or Philosophy; but whether we have liv'd virtuously and piously" (P 7: 89). (Again, it is necessary to recognize Franklin's own limitations in virtue and piety, especially with regard to America's treatment of its native population and the imported slaves.) His is also an intense – perhaps even "puritan" – morality in that it brings home to all who consider it seriously the necessity for increasing efforts to expand a social and naturalistic conception of human well-being. For Franklin, expanding happiness in life was an end in itself, the goal of pragmatic morality.

Franklin's pragmatic work in science or natural philosophy shows him to be a dedicated and successful experimentalist. His brief research periods, coming only when his efforts were not needed elsewhere, addressed clearly recognizable scientific issues and problems – in aeronautics, agriculture, electricity, geology, heating, mathematics, medicine, meteorology, music, navigation, and so forth – in the hope of advancing the happiness of his fellows. Without such pragmatic advances, he thought that the scientist's efforts might be personally rewarding, even fulfilling, but they would remain a social loss. Franklin wrote to Cadwallader Colden of the dangerous temptation of what he called "Philosophical Amusements": "Had Newton been Pilot but of a single common Ship, the finest of his Discoveries would scarce have excus'd, or atton'd for his abandoning the Helm one Hour in Time of Danger; how much less if she had carried the Fate of the Commonwealth" (P 4: 68).

Franklin, of course, did not reject the potential usefulness of learning all that we can. He writes, for example, that a new piece of data, "if it cannot be explain'd by our old principles, may afford us new ones, of use perhaps in explaining some other obscure parts of natural knowledge"

(P 10: 159–60). His primary emphasis, however, was more pragmatic. We have a limited amount of time and energy, and we should concentrate our inquiries on achieving beneficial practical results. As he recommended to another colleague, "employ your time rather in making experiments, than in making hypotheses and forming imaginary systems, which we are all too apt to please ourselves with, till some experiment comes and unluckily destroys them" (Smyth 9: 53). Science as a tool for advancing the common good should not be misused to produce only "philosophical amusements." This pragmatic emphasis led, for example, both to Franklin's development of the Pennsylvania fireplace and the lightning rod, and to his refusal to seek a patent on either. Throughout his life, his scientific work remained the imaginative attempt to use rationality to advance the common good. His hope remained that, through increasing our control of nature, we might be able "to extend the Power of Man over Matter, avert or diminish the Evils he is subject to, or augment the Number of his Enjoyments" (Smyth 8: 593).

At times, Franklin's scientific formulations may seem myopic or optimistic. He offers, for example, with regard to the criticism regarding potential myopia, the seemingly short-sighted comment that it is of little importance "to know the Manner in which Nature executes her Laws; 'tis enough, if we know the Laws themselves" (P 4: 17). Surely, we are not likely to attain much control of nature without uncovering *why* things work as they do. A fuller reading of this and similar passages, however, must incorporate Franklin's moral theme of facing the necessary constraints on our time. It would be a mistake, he tells us, to keep searching fruitlessly for the *why* when the *how* is already usable. It is, moreover, an even greater mistake if, as often happens with "philosophical amusements," we forget that we were looking for a *how* in our ongoing searches for the *why*, and the *why* of the *why*. With regard to the latter question of whether Franklin was excessively optimistic, it is important to note that he was a meliorist rather than an optimist. This means that Franklin believed in potential, not necessary, progress. He writes toward the end of his long life of "the growing felicity of mankind, from the improvements in philosophy, morals, politics, and even the conveniences of common living, by the invention and acquisition of new and useful utensils and instruments" (Smyth 9: 651). Behind all of these advances, however, stood dedicated human effort; and, as a meliorist, he anticipated that these human efforts would continue this progress. His recognition of the expanding work of scientific organizations and of increasing technological breakthroughs led him to write, at least half-seriously, "I begin to be almost sorry I was born so soon, since I cannot have the happiness of knowing what will be known 100 years hence" (Smyth 9: 74–75).

In the back of Franklin's mind was always the belief that scientific discoveries would eventually prove useful. In the front of his mind, in any particular case, was some specific and attractive natural problem. This attitude of long-term practicality combined with short-term fascination would seem to be what drives any working scientist. We can attack a crippling disease, for example, knowing in advance that its elimination will increase human well-being; but we cannot know in advance what particular line of attack will succeed. Franklin offers us a vision of the role of science, tempered by fallibility and committed to public inquiry, as a tool in the advancement of humankind. This aspect of Franklin's thought and work is pragmatic.

Franklin's pragmatism in historical perspective

With a fuller sense of how pragmatic Franklin was in his political and religious and moral and scientific thought, it is possible to take up the second theme of this essay: his close relationship with philosophical pragmatism. Franklin was a thinker who presented the advancement of a richly conceived model of human well-being as his goal; and, as such, he was offering a model of wisdom, a philosophy. His was, of course, a pragmatic philosophy, one that needs to be appreciated for its attachments to what Ralph Waldo Emerson called "the common . . . the familiar, [and] the low." Emerson praised Franklin as "one of the most sensible men that ever lived . . . a transmigration of the Genius of Socrates – yet more useful, more moral, and more pure, and a living contradiction of the buffoonery that mocked a philosophy in the clouds . . ."[7] This pragmatic spirit also connects Franklin – and Emerson – with later pragmatic figures like William James and John Dewey. Pragmatism, as one historical strand within American philosophy, is acutely concerned with a number of values. One is our place within the systems of nature and our role as experimenters attempting to understand the limits and possibilities of our natural situation. Similarly, pragmatism is concerned with experience as our criterion of belief and action, as a means of directing ourselves to a better future. Pragmatism also presents a world of possibility, in which melioristic efforts make sense. Finally, pragmatism emphasizes community as the source of human well-being and as the focus of our efforts to enact long-term improvements.

Overall, Franklin's pragmatism, like this philosophical version of pragmatism, represents a rejection of metaphysical inquiry and its replacement with inquiries that are aimed at improving common experience and advancing the common good. While the notion of "metaphysics" often carries a vague meaning, we have a fairly clear sense of what Franklin meant when he considered the topic. In the *Almanack* for 1743, Poor Richard writes for example: "Men differ daily, about things which are subject to Sense, is it likely then they should agree about things invisible" (P 2: 368). The metaphysical enemy that Franklin opposed was the interminable speculative discussion of matters invisible and unknowable, especially as this discussion was able to draw us away from our service obligations and into discord. Later, he continues: "The great Uncertainty I have found in that Science [i.e., metaphysics]; the wide Contradictions and endless Disputes it affords; and the horrible Errors I led my self into when a young Man, by drawing a Chain of plain Consequences as I thought them, from true Principles, have given me a Disgust to what I was once extreamly fond of" (P 3: 88–89). Even when these negative consequences were not apparent, Franklin was indifferent to questions that had no practical impact. In a limited world where we must decide how to direct our finite energies, indifference to what offers no advantage to practical conduct – especially when "practical" is broadly conceived – is not an intellectual or philosophical vice. It seems clear, then, that for Franklin arguments about speculative topics like freedom (and immortality and the Divine) are "metaphysical," because they begin without any initial agreement on the interpretation of evidence, and they drag on unable to agree on what would constitute a decisive conclusion. For the pragmatist Franklin, experience is our criterion, and "Opinions should be judg'd of by their Influences and Effects" (P 2: 203).

There are comments scattered throughout the Franklin literature suggesting that he was a precursor of later pragmatism. Many of these commentators demonstrate only a casual familiarity with the complexity of philosophical pragmatism, and they equate it with any interest in action, whether socially useful or not. Other commentators on Franklin, however, are quite well informed about the philosophical pragmatism that developed later. These writers focus upon the importance of deliberately evaluating beliefs and policies based upon their results. Thus, whether our interest is in deciding on the value of religious doctrines, or moral rules, or metaphysical hypotheses like determinism, they recognize that Franklin's pragmatism emphasizes the necessity for grounding these debates in experienced facts. Speculation is, on its own, valueless. These informed writers indicate as well that Franklin's pragmatism also emphasizes that we must consider what sort of people we are making ourselves into by adhering to these doctrines and rules and hypotheses. We cannot exclude the effects of living according to these beliefs from a consideration of their truth; and, since intellectual resolutions often remain indeterminate, Franklin notes that we seldom have much upon which to base our decisions of their value except their workings in human life. In other words, in a context very different from the familiar academic one a century ago, in which professors explored the nature of the possible integration of intellectual work with life outside of the university through the formulation of a pragmatic philosophy, Franklin developed an intellectual spirit or a way of life that was equally pragmatic.[8]

This understanding of Franklin as connected with later philosophical pragmatism has not been widely accepted. Perhaps much of the reluctance to recognize Franklin's close connections with philosophical pragmatism comes from our unwillingness to see Franklin as a "philosopher." For some, of course, this resistance is an attempt to defend Franklin's importance from those who would turn him into an "intellectual." In any case, it was not always so difficult to see Franklin as a philosopher. For Thomas Jefferson, for example, Franklin was "the father of American philosophy." In his *Notes on the State of Virginia*, Jefferson writes that "no one of the present age has made more important discoveries, nor has enriched philosophy with more, or more ingenious solutions of the phaemonena of nature," than Franklin. The Scot David Hume similarly seems untroubled in his evaluation of Franklin as a philosopher when he writes to him in 1762: "America has sent us many good things, Gold, Silver, Sugar, Tobacco, Indigo, &c.: But you are the first Philosopher, and indeed the first Great Man of Letters for whom we are beholden to her."[9] Such liberal uses of the term "philosophy" indicate, of course, the broad historical conception of the term as the pursuit of wisdom to render human life more secure and fulfilling. In the eighteenth-century world, where philosophy's inclusion of the moral and natural sciences fostered the wide-ranging application of reason to advance human well-being, Franklin offered a complex vision of the pursuit of wisdom and clearly belongs within this broad understanding of "philosopher."

The meaning of the term "philosophy" has since narrowed. For about a century, it has carried a more constricted meaning, concerned with technical questions related to isolated topics of interest primarily to professionalized academics. In this context, discussions of Franklin as a philosopher are, as might be expected, infrequent. The approach adopted by most historians of the American philosophical tradition over the last century has been to allude to his significant intellectual and political importance, but to avoid discussing him as a "philosopher." That term is generally reserved for such thinkers as Cadwallader Colden (1688–1776), Samuel Johnson (1696–1772), Jonathan Edwards (1703–58), and John Witherspoon (1723–94). Unlike Franklin, these thinkers were interested in questions like the existence of God, the nature of knowledge, the possibility of free will, and other topics often classified as "metaphysical."[10] For Franklin, on the contrary, practical questions with possible answers remained at the center of his thinking.

The position that Franklin was not a philosopher has remained the dominant one. Franklin thus plays a very minor role in contemporary discussions of the history of American philosophy. The question remains, however, unsettled. If we decide to limit the term to its current academic meaning, focusing upon technical questions related to the meanings of concepts and the machinery of reasoning, and emphasizing the abstract and the "meta-physical," then regardless of Franklin's merits, he would be dismissed as a philosopher. If, on the other hand, we allow for a sense of the term that incorporates the broad pursuit of wisdom and the inherited sense of natural philosophy that connects our pursuit of wisdom with inquiries into our natural place, then Franklin's status as a philosopher would seem secure. In addition, any reconstruction of our understanding of the American philosophical tradition that would yield a significant place for Franklin would also offer us a chance to rethink our present understanding of the term "philosophy" itself.

Perhaps the beginning of this rethinking of philosophy, and of Franklin as philosopher, would come from emphasizing, as I have done, his continuities with philosophical pragmatism. Franklin's political, religious, ethical, and scientific work presents a vision that is both fundamentally pragmatic on its own terms and clearly within the broad stream of American philosophy that sought the wisdom necessary to advance a natural and social conception of human well-being. Franklin's vision is thus continuous with those of Emerson, James, and Dewey, all central pillars of American pragmatism. Each of them saw the proper aim of the philosophical endeavor to be the advance of the common good and the overall well-being of the average individual. In particular, they addressed the creating and shaping power of social institutions and the place of the individual as interpreter and modifier of this process.

It is possible to sketch out this pragmatic vision a bit further by considering the manner in which Franklin, Emerson, James, and Dewey each address its four central themes of nature, experience, possibility, and community. The first is the attempt to understand our natural place. Franklin presents humans as experimenters striving for control of our natural situation, while Emerson celebrates our relationship with nature. Understanding our place in nature is also central to the post-Darwinian explorations of James and Dewey, the former discussing the embodiment of the live organism, and the latter the meaning of evolutionary thinking for our reconception of our place in existence. The second aspect of this pragmatic vision is our understanding of experience. Franklin offers us experience as the hypothetical and cooperative criterion for overcoming the tyranny of entrenched dogma. Experience is central to Emerson, as well, for experience enables us to find value in a world inclined toward routinization. For James, what matters is our attendance to the stream of experience so that we can grasp its meaning. Dewey's emphasis lies in adopting a critical stance toward experience and hunting for true values amid the ever-present apparent goods available to us. The recognition of possibility is the third theme central to American pragmatism. Franklin focuses on how the individual's life can be more fulfilling in a practical sense; Emerson, in a more transcendental sense. For James, possibility is something that the individual uses to create a system of living beliefs. Dewey's focus is on educational possibilities, by means of which society can present the next generation with a more vibrant future. The fourth theme central to an adequate understanding of American pragmatism is community. Franklin's emphasis is on the importance of creating and maintaining political unity; Dewey's, on the ongoing need for social reconstruction. Both of them concern themselves with the importance of institutions of cooperative living. Emerson and James, although often seen as "individualists," were both intensely public figures who participated in the intellectual life of their society.

Franklin's broad sense of pragmatism envisioned advancing the common good through attempts to improve science, religion, ethics, and politics, and through rebuilding social institutions by means of cooperative inquiry and education. He offers us a living intellectual perspective that began with the attempt to address specific problems in a tentative and cooperative fashion, that emphasized the importance of duty and service, and that fostered a criterion of weighing the social consequences of our actions as the key to determining proper conduct. It would not be inaccurate to suggest that Franklin's vision of life grew in the hands of the others into a self-conscious, articulated philosophy. Admittedly, Emerson and James and Dewey performed this task without being particularly cognizant of Franklin's contribution.[11] Still, this pragmatic vision of human well-being is fundamental to his – and their – way of thinking and acting, and it does seem fair to categorize him as a pragmatist. If he is a pragmatist, it would also seem sensible to categorize him as a philosopher, as well, and to treat him as one who deserves a more central place in our discussions of American philosophy. Over the years, philosophers have drifted from his broad social conception of philosophy and from this pragmatic focus upon the common good. Philosophy has too often become an inward-looking pursuit of the preconditions of the means to begin to prepare to attempt to understand. Similarly, the common good, when it appears as a value at all, is too often simply assumed to be connected to whatever philosophers are interested in exploring.

We might well wonder how the pursuit of wisdom, philosophy's historic mission, was ever allowed to separate from a broad sense of human well-being. Franklin himself poses the question this way: "What signifies

Philosophy that does not apply to some Use?" (P 9: 251). When he busied himself with such practical problems as inventing a more efficient stove, or developing procedures to minimize theological disputes, or constructing an algebra for simplifying moral dilemmas, or establishing an institution to better organize the availability of books, he was applying philosophy to some use. While Franklin admits that these problems may appear to some as "trifling Matters" or affairs of a "seemingly low Nature" (A 207), for him they are the elements of human life, and their solutions represent a part of the advancing of wisdom that has always been philosophy's task. Our narrower conception of philosophy leaves philosophers largely blind to the vision of a thinker like Franklin; but, by returning to this historical task of philosophy, philosophers and others might come more easily to recognize the pragmatist in Franklin.

Notes

1. Edmund S. Morgan, "The End of His Pragmatism," in *Benjamin Franklin: In Search of a Better World*, ed. Page Talbott (New Haven: Yale University Press, 2005), 299.
2. For an example of each position, see Adrienne Koch, *Power, Morals, and the Founding Fathers: Essays in the Interpretation of the American Enlightenment* (Ithaca: Cornell University Press, 1961), 14–22; and Carl L. Becker, "Benjamin Franklin," in *Dictionary of American Biography*, ed. Allen Johnson and Dumas Malone (New York: Scribners, 1931), 6: 585–98.
3. Morgan, "The End of His Pragmatism," 300.
4. Franklin, *Plain Truth*, P 3: 188–204; *Observations Concerning the Increase of Mankind*, P 4: 225–34; *Causes of the American Discontents before 1768*, P 15: 3–13; "An Edict by the King of Prussia," P 20: 414–18; and the essay on the slave trade, Smyth 10: 87–91.
5. For the Hemphill discussions of 1735, see A 167–68, P 2: 37–126. "A Parable against Persecution," P 6: 122–24. For the comments on lighthouses, see: A 259 and P 7: 243–44.
6. *The Way to Wealth*, P 7: 340–50; "A Man of Sense," P 2: 15–19; "The Speech of Miss Polly Baker," P 3: 123–25. For the moral algebra, see P 19: 299–300.
7. Ralph Waldo Emerson, "The American Scholar," in *The Complete Works of Ralph Waldo Emerson*, 12 vols., the Centenary Edition, ed. Edward Waldo Emerson (Boston: Houghton Mifflin, 1903–04), 1: 111; *The Journals of Ralph Waldo Emerson*, 10 vols., ed. Edward Waldo Emerson and Waldo Emerson Forbes (Boston: Houghton Mifflin, 1909–14), 1: 375–76.
8. For some helpful discussions of Franklin's pragmatism, see Robert E. Spiller, "Benjamin Franklin: Promoter of Useful Knowledge," in *The American Writer and the European Tradition*, ed. Margaret Denny and William H. Gilman (Minneapolis: University of Minnesota Press, 1950), 29–44; Spiller, "Benjamin Franklin: Student of Life," in *Meet Doctor Franklin* (Philadelphia: Franklin Institute, 1943), 83–103; and Elizabeth Flower and Murray G. Murphey, *A History of Philosophy in America* (New York: Putnam's, 1977), 1: 99–115.

9. Jefferson to Jonathan Williams, July 3, 1796, in *The Writings of Thomas Jefferson*, 10 vols., ed. Paul Leicester Ford (New York: G. P. Putnam's Sons, 1892–99), 7: 87; Jefferson, *Writings*, ed. Merrill D. Peterson (New York: Library of America, 1984), 190. Hume's comments are reprinted in P 10: 81–82.

10. In 1925, Herbert W. Schneider asserted, "Although Benjamin Franklin was regarded by his contemporaries both here and in Europe as the foremost philosopher of America, he is rarely mentioned in philosophical circles today": "The Significance of Benjamin Franklin's Moral Philosophy," in *Studies in the History of Ideas*, 3 vols. (New York: Columbia University Press, 1925), 2: 293–312, quotation at 293. For discussions of Franklin as a non-philosopher, see Isaac Woodbridge Riley, *American Philosophy: The Early Schools* (1907; New York: Russell and Russell, 1958), 229–65; and Vincent Buranelli, "Colonial Philosophy," *William and Mary Quarterly* 3rd ser. 16 (July 1959): 343–62.

11. Some of Emerson's references to Franklin have been cited previously. James, in a rare reference to Franklin, points to our need to get beyond "the coarser and more commonplace moral maxims" of *Poor Richard*, in *The Will to Believe, and Other Essays in Popular Philosophy* (1897; Cambridge, MA: Harvard University Press, 1979), 143. Dewey's interest in Franklin was primarily as a contemporary of Jefferson, whose writings, he notes, were "without that tinge of smugness that sometimes colors Franklin's reflections on life": "Presenting Thomas Jefferson," in *Later Works of John Dewey*, 17 vols., ed. Jo Ann Boydston, *et al.* (Carbondale: Southern Illinois University Press, 1981–90), 14: 201–23, quotation at 204.

9

LESTER C. OLSON

Franklin on national character and the Great Seal of the United States

For my own part I wish the Bald Eagle had not been chosen as the Representative of our Country. He is a Bird of bad moral Character.
Benjamin Franklin, letter to his daughter, Sarah Bache, January 26, 1784

Character was a preoccupation of men in Britain and colonial America throughout the eighteenth century – not only the character of the individual men in prominent roles within each community, but also the character of entire nations in evidence in their manners.[1] Reputation was a vital factor determining one's place in British colonial hierarchy, the society in which Benjamin Franklin was raised and entered public life long before the American Revolution. Yet, Franklin, who worked as the printer of *The Pennsylvania Gazette*, was not a "gentleman" in the eighteenth-century sense of a man who did not need to work for a living, a man of leisure. Even after he had retired from publishing *The Pennsylvania Gazette*, his opponents criticized his class origins and resources. Finding himself vilified during the mid-1760s, for example, he assured himself and his allies, when writing that "Dirt thrown on a Mud-Wall may stick and incorporate; but it will not long adhere to polish'd Marble" (P 13: 488). Subsequently, at times, he sought to cultivate an image of his own character as a gentleman worthy of leadership in British America.

Franklin was likewise preoccupied with the perceived national character of the new United States in evidence in its manners. In his various pictorial representations of British America over the decades, one constant was his emphasis on the character of the American community, character that he hoped his works would assist in imparting to his audience. Franklin's concern with national character shaped his emphatic rejection of the bald eagle as the new nation's symbol on the Great Seal of the United States. Toward the conclusion of the American Revolution, the Continental Congress had selected the eagle's image to become the national emblem, because, to the delegates, the eagle emphasized an American commitment to classical republicanism in keeping with certain iconographic traditions. When Franklin learned about the Congress's choice of the eagle for the national emblem, he lamented in a letter to his daughter, Sarah Bache, during January 1784, that the eagle would rather steal fish caught by a fishing hawk – better known today as an osprey – than endeavor to catch the fish itself. Despite his expression of dissatisfaction, the eagle is the most enduring of the eighteenth-century images designating the United States.[2]

To understand Franklin's letter concerning the Great Seal in its historical context, it is important to remember that he devoted the first several paragraphs to ridiculing the entire idea of descending honors, concerned as he was that the recently formed Society of the Cincinnati could become a vehicle for the creation of a noble order in the United States. The Cincinnati, an honorary society composed of officers who had served under George Washington during the Revolution, had employed the eagle's image on its symbolic artifacts, because the Great Seal had featured the eagle. So Franklin's concerns in the letter were overtly about the Society's device and, only in the course of developing those concerns, about the seal that had inspired it. This slight difference in primary focus is consequential, because, situated within an international public controversy over the Cincinnati, the eagle's image would have emphatically resonated with the history of privileged classes.

This chapter will explore Franklin's perspective concerning the design of the Great Seal to underscore his plea for cultural and class simplicity in forming the new nation's character and to explore the complicated history informing the Great Seal's meanings during its initial circulation. Franklin meant the substance of his objections to the seal's design to be taken seriously, not merely as humor calculated to amuse his daughter, however playful the style of the criticism. Various factors underscored his genuine dissatisfaction with the eagle's image on the Great Seal. First, his earlier political writings and pictorial symbolism represented Britain as a predatory eagle. Second, his earlier proposals for specific images to represent the British American colonies involved particular criteria that he later evoked to disavow the eagle's image on the Great Seal. Finally, his queries about publishing his criticism of the Great Seal's design in a political pamphlet at the time suggested the depth of his concern over the specific cultural values to be promoted by the pictorial design. Attention to this last factor entails examining Franklin's reliance on ridicule during an international controversy over the recent formation of the Cincinnati, whose use of the eagle's image had prompted Franklin's letter.

Franklin's disavowal of the eagle's image

During the eighteenth century, the image of the eagle for the Great Seal received the most careful scrutiny of any image representing the United

States. Congress endorsed the seal because it was based, in part, on collections of emblems and devices, on the rules governing heraldry, and, above all, on the iconographic traditions associated with flag designs during the Roman Republic. To Congress, the eagle's image emphasized an American commitment to classical republicanism, the authority and power to promote republicanism, and the predisposition of the American people toward peace through military strength.[3]

However, Franklin was not pleased with the result of the congressional deliberations. On January 26, 1784, he articulated a now famous criticism of the decision by Congress to use the eagle for the Great Seal. In a letter to his only daughter, Sarah Bache, he commented at length on the ramifications of the eagle's image for national character, because this image was now to appear on the medallions of the Cincinnati. In the letter, Franklin mentioned dissatisfaction with the quality of the Latin motto "as wanting classic Elegance & Correctness," the questionable decision to use Latin rather than English for the motto, and the pretentiousness of suggesting that American soldiers were like Cincinnatus, who had served without pay, since only General Washington had done so. Among the shortcomings, Franklin expressed to his daughter his dissatisfaction with Congress's choice of the bald eagle to represent the United States by concentrating on honesty, industriousness, and courage as features of national character:

> For my own part I wish the Bald Eagle had not been chosen as the Representative of our Country. He is a Bird of bad moral Character. He does not get his Living honestly. You may have seen him perch'd on some dead Tree near the River, where, too lazy to fish for himself, he watches the Labour of the Fishing Hawk; and when that diligent Bird has at length taken a Fish, and is bearing it to his Nest for the Support of his Mate and young Ones, the Bald Eagle pursues him and takes it from him. With all this Injustice, he is never in good Case but like those among Men who live by Sharping & Robbing he is generally poor and often very lousy.

As for the attributes of courage that Franklin had long associated with the United States, he lamented that the eagle "is a rank Coward: The little *King Bird* not bigger than a Sparrow attacks him boldly and drives him out of the District." Franklin next contrasted the eagle's character with that of the Society of the Cincinnati, complaining to Sarah that the eagle "is therefore by no means a proper Emblem for the brave and honest Cincinnati of America who have driven all the *King birds* from our Country, tho' exactly fit for that Order of Knights which the French call *Chevaliers d'Industrie*," a French expression designating crooks or swindlers.

Franklin confided to his daughter that the design's mediocre execution had made the bald eagle look like a turkey. He then developed a sustained comparison of these birds to explain his own preference for the turkey as an emblem:

> I am on this account not displeas'd that the Figure is not known as a Bald Eagle, but looks more like a Turkey: For in Truth the Turkey is in Comparison a much more respectable Bird, and withal a true original Native of America. Eagles have been found in all Countries, but the Turkey was peculiar to ours, the first of the Species seen in Europe being brought to France by the Jesuits from Canada, and serv'd up at the Wedding Table of Charles the ninth. He is besides, tho' a little vain & silly, a Bird of Courage, and would not hesitate to attack a Grenadier of the British Guards who should presume to invade his Farm Yard with a red Coat on.

Franklin was dissatisfied with the image of the bald eagle representing America for a number of specific reasons derived largely from his observations of the bird's behavior in the wild. His criteria were also overtly cultural in that they were derived from emblem books and heraldic traditions. The values guiding his assessment – courage, honesty, industriousness, magnanimity, and self-reliance – were as cultural as the language that he employed to express his dissatisfaction.

Franklin's frank assessment has become a source of embarrassment to some, who have dismissed the remarks as merely whimsical or as a humorous commentary calculated to amuse his daughter, not a substantive criticism of the national character that the eagle's image promoted to Americans. While he employed clever puns and amusing images to make his criticism palatable, these stylistic elements may have undercut the substance of the criticism, which concentrated on the implications of the eagle's image for national character. As evidence that Franklin was just being playful, interpreters of his letter have underscored that he himself had used the eagle's image on earlier occasions in the imperial dispute and, further, that he immediately used the Great Seal's image prominently on two publications concerning the recent peace agreement and the resulting nation's form of government.

Despite Franklin's displeasure with the design on the Great Seal, he later included the image in two publications: *Constitutions of the Thirteen United States of America*, published under the title, in French, *Constitutions des Treize Etats-Unis de l'Amérique* (Figure 1) and *The Definitive Treaty between Great Britain, and the United States of America, Signed at Paris, the 3d day of September 1783* (Figure 2). His use of the seal on these publications was not dependable evidence that he was "not writing seriously." Nor was it conclusive "evidence that his later expression of

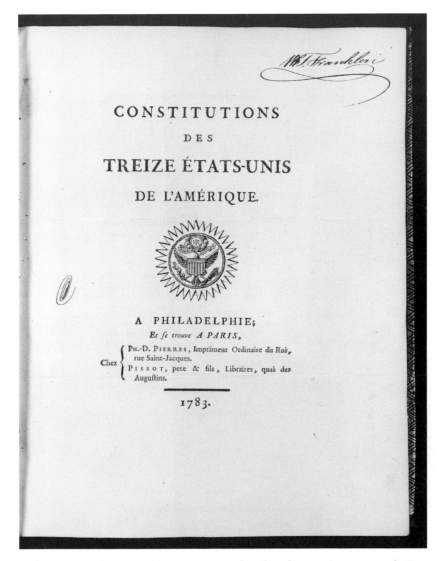

CONSTITUTIONS

DES

TREIZE ÉTATS-UNIS

DE L'AMÉRIQUE.

A PHILADELPHIE;
Et se trouve A PARIS,

Chez { Ph.-D. Pierres, Imprimeur Ordinaire du Roi, rue Saint-Jacques.
Pissot, pere & fils, Libraires, quai des Augustins.

1783.

1 The Great Seal of the United States, as engraved on the title page, *Constitutions des Treize Etats-Unis de l'Amérique* [translated by Louis-Alexandre, duc de la Rochefoucault], (Paris and Philadelphia: [Philippe-Denis] Pierres, 1783).

preference for the turkey as a symbol of the United States Government is not to be taken seriously." Richard S. Patterson and Richardson Dougall, who made these dismissive comments, observed accurately in *The Eagle and the Shield: A History of the Great Seal of the United States*, perhaps the most comprehensive study of the design for the Great Seal, that "Historically, a seal established the authenticity of a document, just as a modern signature

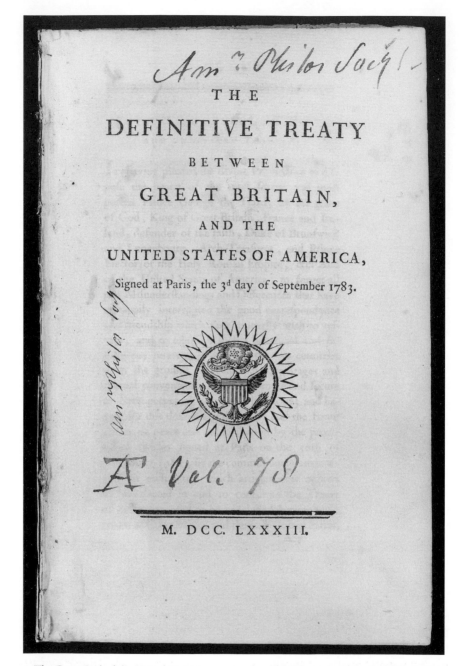

THE

DEFINITIVE TREATY

BETWEEN

GREAT BRITAIN,

AND THE

UNITED STATES OF AMERICA,

Signed at Paris, the 3ᵈ day of September 1783.

M. DCC. LXXXIII.

2 The Great Seal of the United States, as engraved on the title page of *The Definitive Treaty between Great Britain, and the United States of America, Signed at Paris, the 3d day of September 1783* ([Passy: Press of Benjamin Franklin], 1783).

does." They added, "A great seal is the principal seal of a nation, state, or other major political entity, used for authenticating documents of high importance or high ceremony issued in the name of the sovereign or chief executive authority."[4] Whatever private reservations Franklin had about the image, he could not have withheld the "signature" of the United States from the documents explaining the new nation's form of government, or the treaty ending the war. Because the Congress had authorized the eagle's image on the Great Seal to be the legitimating signature of that governing body, he was obligated in his role as plenipotentiary minister to use the image to authenticate the later publications.

The eagle in Franklin's earlier designs

Franklin's criticism of the Great Seal's design was minimized in another account by J. A. Leo Lemay, because Franklin had employed the eagle's image on two earlier occasions, first in his 1747 design for the flags for the Pennsylvania Associators, and then in his 1775 proposal for the paper currency of the Continental Congress. Although Franklin did use the eagle on flags in 1747 to represent the Associators, he never used it to represent either the united colonies or the United States. In 1747, Franklin was still loyal to the British Crown, and he would not have had reservations about the eagle's aristocratic associations. But he had changed markedly during the thirty-seven intervening years, which included the period of the French and Indian War, the decade of colonial dissent, the "Declaration of Independence," the bloody American Revolution, and national independence. Moreover, near the end of that period, he consistently employed the eagle's image as an embodiment of an abusive and predatory British government. As J. A. Leo Lemay has accurately noted, "The eagle was traditionally a symbol of military prowess, of aristocracy, and of feudalism. Franklin knew the traditional associations and chafed at them."[5]

Franklin employed the eagle's image on the three-dollar Continental currency in 1775, but he used it to represent Britain's abusive and predatory power, not to embody the United States. At least three contemporaneous publications printed commentaries regarding the eagle's image on the paper currency in a similar light that associated the eagle with the monarchical and aristocratic power of Britain. Indeed, Franklin had employed the eagle's image on the currency, but that usage does not discount his later letter to his daughter concerning the Great Seal. To the contrary, the currency is evidence that he was serious about his dissatisfaction.

Consider a pseudonymous commentary on Franklin's use of the eagle before turning next to two poetic verses about it, because, taken together, these three commentaries provide evidence of contemporaneous under-standings of the eagle's meanings shortly before its use on the Great Seal. One such commentary circulated initially in the *Pennsylvania Gazette* for September 20, 1775, and, later, in the *Pennsylvania Magazine* for December 1775:

> On another [denomination of the Continental currency] is drawn an *eagle* on the wing, pouncing upon a *crane*, who turns upon his back, and receives the eagle on the point of his long bill, which pierces the eagle's breast; with this motto, EXITUS IN DUBIO EST; – *The event is uncertain.* The eagle, I suppose, represents Great-Britain, the crane America.

This widely distributed description of the design was sometimes attributed to Franklin. If the attribution were accurate (which is unlikely), then the case for the seriousness of his concerns about national character was amplified by the earlier uses of the eagle imagery, not diminished.[6]

Two additional eighteenth-century commentaries, both in the form of poetic verses but by authors with opposing views of the war, identified the eagle on the three-dollar bill as the embodiment of Britain, not the United States. Joseph Stansbury, an American who remained loyal to the British crown, commented on the currency design in "The History of Peru, &c.," which he wrote over the pseudonym "R. R." at Philadelphia in 1776. The Loyalist writer took poetic license with the pictorial elements by alluding to the eagle and the crane in two separate stanzas and in combination with the pictorial elements from other bills. Stansbury recognized the eagle as an aggressive embodiment of Britain: "The Eagle was *Britain*." Another writer with views supporting the American colonists also identified the eagle as Britain and the crane as the United States in "A Contest between the Eagle and the Crane," published in the Rev. Wheeler Case's collection of *Poems occasioned by several circumstances* in New Haven in 1778. This poetic verse recounted a recollection made by a witness of a predatory eagle's attack on a crane, which ended with the eagle mortally impaled through the throat by the crane's bill. Then the poem turned to the allegorical implications for the British Empire, unequivocally identifying the eagle with Britain's misuse of power. Thus, Franklin's use of the eagle's image on the paper currency was recognized by his contemporaries as an emblem of predation, regardless of political sympathies.[7]

Franklin employed the eagle's image to represent Britain in other notewor-thy instances that, consistent with his use of the eagle's image on the currency in 1775, reflected the negative connotations he associated with the eagle. He used the image again in the article, "NEW FABLES, *humbly inscribed to the S - - - - - y* [Secretary] *of St - - e* [State] *for the* American Department," published initially in the *Public Advertiser* of London on January 2, 1770: "AN Eagle, King of Birds, sailing on his Wings aloft over a Farmer's Yard, saw a Cat there basking in the Sun, *mistook it for a Rabbit*, stoop'd, seized it, and carried it up into the Air, *intending to prey on it*. The Cat[,] turning, set her Claws into the Eagle's Breast; who, finding his Mistake, opened his Talons, and would have let her drop; but Puss, unwilling to fall so far, held faster; and the Eagle, to get rid of the Inconvenience, found it necessary to *set her down where he took her up*" (P 17: 3). Written by Franklin during the controversy after the Townshend duties of 1767, this fable condemned Britain's abusive power by using the eagle's image to describe predation.

In addition, Franklin's contemporaries recognized his strong convictions concerning the eagle. While he resided in France as an official representative, he was presented with various verses written in French by an anonymous author using the initials, "L. A." One of these French verses was derived from Franklin's "Fable of the Eagle and the Cat," as indicated in the title, "L'Aigle et le Chat. Fable allégorique de M. Franklin." In this poem, the author sustained the eagle's associations with Britain by such phrases as "A sa Majesté l'Aigle [To His Majesty the Eagle]," and the cat with the United States, "Chat Américain [American Cat]."[8] Not only had Franklin continued to regard the eagle as a symbol of predatory and abusive power, but his convictions about the image were well known to his French contemporaries. If Franklin's earlier uses of the eagle's image are indicative of the depth of his later dissatisfaction with the Great Seal, they suggest that his concerns were genuine and of long duration.

Franklin's rhetorical style of ridicule

Additional factors suggest that Franklin's letter to his daughter articulated substantive objections to the eagle's image on the Great Seal, because of its implications for national character. These factors were his use of ridicule, which characterized the letter's rhetorical style as a whole; his choice of audience, his only daughter; and the broad context of the ongoing public debate over the formation of the new Society of the Cincinnati.

Interpretations of his letter as private humor within the Franklin family rest on an assumption that he intended the document only for his daughter, or, possibly, for later generations of Americans. But there is evidence that he considered publishing his criticisms at the time and that certain elements from his letter found their way into the public discourse of the time. Moreover, the interpretations of the letter simply as humor assumed that ridicule was a means of amusement in the eighteenth century, not a style of substantive argumentation. However, during the eighteenth century, deists regarded ridicule as a powerful mode of argument for exposing the deficiency of an opposing point of view.

Franklin, who admired the writings of Anthony Ashley Cooper, third Earl of Shaftesbury (1671–1713), viewed ridicule, as Shaftesbury did, as a means of testing truth: truth or worthiness, to Franklin, can always withstand the test of ridicule. Ridicule was not merely a style of humor calculated to amuse; rather, ridicule could serve as a legitimate mode of argumentation. In 1708, Shaftesbury suggested that truth "may bear all lights; and one of the principal lights or natural mediums, by which things are to be viewed, in order to a thorough recognition, is ridicule itself, or that manner of proof by which we discern whatever is liable to just raillery in any subject." He inquired in his *Letter Concerning Enthusiasm* (1708), "Now what rule or measure is there in the world, except in the considering of the real temper of things, to find which are truly serious, and which ridiculous? And how can this be done, unless by applying the ridicule to see whether it will bear?" The laughter evoked by ridicule constituted proof that the described choice or belief was unacceptable to discerning people. Franklin had read Shaftesbury and spoke highly of his writings.[9]

Further, at the time, Franklin considered publishing his letter in a pamphlet translated into French. But he decided not to do so, out of deference to the political judgment of his intimate friend, Abbé Morrellet. When he returned a translated version of the letter to Franklin, Morrellet, whose profession placed him in one of the privileged orders, enclosed a note explaining his reservations about publishing the letter: "If you permit me to say so, this paper, though excellent, may cause irritation to some people you do not want to antagonize; and for this reason you ought not to give it, unless you think otherwise, except to persons who have enough philosophy to know and feel all the absurdity and ridiculousness of the harmful bias you fight so well." To this advice, Franklin responded, "Your Sentiments and mine, my dear Friend, are exactly the same respecting the Imprudence of showing that Paper; it has therefore, tho' written some Months past, never been communicated to anyone but yourself, and will probably not appear till after my Decease, if it does then." Political considerations of propriety convinced Franklin to suppress publication of the letter under his name during his lifetime, because his comments concerning the Cincinnati might have offended people in France as well as in America. As the ambassador from the United States to France, he could not with propriety in public ridicule French institutions such as the nobility. In any event, French censors would not have permitted the letter's publication in France.[10]

But Franklin nonetheless indirectly engaged in the public controversy over the Cincinnati by providing materials and encouragement to other polemicists. He framed the entire letter to his daughter as a response to "the Newspapers," which his daughter had sent to him. These newspapers were filled with articles concerning the Cincinnati. Accordingly, Franklin wrote his letter during an ongoing public controversy that arose in response to the society's preliminary plans: "Membership was to be hereditary in the line of the eldest son, like titles of nobility."[11] Many of those involved in the controversy associated such descending honors with the institution of the nobility. Joining their opposition, Franklin wrote to his daughter: "Honour worthily obtained (as for example that of our officers) is in its nature a personal thing and incommunicable to any but those who had some share in obtaining it." He amplified, "Descending honor, to posterity who could have no share in obtaining it, is not only groundless and absurd but often hurtful to posterity, since it is apt to make them proud, disdaining to be employed in useful arts and thence falling into poverty."

This view concerning the descent of privilege was a constant in Franklin's outlook, having been affirmed as early as 1751 in his *Poor Richard's Almanack* and recurring in his later personal correspondence with other family members. In the *Almanack*, he had summarized a mathematical calculation to prove "that the Pretension of such Purity of Blood in ancient Families is a mere Joke" (P 4: 98). In the letter to his daughter over thirty years later, he likewise did a mathematical calculation: "A man's son, for instance, is but half of his family, the other half belonging to the family of his wife. His son, too, marrying into another family, his share in the grandson is but a fourth." After nine such generations of biological reproduction, Franklin concluded, "which would not require more than three hundred years (no very great antiquity for a family), our present Chevalier of the Order of Cincinnatus's share in the then existing knight will be but 512th part." The society's plans for hereditary membership and its use of the eagle's image would have magnified for Franklin the association of the eagle with the aristocracy and nobility.

When Aedanus Burke's *Considerations on the Society or Order of Cincinnati... Proving That It Creates a Race of Hereditary Patricians, or Nobility* (Philadelphia, 1783), came to Franklin's attention, he encouraged the translation of it into French by Honoré-Gabriel de Riquette, comte de Mirabeau.[12] In 1783 alone, Burke's pamphlet went through three editions published at Charleston, Philadelphia, and Hartford. Burke had criticized the Cincinnati's creation of inherited honors as the institution of a nobility that was inconsistent with the new republic's commitment to equality among men. The tenor of Burke's pamphlet, which sounded an alarm on behalf of the young republic, was suggested by the biblical epigraph: "Blow ye the trumpet in Zion." Burke summarized his objections: "However pious or patriotic the pretence, yet any political combination of military commanders, is, in a republican government, extremely hazardous, and highly censorable. But that instituting exclusive honours and privileges of an Hereditary Order, is a daring usurpation on the sovereignty of the republic." To Burke, the society threatened the "principle of equality, which forms the basis of our government," because it instituted an order of nobles or a hereditary aristocracy.[13] Burke's criticisms were expanded and amplified in Mirabeau's *Considérations sur l'ordre de Cincinnatus*, which Franklin had a role in publishing in London during late 1784 "as a covered satire against *noblesse* in general" (Smyth, 10: 354).

After commenting in his July 1784 journal entry that the translation was "well done," Franklin commented, "They say General Washington missed a *beau moment*, when he accepted to be of that society (which some affect to call an *order*). The same of the Marquis de la Fayette" (Smyth 10: 354).[14] The two leaders had missed a "beautiful moment" in that the entire idea of Cincinnatus, the Roman military leader who left his plow to rescue Rome only to return modestly to his fields after the danger had passed, was incompatible with the Society as it was depicted in the pamphlets and newspapers. Washington's decision to accept leadership of the Cincinnati was inconsistent with the modest and unassuming character of the legendary Cincinnatus, who had declined public recognition and a prominent leadership role after the danger had passed. Then, too, there was the irony of having fought a revolution, whose Declaration of Independence asserted that all men were created equal, only to place some men and their offspring honorifically above others because of their blood lines.

So the ensuing international controversy was intense and emotional, to judge from pamphlets and newspaper articles in Britain, France, and the United States. If, at the outset, the United States's most prominent military leader so flagrantly discarded the country's professed commitment to equality among men, the prospects for the republic were bleak, partisans argued. Washington was keenly aware of some public criticisms of the Cincinnati. Subsequently, he used his leadership role in the society explicitly to blunt its use to perpetuate descending honors and nobility in America.[15]

Conclusion

The newly born nation had a very recent history of well-established institutions and habits of thought militating against the new practices it was attempting to institute. If only for this reason, but likely for many other reasons, the public controversy over the Cincinnati was heartfelt and serious. In Franklin's letter to his daughter about the use of the eagle on the

Great Seal's design and in the artifacts of the Cincinnati, Franklin's concerns about the eagle's aristocratic associations formed a crucial element, one that underscored gravity beneath bemused humor. Of course, despite Franklin's concerns about inherited honor among the Cincinnati, the eagle's image was widely reproduced on an immense variety of housewares – not only on plates, pitchers and bowls featuring Liverpool transfer designs and imported china, but also on furniture decorated with carvings – that were sought after and used among the general public and especially among the Cincinnati, because the eagle was the official emblem of the United States.

Although Franklin drew upon the European tradition of emblems and devices in his own imagery representing America, and although he was familiar with the cultural traditions that informed the Congressional decision to use the eagle's image to represent the United States, Franklin objected to the image. To Franklin, the eagle's behavior in nature was objectionable. And Franklin's commitment to the values of industry, courage, and national distinction collided with what he perceived to be the reprehensible, aggressive posturing of this bird chosen to represent the nation. On no fewer than three occasions, Franklin had employed the eagle's image as the perfect embodiment of Britain – not the United States – precisely because the eagle was a predator whose most recent cultural associations had been with monarchy and aristocracy. Finally, he regarded the eagle as a thief that survived by seizing the product of the fishing hawk's labor. The content of the criticism reiterated his abiding concerns about the abuse of power and the ability of individuals to profit from their own thrift and industry. A few years later, after Franklin had returned to the United States and had participated in the Constitutional Convention, he hinted again at the problems a hereditary aristocracy might pose for the new government. As Franklin was leaving the scene of the ratification of the Constitution of the United States, Mrs. Samuel Powel had called out to him, "Doctor, what have we got, a Republic or a Monarchy?" Franklin replied, "A Republic, if you can keep it."[16]

More appropriate than the eagle on the Great Seal, in Franklin's estimation, was the image of the birth of the nation as the infant Hercules, whose youth, courage, industry, promise, and strength boded well for the new nation's character. Franklin himself identified closely with these qualities, and he sought to inculcate them in his grandson, whom he once described as an "Infant Hercules." Franklin's *Libertas Americana* medal represented the birth of a new nation depicted as infant Hercules, whose stature as a youthful, male god made an emphatic, classical allusion to a republican system of government. Years earlier, during June 1775 on the eve of the American Revolution, Franklin described his grandchild, William Bache, in a letter to his sister, Jane Mecom, as "the strongest and stoutest Child of his Age that

I have seen: He seems an Infant Hercules" (P 22: 67). In 1782–83, by using the image of the infant Hercules on the medal that Franklin consciously designed to represent a new republic and the emblem that he endeavored most assiduously to distribute internationally as a symbol designating the United States, the aging grandfather perhaps identified his own descendants' lives, strength, and future with the birth, character, and promise of the new nation. Less than a decade before his death, Franklin devised a symbol of his legacy to the United States in the form of *Libertas Americana*'s emblem of the infant Hercules – a powerful youth with a legendary life.

Notes

1. For background on this issue, see Lester C. Olson, *Benjamin Franklin's Vision of American Community: A Study in Rhetorical Iconology* (Columbia: University of South Carolina Press, 2004), 232–52, which provides additional documentation and lines of argument.
2. BF, autograph letter, signed, to Sarah Bache, January 26, 1784, currently on deposit in the Library of Congress and used by permission of the Library. All subsequent citations for Franklin's letter are taken from this source, although the letter is available in Smyth 9: 161–68.
3. Richard S. Patterson and Richardson Dougall, *The Eagle and the Shield: A History of the Great Seal of the United States* (Washington, DC: Government Printing Office, 1976), 6, 30.
4. *Ibid.*, 31, 384, 2.
5. J. A. Leo Lemay, "The American Aesthetic of Franklin's Visual Creations," *Pennsylvania Magazine of History and Biography* 111 (1987): 465–99, esp. 497, 499.
6. Eric P. Newman, "Benjamin Franklin and the Chain Design: New Evidence Provides the Missing Link," *The Numismatist* 96 (1983): 2272–73; J. A. Leo Lemay, *The Canon of Benjamin Franklin, 1722–1776* (Newark: University of Delaware Press, 1986), 122–24. I discuss my misgivings about the attribution in *Franklin's Vision*, 4.
7. Stansbury's entire poem was reprinted in Eric P. Newman, *The Numismatist* 96 (1983): 2282–84. Wheeler's poem was reprinted in Henry Phillips, Jr., *Historical Sketches of the Paper Currency of the American Colonies: Prior to the Adoption of the Federal Constitution*, 2 vols. (Roxbury, MA: W. Elliot Woodward, 1865–66): 2: 256–58.
8. "L'Aigle et le Chat. Fable allégorique de M. Franklin," circa 1778, American Philosophical Society.
9. For the quotations from Shaftesbury, see James A. Herrick, "Miracles and Method," *Quarterly Journal of Speech* 75 (1989): 323; and James A. Herrick, *The Radical Rhetoric of the English Deist* (Columbia: University of South Carolina Press, 1997), 53. See Douglas Anderson, *The Radical Enlightenments of Benjamin Franklin* (Baltimore: Johns Hopkins University Press, 1997).
10. Both men are quoted in Claude-Anne Lopez, *Mon Cher Papa: Franklin and the Ladies of Paris* (New Haven: Yale University Press, [1966]), 288–90.

11. See Carl Van Doren, *Benjamin Franklin* (New York: Viking, 1938), 707, for details concerning the international controversy, 709–10.

12. Bernard Faÿ, "Franklin et Mirabeau collaborateurs," *Revue de littérature comparée* 8 (1928): 5–28.

13. Aedanus Burke's *Considerations on the Society or Order of Cincinnati* was published at Charleston by A. Timothy, at Philadelphia by Robert Bell, and at Hartford by David Webster [Evans numbers 17862–64], quotations from p. 14 of Philadelphia edition.

14. See Van Doren, *Franklin*, 710.

15. Garry Wills, *Cincinnatus: George Washington and the Enlightenment* (New York: Doubleday, 1984).

16. Max Farrand, ed., *The Records of the Federal Convention of 1787*, rev. edn., 4 vols. (New Haven: Yale University Press, 1937), 3: 85. See also William G. Carr, *The Oldest Delegate: Franklin in the Constitutional Convention* (Newark: University of Delaware Press, 1990), 122.

10

WILSON J. MOSES

Protestant ethic or conspicuous consumption? Benjamin Franklin and the Gilded Age

"Protestant Ethic" is a widely misapplied term, invented by Max Weber, the German sociologist who relied heavily on the writings of Benjamin Franklin to define that concept in his celebrated work, *The Protestant Ethic and the Spirit of Capitalism* (1905). Weber demonstrated boundless imagination and covert irony, slyly deforming Franklin's jolly image, and transforming Poor Richard into Ebenezer Scrooge. In fact, the man behind the playful mask of Poor Richard was a precursor of the lavish "Robber Barons," especially Andrew Carnegie, who so consciously emulated Franklin. The Robber Barons were central archetypes for the American sociologist, Thorstein Veblen, who formulated *The Theory of the Leisure Class* (1899), and Veblen, who is celebrated for his irony, would have been more justified than Weber in using Franklin to illustrate his thesis. In fact, Franklin, who made such enviable use of his leisure, personified Veblen's complicated, and frequently oversimplified concept of "Conspicuous Consumption." Undeniably, certain prophets of the Gilded Age skillfully developed a rhetoric resembling that of Franklin's mythical Poor Richard, among them, Booker T. Washington, the wily adviser to striving African Americans, and a notable beneficiary of the American tradition of private philanthropy that Carnegie inherited from Benjamin Franklin. Henry Ford was another baron who became a philanthropist. He played the role of a Poor, penny-pinching Richard, but he lived well, and while preaching thrift, he promoted inflation in order to encourage consumer spending.

Indelible Calvinism or colorless deism

Weber's ironic, imaginative, and somewhat wistful interpretation of Franklin is so complicated that several steps are required to fully appreciate it. Weber's goal was to offer a sociological explanation for the rise of capitalism in Western Europe and North America.[1] He argued that the Protestant ethic arose from Martin Luther's and John Calvin's doctrine of predestination. If an omniscient God knew the destiny of every soul, He must have intended some for salvation and others for damnation. This doctrine should have led to fatalism, but real-world Protestants seemed to be anything but fatalistic. How might the sociologist explain the flourishing of a vigorous bourgeois culture on the rocky soil of Calvinist self-denial and fatalism? Weber used Franklin to illustrate how these opposites might be reconciled.

Franklin was born in Boston, a small town of only 8,000 inhabitants, dominated by Puritan elders like Cotton Mather. Bostonians were expected to dress soberly, worship in a simple church, and eschew flagrant displays of worldly goods. They must husband the monetary proceeds of their labors, for they could not spend them. Thus Boston's Protestant ethic implied not only hard work but saving and investment. It led to the constant accumulation of capital, which could never be enjoyed, only multiplied. The Protestant ethic evolved into what Weber called "the spirit of capitalism," a compulsion to multiply money constantly and to accumulate capital for its own sake, or at least to impress one's neighbors. In order to convince spectators of their election, Puritans felt pressure to live exemplary lives, but often the result of their straight-living was an economic prosperity that carried with it the temptation to luxurious display. Seventeenth-century Protestantism produced in Benjamin Franklin an eighteenth-century capitalist who preached seventeenth-century thrift. This device enabled Weber to use Franklin as a symbol of his "Protestant ethic," while describing him as "a colorless deist."

The spirit of capitalism, in Weber's definition, was not Protestantism, but its evolutionary product. Quoting extensively from Franklin's *The Way to Wealth*, Weber argued that the "*summum bonum*" of Franklin's ethic was "the earning of more and more money, combined with the strict avoidance of all spontaneous enjoyment of life"[2] He acknowledged that these maxims did not represent the totality of Franklin's economic creed, but treated them as if they did. Furthermore, he ignored the fact that Franklin, having amassed a comfortable fortune by the age of forty-two, retired from business and focused his attention thereafter on civic affairs and scientific pursuits. The real Franklin conformed neither to the image of the Puritan nor to the mechanical deist; he was the comfortable burgher, leisurely and conspicuously consuming his supper in the jovial atmosphere of his London club.

But Franklin never shook loose from the doctrine of Mather's *Bonifacius: An Essay upon the Good* (1710).[3] As a teenager, he employed the alias, Silence Dogood, with gentle mockery, but Franklin never outgrew Mather's doctrine that stewards of whatever talent, whether mental or material, should strive "to love the public, to study an universal good." He seems never to have questioned the central doctrine of *Bonifacius*, which, he said, "perhaps gave me a Turn of Thinking that had an Influence on some of the principal future Events of my Life" (A 58).[4]

Weber was correct in asserting that Franklin the deist never forgot the Protestant ideology, which he recycled in his numerous successful advice books, replete with counsels that abstemiousness was "the way to wealth." Unfortunately, he perceived these maxims as the totality of Franklin's economic philosophy, rather than as sophisticated literary exercises in household micro-economics. In fact, Franklin experimented with a sequence of macro-economic ideas throughout his life, and the ideas that he circulated in the literary marketplace were often contradicted by his public policies.

Weber, by narrowly focusing on the domestic parsimony of the fictional characters Poor Richard and Father Abraham, failed to observe that Franklin had once advocated a comprehensive economic policy to encourage consumption. Franklin's *A Modest Enquiry into the Nature and Necessity of a Paper-Currency* (1729), published when he was twenty-three, viewed money as a medium of exchange rather than a means of storing wealth. Not surprisingly, Mather and Franklin agreed that money represents labor, and that work is the source of all value. Franklin's labor theory of value bore the influence of William Petty, who also influenced Adam Smith.[5] In any case, the labor theory of value was hardly original with Petty; it was fundamental to the economic thought of Aristotle and Thomas Aquinas and reflected both their moral and economic principles. Franklin's early economic theory accepted such traditional concepts as the labor theory of value. He supped with David Hume and Adam Smith and may possibly have had some influence on the latter.[6]

Franklin's economic theories, before the revolution, were congruent with the labor theory of Adam Smith, and others who reviled the physiocrats. But in his final days, he fell under the influence of the physiocrats, who believed that land was the only source of wealth. In 1769 Franklin called "*Agriculture* the only *honest Way*" for a nation to acquire wealth (P 16: 109).[7] Nonetheless, even after his supposed conversion, he continued to support the artisan class, and argued against property restrictions on voting rights. Like Adam Smith, who began the first chapter of his *The Wealth of Nations* (1776) with a description of industrial processes on the factory floor, Franklin recognized the economic worth even of unskilled workers. The *Encyclopedia* (1751–80) of Denis Diderot and Jean le Rond d'Alembert exalted the skilled trades, a practice alien to the courtly tradition of physiocracy. This was revolutionary, a recognition not only of workmanship, but of the rising prestige of technical competency. Franklin, as did the encylopedists, recognized the centrality of technical craftsmanship to modern civilization. As a man proud of his "leather apron" status, he rejected at least one physiocratic notion, Thomas Jefferson's aristocratic disdain for "the class of artificers as the panders of vice & the instruments by which the liberties of a country are generally overturned."[8] Franklin, more faithful to the tradition of Mather than to the novelties of Jefferson, believed that all labor built character.

Before the Revolution, he had encouraged the domestic manufacturing economy and protested the scarcity of money in the colonies that had resulted from the British government's mercantilist policies of hoarding precious metals in the national treasury. England discouraged the colonies from printing paper money, with the result that American merchants and traders, lacking both hard and paper money, were often forced to compensate their employees with "Goods in Pay," Franklin said in *Paper-Currency* (P 1: 145). These manufactures, largely imported from Britain, were often luxury items, Franklin opined, and "Working Men and their Families are thereby induced to be more profuse and extravagant in fine Apparel and the like" (P 1: 145).

The young Franklin piously disparaged conspicuous consumption with one stroke of the pen, but with the next, he acknowledged the necessity of keeping cash in circulation. In the long run, it was not money, but the lack of it, that threatened to corrupt society. He argued that the scarcity of money in colonial America encouraged carpenters, bakers, and shoemakers in *"Pride and Prodigality"* (P 1: 145) but the circulation of paper money would encourage thrift and sustain capital accumulation at the micro-economic level. Expanding the money supply would also have the macro-economic effects of supporting domestic manufactures, sustaining the price of labor for "Artificers and labouring Men" and "making the Balance of our Trade more equal than it now is" (P 1: 145).[9] He admitted, in later years, that he benefited from the expression of these opinions, which helped him to increase his credit, to enlarge his savings, and to win more than one contract for the printing of paper money.

Franklin's inconsistency on the land theory, versus the labor theory of value, was one of many areas in which he was annoyingly difficult to pin down. For many years, he "went on swimmingly," as he put it, advocating savings accumulation for the laboring class, but also a policy of inflation that would encourage consumption by that same class, ostensibly for the benefit of all. He claimed to have the interests of the common people at heart, and recalled many years later that his pamphlet "was well receiv'd by the common People in general; but the Rich Men dislik'd it; for it increas'd and strengthen'd the Clamour for more Money" (A 124). America had not yet developed the consumer economy in which the "rich men" would support inflation in order to bolster "consumer confidence." Inflating the money supply to increase the purchasing power of ordinary working people, whether enacted by government or by the private sector, is a modern idea. Inflation is always more attractive to the extravagant commercialist than to the parsimonious Puritan of Weber's thesis.

A limited and superficial reading of Franklin's works, and a failure to appreciate his canny vacillations, was Weber's most serious error. Franklinean economics had both micro-economic and macro-economic components. True enough, on the micro-level, Franklin expressed a common-sense view of how a prudent *bourgeoisie* might husband their resources and practice an efficient *huswifery* in their homely affairs. On the macro-level, however, he offered a prescription for how a colonial system might hope to prosper within the restricted freedom of a mercantile economy. Franklin's economic thought was complicated and global. Franklin's *Paper-Currency* defined national wealth as "the Quantity of Labour its Inhabitants are able to purchase, and not by the Quantity of Silver and Gold they possess" (P 1: 149). In this he agreed with Adam Smith, so strangely absent from Weber's essay.

But the Franklin that Weber invented in *The Protestant Ethic* was not Franklin; in fact, he was not even Poor Richard, Franklin's literary persona. He was a monochromatic and two-dimensional reconstruction of Father Abraham, a character in *The Way to Wealth*. The man Weber quoted was a fiction within a fiction – viz., Father Abraham, quoting Poor Richard – and neither should be confused with Benjamin Franklin, the creator of both. For reasons that he adequately justified, Weber tied his "Protestant ethic" to a spirit of capitalism that he defined, not in the words of any Protestant, but in those, as he admitted, of a "colorless deist." This was curious, since the religion of Benjamin Franklin was no less colorful than the rest of his personality. Franklin's "deism" bore the subtle tonalities of Methodist pietism, Newtonian mechanism, Scottish common sense, and an almost Panglossian optimism. Weber took little note of the urbane *bon vivant*, philosopher, and civic philanthropist who cut his intellectual teeth on Mather's *Bonifacius, An Essay upon the Good*.

Franklinism, philanthropy, and Carnegie

"One truth I see. Franklin was right," said Andrew Carnegie in his capitalist manifesto, *The Gospel of Wealth* (1889). The "Master of Steel" was referencing his model's famous refrain that "The highest worship of God is service to Man."[10] Carnegie was right when he asserted a continuity between his goals and those of his fellow Pennsylvanian, and he was happy to profit from his ties to the Franklin tradition. Although his and Franklin's lives were not altogether parallel, there were, nonetheless, striking similarities in the two men's lives. Obvious similarities were their dedication to public libraries, and their encouragement of the virtues of self reliance and civic responsibility. Both were committed to improving American race relations, as was evident in Franklin's support for the school instruction of the children and youth of the Free Africans, and in Carnegie's support for Booker T. Washington's Tuskegee Institute.

Similarities to the life of Franklin, who retired at forty-two and devoted the rest of his life to intellectual and civic duties, are striking. Carnegie remained an active businessman much longer than Franklin, although at the age of thirty-three he recorded a desire to retire early, as Franklin had, and devote the rest of his life to the service of mankind, as his breathless jottings reveal:

> Thirty-three and an income of $50,000 per annum! By this time two years I can so arrange all my business as to secure at least $50,000 per annum. Beyond this never earn – make no effort to increase fortune, but spend the surplus each year for benevolent purposes. Cast aside business forever, except for others ... Man must have an idol – the amassing of wealth is one of the worst species of idolatry – no idol more debasing than the worship of money.[11]

Carnegie well knew that Franklin had never viewed money as an end in itself, but as a means of buying a "gentlemanly" leisure to be spent on philanthropy and scientific inquiry.[12] After all, the mature Franklin was not a Puritan – not even a Protestant. Despite Carnegie's obvious genius for business and industrial organization, similarities between him and Franklin should not be overstated. Carnegie never demonstrated unusual brilliance as a scientist, a politician, or a political satirist. Although Carnegie's philosophy and opinions were lucid, they were not sublime. His philosophy at times merely recycled Herbert Spencer's doctrine of "survival of the fittest," in the vocabulary of triumphant capitalism, and argued that "the law of competition" between commercial and industrial behemoths was "essential for the future progress of the race."[13] The more egalitarian, democratic, and ribald elements of Franklinism were absent from Carnegie's literary and intellectual cosmos.

But the continuity between his legacy and that of Franklin was fixed when Carnegie became aware that his predecessor had bequeathed a fund to the city of Boston to help educate apprentices in the technical trades. Carnegie supplemented the endowment, when the managers of the fund decided in 1906 to establish a technical institute, which exists at present as the Benjamin Franklin Institute of Technology. Interestingly, the Institute currently has a high African American enrollment, which is a matter of at least sentimental interest, when we recall Carnegie's well-known generosity to Tuskegee Institute, and Franklin's support for African American education.

Carnegie finally gained his long-awaited admission to the university world in 1902, when he was elected to the Lord Rectorship of St. Andrews University in Scotland. Occasionally he received St. Andrews dignitaries at his estate, Skibo Castle, and as he wrote in his *Autobiography*:

> One of the memorable results of the gathering at Skibo in 1906 was that Miss Agnes Irwin, Dean of Radcliffe College, and great-granddaughter of Benjamin Franklin, spent the principals' week with us and all were charmed with her. Franklin received his first doctor's degree from St. Andrews University, nearly one hundred and fifty years ago. The second centenary of his birth was finely celebrated in Philadelphia, and St. Andrews, with numerous other universities throughout the world, sent addresses. St. Andrews also sent a degree to the great-granddaughter. As Lord Rector, I was deputed to confer it and place the mantle upon her.[14]

Unfortunately, Carnegie recorded only a few of his thoughts on Franklin, but these are significant enough to bear prominent inclusion in every Benjamin Franklin casebook. Carnegie's observations are a more useful interpretation than those of D. H. Lawrence, whose views are continually recycled in American Studies courses. And they are more accurate than those of Weber, whose opinions on Franklin have received greater exposure in the intellectual world. Indeed, Franklin's gospel of wealth set the pattern, not for Spartan abstinence, but for what one historian has called "The Age of Excess." In that regard, Weber's contemporary, Thorstein Veblen, also a sociologist, was capable of making more useful reflections on the cultural symbolism of Franklin, had he thought to do so.

Conspicuous consumption of leisure

Although Franklin played no major symbolic role in *Theory of the Leisure Class*, Veblen seemingly understood better than Weber, how American capitalists of the Gilded Age, following in Franklin's footsteps, were conspicuous consumers, who shrewdly presented themselves as public servants. Uneasy with their image as "Robber Barons," the great entrepreneurs began to display their wealth in philanthropic endeavors, and at least one of them, Andrew Carnegie, conspicuously and deliberately modeled himself on Franklin.

Veblen argued that Western economies were driven not by parsimony but by the conspicuous consumption of wealth and symbols of wealth. The gaudiness and extravagance of the Gilded Age were logical expressions of human nature. Veblen was contemptuous of "conspicuous consumption," but argued that it was deeply embedded in natural instinct. With acerbic accuracy, he described the behaviors of the wealthy, and his theory offered a better explanation for the lavishness of Carnegie's Castle than Weber's did. Franklin was as critical of extravagance as Veblen, but understood, no less than Veblen, the importance of consumption to the economic system of which he was a part. Some of Franklin's contemporaries had viewed him as a *bon vivant*, a point that Weber's thesis conveniently overlooked. John Adams referred to him as "debauched" and a "hypocrite." His sober garments were fashioned from the most excellent fabric, and he could, by his own admission, be self-indulgent when it came to good food.[15]

But Franklin was hardly an example of the profligacy and cynicism that Veblen later attributed to the Gilded Age leisure class. His scientific and philanthropic contributions were as genuine as the status they brought him. In the eighteenth century, science was very much a gentleman's preserve, and Franklin conspicuously consumed leisure in such a way as to validate his position as a gentleman of the Enlightenment. He enjoyed the status symbol of leisure in order to pursue "useful knowledge." It was after his early "retirement" that Franklin fortified his reputation as a man of letters and of science.[16] The practical uses to which he put his leisure would seem to undermine Veblen's association of leisure with parasitism, wastefulness, and extravagance.

One prophet of the Gilded Age whose hostility to conspicuous consumption was as strong as Veblen's, and whose Protestant stoicism exemplified Weber's thesis, was Booker T. Washington. The sociologist E. Franklin Frazier once compared Washington's autobiography *Up from Slavery* (1901) to the Autobiography of Benjamin Franklin.[17] Frazier was among the fiercest critics of Washington, although, ironically, Frazier's most famous work, *Black Bourgeoisie* (1957), borrowed its central thesis from Washington's autobiography. Frazier contended that the black American middle class was obsessed with conspicuous consumption and would be better off adhering to a Protestant ethic. They should focus on the multiplication of capital, along with the political leverage that would theoretically accompany black capital accumulation. Frazier might have added that Washington's *Black Belt*

Diamonds (1898), a little book of homely maxims extracted from Washington's speeches and addresses, was similar in form and content to Franklin's *The Way to Wealth*.

Booker T. Washington's Protestant ethic

As a model of the Protestant ethic, Booker T. Washington might have served Max Weber much better than Franklin. Washington literally preached sermons against extravagance. The "Sage of Tuskegee" (as he was called) was appalled to observe that the sparse monies passing through the hands of black laborers seemed to be squandered on overvalued luxury items. Washington anticipated Weber in presuming a connection between Christian stoicism and the accumulation of wealth. Washington, unlike Weber, was not concerned with constructing a sociological theory of the Protestant ethic, only with a pragmatic application of it. He offered a plan for escaping an inferior economic and social status. The Protestant values of work and thrift that had served him so well should be useful to anyone intelligent enough to appreciate Franklinean common sense. The Tuskegeean had little patience with those who wasted their weekends on window shopping, or their evenings in public places of amusement.[18]

Washington pursed his lips at the improvident consumerism of the black peasantry. The frenzy and the spirit possession characterizing rural black religion, which folklorists found quaint and pleasing, was nothing more than an obstacle to progress in the theories of Washington. He ridiculed the enthusiastic religion of the Black Belt, hoping to supplant it with his own version of the "Protestant ethic" as a means of large-scale social reform. His most prominent critic, W. E. B. Du Bois, rightly accused him of thoroughly adopting "the speech and thought of triumphant commercialism."[19] Washington's writings allude only indirectly to Franklin and never mention Weber, but he attempted to institutionalize the Protestant ethic and hoped to discourage the thriftless consumerism that he associated with the sharecropping system of perpetual debt. African Americans should be encouraged to view money not as a medium of exchange but as a means of storing wealth. The Tuskegee doctrine disparaged conspicuous consumption just as Poor Richard had done in ages past. Good Calvinist doctrine was preached during the compulsory Tuskegee Chapel hours, but this was a Calvinism, like that of Franklin, stripped of its fatalistic aspects, and preserving only the elements of austerity and work ethic.[20]

Washington never mentioned any Weberian underpinnings for his practical program, nor did he seem aware of Thorstein Veblen's theories regarding its futility. Washington's gospel of thrift and saving anticipated what

Weber identified as the Protestant ethic, and Washington's many attacks on conspicuous consumption, unlike Franklin's, left no room for the irony and fatalism that pervaded Veblen's work. Black peasants must be changed through education, must be converted to the belief of Weber's hypothetical Puritans that money was primarily a means of demonstrating respectability. They must be taught that spending was frivolous and wicked, justifiable only in cases of pragmatic necessity. Benjamin Franklin had viewed money primarily as a medium of exchange, that must flow liberally throughout the world in order to do good. Booker T. Washington viewed money as a means of storing wealth, that must remain in black communities to increase political leverage.

Poor Richard and conspicuous philanthropy

Before Thorstein Veblen introduced the term, "conspicuous consumption," to explain a society based on industrial capitalism, Franklin, and then Washington, had expressed hostility to the processes represented by that term. Neither Washington nor Franklin appreciated the ideas on which Veblen was to base his theory. Veblen did not see industrial capitalism as the result of exceptional traits of the American character nor even as the product of Protestant Christianity. The tendency to display was the result of a competitive instinct inherent in the human species. Veblen's theory of capitalism was irreconcilable with Weber's, for where Weber defined the spirit of capitalism as saving for the sake of saving, Veblen asserted that it was spending for the sake of spending. In *The Theory of Business Enterprise* (1904), Veblen recognized the existence of the Franklinean "instinct of workmanship," but insisted that it was weaker than the "instinct of sportsmanship."

Veblen cynically argued that men were the original leisure class, who gained honor through sports, hunting, and other "exploits," such as seizing women as trophies. Women and slaves lost honor by performing drudgery.[21] Since the leisure class gained status by "conspicuous consumption," work conferred lowly status on those who performed it. If Veblen was right, then Booker T. Washington's program, based as it was on industrious and Spartan habits, ran counter to the normal instincts that black people shared with the rest of humanity.[22] The Tuskegee philosophy was exceedingly critical of the black bourgeoisie, the pseudo-plutocrats who squandered time and their wealth by driving expensive carriages, and wearing expensive clothes in the streets of Washington DC on Sunday afternoons. Washington, who fought vainly against human nature by discouraging leisure pastimes, had once written, "Games, I care little for."[23]

Carnegie, who was known to preach sparse living to the working classes, encouraged such grim thinking. Philanthropic gifts to Booker T. Washington's Tuskegee Institute were based on the rationalization that workers benefited more from libraries and educational institutions such as Tuskegee than from high wages, which they would almost certainly squander on beads and trinkets. Booker T. Washington's descriptions of the profligate spending habits of the black *petite bourgeoisie* seemed to bear out Carnegie's assumptions in this regard. As for the black peasantry, the very fact that they did not have much in the way of disposable income convinced Washington all the more that they should not spend it on flashy clothing or musical instruments.

Franklin, who believed in putting inflated currency in the hands of consumers, like those who support the minimum wage today, sought to boost the economy by increasing the amount of money in circulation. Andrew Jackson had sought to boost the economy by increasing the money supply. William Jennings Bryan had sought to do it through free coinage of silver. The New Deal pumped money into the economy by government spending, a policy described as the monetarist element in Keynesean economics. Obviously Franklin was not the last American to encourage inflationism in the private sector. Henry Ford was criticized by rival capitalists for his policy of inflating the salaries of minimally skilled factory workers. In response he said, "Everyone can afford a Ford," cunningly transmogrifying Veblen's ironically stated principle into the serious claim that conspicuous consumption was good. It was good to put money in the hands of workers, precisely so that they could purchase such luxuries as Model T. Fords.

Ford's tactic of inflating workers' incomes, and encouraging them to consume, resembled the strategy of Franklin's proposal in *The Nature and Necessity of a Paper-Currency*. And when entrepreneurs like Ford and Carnegie committed portions of their wealth to public service, they took possession of Franklin's legacy, the American philanthropic tradition. The essence of American capitalism in the twentieth century was much closer to the ironic observations of Thorstein Veblen than to the Puritan models of Max Weber or the ascetic practices of Booker T. Washington. Although oblivious to the theories of Weber or Veblen, the great industrialists utilized similar concepts towards their own ends, following the pattern of Benjamin Franklin, who simultaneously preached the doctrines of self-denial and good living. Franklin was a prophet of both the Protestant ethic and the conspicuous consumption of America's Gilded Age. His theories, while opportunistically shifting throughout his lengthy public life, consistently supported the expansion of the power of the American people to consume. He was the builder of a bourgeois civilization that saw spending, not saving, as the ultimate good, and which encouraged philanthropy as the ultimate symbol of status within a society based on conspicuous displays of wealth.

Notes

1. Weber's work was originally published in German 1904–05. I have used the classic second English edition, *The Protestant Ethic and the Spirit of Capitalism* (New York: Scribners, 1958), translated by the distinguished sociologist Talcott Parsons, in 1930, with its introduction by R. H. Tawney, author of *Religion and the Rise of Capitalism* (New York: Harcourt, Brace, and World, 1926), the most celebrated critique of Weber's thesis. Weber discounted genetic theories of European dominance (*Protestant Ethic*, 31), but also implicitly attacked the materialist determinism of Karl Marx by emphasizing ideologies, charismatic personalities, and evangelical movements as historical forces.

2. Max Weber, *Protestant Ethic*, 53.

3. Originally published in 1710 as *Bonifacius. An Essay Upon the Good, that is to be Devised and Designed, By Those Who Desire to Answer the Great End of Life, and to Do Good While they Live*... The volume was often reissued as *Essays to Do Good*. Franklin did not specify the edition in the Autobiography (A 58).

4. Selections from Cotton Mather's *Bonifacius* (1719) appear in *The American Intellectual Tradition: A Sourcebook*, 2 vols., ed. David A. Hollinger and Charles Capper (Oxford University Press, 2001), 1: 48–61. Franklin on Mather in Autobiography (A 58).

5. Franklin paraphrases William Petty in *A Modest Enquiry into the Nature and Necessity of a Paper Currency* (1729): P 1: 149–50, 153.

6. Adam Smith opposed paper currency, but was somewhat more tolerant in the case of Pennsylvania. Whether this was due to his contact with Benjamin Franklin, Pennsylvania's most distinguished economist, is uncertain. See Smith, *The Wealth of Nations* (1776; Oxford: Clarendon Press, 1979), 327.

7. Carl Van Doren, *Benjamin Franklin* (1938; New York: Penguin, 1991), 372, presents evidence that, during his years in Paris, Franklin was converted to physiocratic notions, swayed by the flattery of French hosts. I think it more likely he was mesmerized by François Quesnay's *Tableau économique* (1758), which presented mathematical proofs as impressive as the epicycles of Ptolemaic astronomy. Quesnay's volume, which served the ideological interests of the *ancien régime*, was, according to legend, typeset by Louis XVI, and reinforced the theories of such royalists as Pierre Samuel Du Pont de Nemours, and his supporter, the agrarian aristocrat Thomas Jefferson.

8. Thomas Jefferson to John Jay, August 23, 1785, in *Thomas Jefferson: Writings*, ed. Merrill D. Peterson (New York: Library of America, 1985), 818–19. Jefferson also remarked, "Carpenters, masons, smiths, are wanting in husbandry; but, for the general operations of manufacture, let our workshops remain in Europe. It is better to carry provisions and materials to workmen there, than bring them to the provisions and materials, and with them their manners and principles... The mobs of great cities add just so much to the support of pure government, as sores do to the strength of the human body": *Notes on the State of Virginia* (1787) in *Writings*, ed. Merrill D. Peterson, 291.

9. Franklin defended the 1729 essay in Part One of the Autobiography, written in 1771 (A 124–25). Franklin's labor theory of value can be found in *Paper-Currency* (P 1: 149–52).

10. Andrew Carnegie, *The Autobiography* (London: Constable, 1920), 340. Franklin wrote: "I never doubted...that the most acceptable Service of God was the doing Good to Man" (A 146).

11. Quoted in Matthew Josephson, *The Robber Barons: The Great American Capitalists, 1861–1901* (New York: Harcourt, Brace, and World, 1962), 105–06.

12. Franklin as gentleman in Gordon Wood, *The Radicalism of the American Revolution* (New York: Vintage, 1991), 85–86.

13. Carnegie devotes chapter 5 of his *Autobiography* to Herbert Spencer, and refers to himself as "his disciple."

14. Carnegie, *Autobiography*, 272–73.

15. John Adams repeated to Thomas Jefferson an amusing story attributed to Franklin, describing the unlikelihood of a scientist's being so immersed in his studies as to scorn his servant's call to dinner: in *The Adams–Jefferson Letters: The Complete Correspondence Between Thomas Jefferson and Abigail and John Adams*, ed. Lester J. Cappon (Chapel Hill: University of North Carolina Press, 1959), 399. Also see "Dialogue Between the Gout and Mr. Franklin," in *Benjamin Franklin: Writings*, ed. J. A. Leo Lemay (New York: Library of America, 1987), 943–50.

16. Joseph Piper's *Musse und Kulture* (Munich: Jakob Hegner, 1948), not a direct assault on Veblen but a thoughtful antidote to his cynical hyperbole, views leisure as the basis of culture. On Franklin's retirement, see Chronology, in *Benjamin Franklin: Writings*, ed. Lemay, 1477.

17. E. Franklin Frazier, *The Negro in the United States* (New York: Macmillan, 1949), 504, disparaged the literary and intellectual merit.

18. Booker T. Washington, *Character Building: Being Addresses Delivered on Sunday Evenings to the Students of Tuskegee Institute by Booker T. Washington* (New York: Doubleday, Page, 1902), 31. For Du Bois's contrasting views on Saturday pastimes of the peasantry, see *The Souls of Black Folk* (Chicago: A. C. McClurg, 1903), 114.

19. Negative references to black popular religion are abundant throughout the 115 pages of *Black Belt Diamonds: Gems from the Speeches, Addresses, and Talks to Students of Booker T. Washington*, Selected and Arranged by Victoria Earle Matthews, "Introduction" by T. Thomas Fortune (New York: Fortune and Scott, 1898).

20. Max Weber, *The Protestant Ethic*, 172: "When the limitation of consumption is combined with the release of acquisitive activity, the inevitable practical result is obvious: accumulation of capital through ascetic compulsion to save."

21. Thorstein Veblen, *The Theory of the Leisure Class* (1899; New York: Mentor, 1953), 30–33. Thorstein Veblen, *The Theory of Business Enterprise* (1904; New York: New American Library, Mentor Books edition, [1958]), 16–36.

22. Veblen, *Theory of the Leisure Class*, 41–60.

23. Booker T. Washington, *Up From Slavery*, in *The Booker T. Washington Papers*, 14 vols., ed. Louis Harlan, *et al.* (Urbana: University of Illinois Press, 1975), 1: 356.

II

NIAN-SHENG HUANG AND CARLA MULFORD

Benjamin Franklin and the American Dream

During the colonial era, British and British North American readers were treated to promotional accounts praising North America and its promise as paradisiacal, beyond anything that anyone before had experienced or could imagine. Arthur Barlowe wrote in 1584, for instance, that the air off present-day Roanoke Island "smelt so sweet" that the mariners at the coastline felt as though they "had bene in the midst of some delicate garden abounding with all kinde of odoriferous flowers." The island, even in midsummer, had, Barlowe reported, "many goodly woodes full of Deere, Conies, Hares, Fowle, . . . in incredible abundance." John Smith wrote about similar abundance in New England. "[W]ho can but approove this a most excellent place, both for health and fertility?" he asked, in *Description of New England* (1616). He described the land as "onely as God made it, when he created the worlde" and concluded that if the land were properly "cultured, planted and manured by men of industrie, judgment, and experience" there was no doubt "but it might equalize any of those famous Kingdomes, in all commodities, pleasures, and conditions."[1] Barlowe's report confirmed the wonders of the Europeans' "new world" first reported by France, Spain, and the Netherlands. Smith's reports repeatedly showed how the land's abundance would reward hard work and careful husbandry. These two, among the best known of the many early British writers who promoted North America, reveal that the now proverbial conception of the American Dream has had a long history in American culture.

In the eighteenth century, when Britain achieved significant maritime power in the Atlantic world, a more modern-sounding version of the American Dream became commonplace. This version emphasized that the land could be highly productive and thus beneficial and lucrative to individuals, if those who came to North America were willing to work hard, save what they earned, live clean and pure lives, and help others achieve. For the promoters of this version of the American Dream, British North America was the antithesis of the status quo of the Old World, where long-established hierarchical structures stifled social mobility. In this American Dream, the land was good, and with due diligence and hard labor, it could be made better and produce both goods and income for everyone's benefit, not just for the benefit of the landed classes. Such a dream appealed to aspiring laborers whose work stagnated in Britain as a result of too many tradesmen, too many rules, and too few different opportunities for selling their labor. The apprenticeship system in England kept laborers within established social ranks and worked to stifle upward mobility. The American Dream of the eighteenth century was an ideal held by those from a laboring situation, wherein a person from the laboring or middling-level classes would be able to improve his lot, based on the availability of land, combined with his – and, increasingly, her – talent, hard work, careful conserving of funds, and simplified, non-luxurious lifestyle.

During the nineteenth century, especially in its latter half, the place of the working person in the machine of capital formation became particularly important. Writers of the nineteenth century increasingly began to ask, What should be the expectations of capitalists and the bourgeois aspiring to wealth? For some, the version of the American Dream associated with the ideal of the presumed self-made man was the epitome of achievement. For others, as we will show, the whole notion of valuing a materialist American Dream was singularly questionable, and, worse, immoral. Of all the self-made men in US history, Benjamin Franklin is perhaps the most famous. And so around Franklin, especially in the nineteenth century, the cult of the self-made man and the American Dream achieved both dominance and derision.

Why have readers considered Franklin a model representative of the American Dream? This chapter begins to address that question by examining some selections from Franklin's own writings. The chapter then examines Franklin's impact in the nineteenth century. Because Franklin's reputation did have its detractors, almost precisely because of the ways in which his memory was being used to display the American Dream, the chapter touches upon the castigations against Franklin by some who did not like the capitalist and bourgeois tendencies in American culture. The chapter concludes with a meditation on the persistence of the culture's association of Franklin with the American Dream.

Franklin writes the American Dream

As might be expected of a superior rhetorician, Franklin's writings are diverse, and they differently addressed multiple audiences, depending on his purposes. One of his preoccupations, in his earliest years, was writing about how colonial Britons of the laboring classes might improve their lot with just a little industry and frugality. Again and again, whether in his almanacs, newspaper essays, or complete pamphlets, Franklin returned to the theme of how individuals could control their own material destinies by practicing thrift, working hard, and living lives of simplicity. Franklin held this line of Whig rhetoric dear to his heart and fostered it among his readers by printing materials (his own, and others') that associated hard work with good, not high (i.e., luxurious), living. His most popular writings from this earliest part of his life promoted the idea that the possibilities of work in British North America seemed limitless, and thus the benefits and virtues of hard work could reap the laborer boundless reward. He was taking up an American Dream theme already existing in American letters but emphasizing the conjunction between work and living the good life, a life both moral and materially successful.

Franklin's autobiography, written late in his life, clarifies the very self-consciousness of this writing, both when he was a younger man and when he was an elder statesman and renowned scientist. Readers should practice caution when reading Franklin's autobiography, because it was written long after the events recounted, and a life, in narrative retrospect, can be emended and changed, as Franklin himself reminds us at the opening of the memoir. As Franklin indicated in Part Three of his autobiography, he wrote several pieces while a printer that proffered advice about personal and financial success (see A 163–66). We need look no further than Franklin's almanacs, his "Advice to a Young Tradesman," and his proposals for schools to see how Franklin created the impression that due diligence in both learning and labor would reap lifelong benefits to those who practiced industry and thrift. Following the theme of the American Dream available from the earliest promotional literature in Britain, Franklin participated in fostering and thus celebrating the potential for everyone's achieving what became known later as the American Dream.

Perhaps the clearest exhortation Franklin offers to young, laboring people occurs in his "Advice to a Young Tradesman" (1748), a broadside that contained much of the advice he gave the young printers who became his printing partners.[2] Here, Franklin advised that the "Way to Wealth" depended "chiefly upon two Words, INDUSTRY and FRUGALITY; . . . He that gets all he can honestly, and saves all he gets (necessary Expences excepted) will certainly become RICH," if "that Being who governs the World" enables it (P 3: 306–08; quotation at 308). A similarly serious compendium of advice regarding working in the trades is Franklin's "Rules Proper to Be Observ'd in Trade," published in the *Pennsylvania Gazette*, February 20, 1750. And Franklin's almanacs for the 1740s yield a plethora of little pieces of advice about saving money, working hard, using time well, and observing charitable thoughts toward others. A sample taken from the May entry in *Poor Richard* of 1749 illustrates the kind of advice Franklin was fond of offering:

> If *Passion* drives, let *Reason* hold the Reins.
>> Neither trust, nor contend, nor lay wagers, nor lend;
>> And you'll have peace to your Lives end.
> *Drink* does not drown *Care*, but waters it, and makes it grow faster.
> Who dainties love, shall Beggars prove. (P 3: 340)

Working by inversion and using complementary qualities, Franklin contrasts potentially negative qualities or actions (passion, trust [in false dealers], contentiousness, betting, lending, drinking) with their implied beneficial opposites (reason, peace, and contentment). The inversions wittily and with brevity illustrate for readers what sermonizers would take hours to deliver.

Franklin's proposals for different kinds of schools – *Proposals Relating to the Education of Youth in Pensilvania* (1749) and *Idea of an English School* (1751) – were formulated during these years. His proposals clarify Franklin's awareness that vernacular (pragmatic) learning rather than "academic" subjects were the studies most needed in the colonies.[3] Believing that most young people required basic training in letters and numbers, Franklin recommended they learn how to speak well the English language and read with insight those materials he conceived the best of polite literature in English. By the later 1740s, Franklin had achieved sufficient income from his printing business that he could retire from the daily work of it and turn his attention more fully to Pennsylvania politics and to his scientific interests. Even this early in his life, Franklin was aware that his success had been remarkable, hard-won, and exemplary, and he offered to others little pieces of advice based on his own methods of achievement.

Perhaps the most often cited of Franklin's writings on bettering oneself by working hard, saving money, and leading a simple life is his famous little Preface to the 1758 *Poor Richard's Almanack*, "Father Abraham's Speech" (1757), now commonly called *The Way to Wealth*. This narrative is an encapsulation of many of the little aphorisms regarding working and saving that had decorated his almanacs. While some readers consider the pamphlet a jest about money-getting and lending, most readers understand the narrative to stand in as Franklin's lightly self-mocking advice, often not listened to, regarding working hard and saving one's earnings rather than spending them on superfluities. Like his writings from the 1740s, the pamphlet evidences Franklin's linking of opportunities to labor with opportunities to gain both fame and wealth, signal markers of the American Dream that his own life came to represent, after his death.

Franklin's autobiography, a rhetorical masterpiece, clarifies his self-awareness regarding the American Dream theme. Franklin included in his plan for publishing his memoir the letters sent him by his friends Abel James and Benjamin Vaughan, who had prompted him to continue writing his life's story. James wrote to Franklin, "I know of no Character living nor many of them put together, who has so much in his Power as Thyself to promote a greater Spirit of Industry and early Attention to Business, Frugality and Temperance with the American Youth" (A 134). Vaughan's letter, more copious, enjoined Franklin to continue his memoir by remarking, "All that has happened to you is also concerned with the detail of the manners and situation of *a rising* people; and in this respect I do not think that the writings of Caesar and Tacitus can be more interesting to a true judge of human nature and society" (A 135). When he started writing his memoir again, Franklin decided that, should the memoir ever be circulated or reach publication, these letters requesting his continuation should be placed right in the text of the memoir itself. The second part, a direct response to the entreaties of his friends, begins with Franklin's explanation of his attempts to improve his conduct and reputation, clarifying his sense that both conduct and reputation directly related to his success as a printing entrepreneur, diplomat, and benefactor of public projects.

Franklin was aware that the circulation of the memoir would complement his other writings in circulation – all working to instruct people in their moral, laboring, and financial ethics. He well knew that existing literature promoting the colonies was influencing more and more people of different backgrounds to come to British North America, attempting to fulfill their own American dreams. By providing writings that would inculcate virtues conducive to personal, fiscal, and social improvement, Franklin was himself participating in writing up his own version of the American Dream, that if one simply worked hard enough, one might become a Benjamin Franklin.

Apotheosis: Franklin becomes the "self-made man" of the American Dream

After Franklin's death in 1790 and through the first half of the nineteenth century, his legacy enjoyed a widespread popularity, because the ethics he symbolically embodied and attempted to promulgate in public culture were construed to underscore the ideology of the American Dream.[4] When Franklin died, his papers were dispersed in the hands of a number of relatives and friends. To celebrate his life's achievement (and, of course, to make money), many printers took it upon themselves to reprint several of Franklin's writings, some that had been published already and some that had, like the memoir, remained in manuscript at the time he died. Among the writings already discussed, Franklin's "Advice to a Young Tradesman" alone appeared eleven times before the year 1822, in towns widespread between Vermont, Massachusetts, Connecticut, New York, Pennsylvania, and West Virginia. In bowdlerized versions, the unfinished memoir, sometimes even then called his *Autobiography*, was reprinted piecemeal nearly one hundred and twenty times before the end of the 1850s. Publishers included not only those in big cities like New York, Philadelphia, and Boston, but also smaller but growing towns, such as Auburn and Buffalo in New York; Cincinnati, Cleveland, and Hudson in Ohio; Milwaukee, Wisconsin; and San Francisco, California. Evidence further suggests that Franklin had his most serious impact on the minds of many young people not from formal textbooks, but from individual readings after school. Silas Felton of Marlborough, Massachusetts, for instance, obtained a copy of Franklin's memoirs as early as 1796 when he was eighteen years old. "I perused them attentively," he said, "and found many very valuable precepts, which I endeavoured to treasure up and follow." Young Felton actively participated in community affairs, became interested in the diffusion of knowledge to the countryside through libraries and newspapers, and even began writing an autobiography at the age of twenty-five.[5]

By 1850, *The Way to Wealth* had been printed more than eighty times, suggesting that during the first half of the nineteenth century this tract was more readily available than any other work by Franklin, second only to his autobiography. Widely regarded to be the antidote to poverty and the best treatise for enterprising youth, *The Way to Wealth* was published as a separate pamphlet, chapbook, or broadside, and it appeared in many journals, newspapers, magazines, anthologies, and other almanacs as well. For less educated readers, simplified and ever distorted versions of this text and others of Franklin's also emerged. Heavily illustrated compendia included *Bowle's Moral Pictures; or, Poor Richard Illustrated, Being Lessons for the Young and Old, on Industry, Temperance, Frugality, etc.,* (1796?) based on *The Way to Wealth* and sententiae from the almanacs; *The Art of Making Money Plenty in Everyman's Pocket* (1811), a similar broadside, published widely; and *The Farmer's Road to Wealth* (1800), based on Franklin's almanacs – all of which were published numerous times during the nineteenth century.[6]

Franklin represented the possibility of personal success to aspiring common people who were as passionate about individual (political) freedom as personal (material) success. They were taught by the print media to embrace Franklin as a personification of American national character in a world of change, where an individual's hard work and self-determination for upward mobility were as important as all citizens' collective striving for independence and self-government. The general culture of the earlier nineteenth century created a favorable environment where Franklin's reputation thrived. Numerous prints of his writings promoted his stories. Many portraits and woodcuts of his likeness made him an icon and a success story. Newspapers carried headlines reporting craftsmen's – and especially printers' – celebrations annually on his birthday.

Indeed, Franklin's legacy was particularly dear to printers, who were proud that a tradesman had in his lifetime enjoyed and continued to experience, after death, international renown. Even when Franklin was alive, some printers in Philadelphia formed an institution called the Franklin Society, which was dissolved shortly after his death. But after his death, a group of New York printers in 1799 founded the Franklin Typographical Society of Journeymen Printers, and in succeeding years, Franklin typographical associations cropped up again and again across the country. These organizations were among the earliest benevolent societies within the craft.

To be sure, emulation of Franklin's life was never a guarantee for success, even among printers, but Franklin's success was taken as the epitome one might reach for. Having learned the printing business and studied Franklin's life, Orion Clemens, a printer in Missouri, wrote to his mother that he was "closely imitating" the great Franklin. For a while he lived on bread and water, and he was amazed to discover how clear his mind had become on such a spare diet. He worked hard and often drove his helpers to do the same, sometimes until midnight. His teenage brother, who was serving as his apprentice, often complained. At these times, Orion would quote to his brother Poor Richard's proverbs, which only led to more resentment. Facing a deteriorating environment, the younger brother, who was never paid a penny, left the print shop to explore a different life. He was Samuel Clemens, an inventive printer but perhaps a better writer, now known, of course, as Mark Twain.[7]

As Franklin's legacy held sway for printing trades, so did it more generally reach notice for most tradespeople. For instance, during the era of normal schools and the Lyceum movement, when public lectures became highly popular, a new series of lectures was established to educate young men in Boston in 1831. Called the Franklin lectures, they were inaugurated by Edward Everett, a prominent orator who was frequently invited to speak at many Lyceums in different states. He emphasized that, as far as happiness was concerned, no goal was greater than the enrichment of the mind.

For those who lacked formal education, Franklin's story could not be told too often, he argued, because Franklin's humble origins never discouraged him from educating himself. Others agreed: Robert C. Winthrop, Henry D. Gilpin, and Horace Greeley in their public speeches expressed similar ideas,[8] and so did Henry Howe in his *Memoirs of the Most Eminent American Mechanics* (1841) and Freeman Hunt in his selection of business ethics called *Worth and Wealth: A Collection of Maxims, Morals, and Miscellanies for Merchants and Men of Business* (1856). They confirmed that Franklin's model showed "the true philosophy of business life, in giving tone and direction to the mercantile mind of America." Or as John L. Blake concluded, in his biographical dictionary of 1856, Franklin was "a philosopher and statesman, and emphatically a self-made man."[9]

Franklin's increasing popularity coincided with a growing availability of artifacts representing him, whether as sculpted busts or full-life figures, printed engravings or paintings, medals, or the numerous forms of tender used, especially in the mid-nineteenth century and later, in the absence of coin (including postage stamps, fractional currency, tokens, railway tickets, and store cards).[10] Franklin's image was circulated by various means throughout the nineteenth century. Especially during the Civil War, when coinage was extremely scarce, the circulation of little Franklins as legal tender – whether on stamps, store cards, tokens, or any other representations then used as money – surely brought delight to the user, a delight both aesthetic and material combined. Whether one were from a longstanding heritage in the US or from an immigrant population whose first glance at Franklin (if the immigrant were literate) might have been in the many translations of his writings (in German, Polish, Italian, French, or Spanish), the figural use of Franklin could have worked to create a kind of "national" solidarity in times of crisis, such as the civil and financial crises experienced throughout the middle and latter parts of the nineteenth century. In this sense, the material cultural use of Franklin's image and his body might have outweighed, in some ways, the literary uses to which Franklin's own writings and writings about him were being put. Holding a Franklin image as legal tender meant one had "money," the common cultural means of exchange used at the national level as currency. Franklin was currency, actually and figurally, and his memory thus was both commodified and served as an emulable example for others.

Skepticism: Franklin and American nightmares

Thus far we have presented a general narrative about the ways in which Franklin's own writings and representations about him worked positively, stitching together a presumed national fabric. Yet there were skeptics about Franklin, during his life and especially after he died, who found means to express their dubious attitudes about him, his legacy, and his achievements. As the nineteenth century wore on, many there were who doubted whether the capitalist direction in American culture was good for most US citizens, for capitalism was driving divisions among the very people who could best benefit from becoming like a Benjamin Franklin. Franklin's seeming homespun sayings about morality and thrift were taken out of context again and again, and they were used, some suggested, to undermine creativity and to consolidate the status quo of big business as a cultural ideal. Mark Twain, in other words, was not the only nineteenth-century American who conceived of Franklin as a tiresome, pompous old fellow whose chief end in life was making money and driving printers' apprentices to bedlam.

Skeptics, who disliked Franklin for political or social reasons, never stopped questioning his model. Even though he was popular among the general public, his legacy was tarnished by events from his own life that, once he died, he could not himself contend against. Almost from the moment he died, venomous attacks against Franklin's character began to appear in Philadelphia newspapers by the English essayist William Cobbett, a Federalist printer opposing Franklin's grandson Benjamin Franklin Bache, a Republican. Another journalist and publisher, Joseph Dennie, a smug Anglophile, insisted that compared with English literature and science, Franklin borrowed more than he invented. Annoyed that many Americans were willing to use Franklin to represent the new nation, Dennie warned that Franklin's model provided no future for the country, but "to lose history by being severed from the traditions of England."[11] Part of Dennie's annoyance, of course, lay in his highbrow notions about himself and England. He disdained Franklin's writings for common people, and he held in contempt working people, whom he considered to be ignorant and untrustworthy. Dennie announced that his paper would be nothing like Franklin offered; rather, his paper, as he said in his *Prospectus of a New Weekly Paper, Submitted to Men of Affluence, Men of Liberality, and Men of Letters* (14 Feb. 1801), "will not strive to please the populace," because "the lower classes of our motley vulgar are too often composed of the scoundrels of all nations, and perpetually restless and rebellious."[12]

Such attitudes became somewhat commonplace among the academic and educated classes seeking an intellectual identity beyond the pragmatic goals of political and material survival of the United States. Well-known New England philosophers and literary figures remained ambivalent about public accolades given Franklin, skeptical as they were about issues such as immigration, social amelioration, and the cultural dominance of manufacturing and business interests. For some, Franklin was more complicated than the popular press suggested. Yet the popular versions of Franklin were those best known, so coming to terms with popular versions of Franklin's activities and his life was essential to coming to a better understanding of the cultural attractions of Franklin's image.

Ralph Waldo Emerson is a good case in point. Emerson again and again contemplated Franklin's attitudes, his virtues, and his beliefs.[13] On the one hand, Emerson found delight in the "extraordinary ease" he discovered in Franklin's mind: Franklin was, he wrote, "unconscious of any mental effort in detailing the profoundest solutions of phenomena & therefore makes no parade." Yet Emerson disparaged in Franklin the utilitarianism of Emerson's own age: "Franklin's man is a frugal, offensive, thrifty citizen, but savours of nothing heroic."[14] What comes to the fore in examining Emerson's attitudes about Franklin is the extent to which Emerson ultimately admired Franklin's wisdom and his "moral philosophy," even though Franklin represented in the more general American culture some of the more reprehensible aspects of money-grubbing and time-keeping.

Emerson's associate, Nathaniel Hawthorne, seems to have viewed in Franklin the possibility of a more heroic fame that was undermined by the popularizations of Franklin's homespun rhetoric from the almanacs. Hawthorne considered Franklin's almanac wisdom "suited to the condition of the country; and their effect, upon the whole, has doubtless been good, although they teach men but a very small portion of their duties."[15] Hawthorne clearly distinguished Franklin's abilities and his accomplishments from the way Franklin's memory was being promulgated in his own day:

> I doubt whether Franklin's philosophical discoveries, important as they were, or even his vast political services, would have given him all the fame which he acquired. It appears to me that "Poor Richard's Almanac" did more than anything else towards making him familiarly known to the public. As the writer of those proverbs which Poor Richard was supposed to utter, Franklin became the counselor and household friend of almost every family in America. Thus it was the humblest of all his labors that has done the most for his fame.[16]

Hawthorne was, thus, not overly critical of Franklin, but he was dismayed that the central story about Franklin was pragmatic, based in the simplified versions of Franklin's wit that were best known among general readers.

While Emerson and Hawthorne, both of them well educated, knew more than many of their contemporaries about Franklin's discoveries and his diplomacy, both seem ultimately to have been responding negatively to the ways in which Franklin's figure was known popularly, as a representative of the American Dream turned into the exaggerated capitalist nightmare. Yet it was in Herman Melville's hands that Franklin reached a sort of nadir of derision by the intelligentsia. In his novel, *Israel Potter* (1855), Melville describes a scene in which the title character is led into the chambers of Franklin to be an audience to the great man. Franklin, "[w]rapped in a rich dressing-gown, a fanciful present from an admiring Marchesa, curiously embroidered with algebraic figures like a conjuror's robe, and with a skull-cap of black satin on his hive of a head," comes off as something of a necromancer. "[T]he man of gravity," Melville's narrator continues, "was seated at a huge claw-footed old table, round as the zodiac." Franklin's table

> was covered with printed papers, files of documents, rolls of manuscripts, stray bits of strange models in wood and metal, odd-looking pamphlets in various languages, and all sorts of books, including many presentation-copies, embracing history, mechanics, diplomacy, agriculture, political economy, metaphysics, meteorology, and geometry. The walls had a necromantic look, hung round with barometers of different kinds, drawings of surprising inventions, wide maps of far countries in the New World, containing vast empty spaces in the middle, with the word DESERT diffusely printed there, so as to span five-and-twenty degrees of longitude with only two syllables, – which printed word, however, bore a vigorous pen-mark, in the Doctor's hand, drawn straight through it, as if in summary repeal of it; crowded topographical and trigonometrical charts of various parts of Europe; with geometrical diagrams, and endless other surprising hangings and upholstery of science.[17]

Here Melville drew an immensely negative portrait of Franklin's knowledge, his impact on the sciences, his diplomacy regarding the American colonies, and his personal achievements, only to remark, some pages later, that Franklin was not a poet! Mocking Franklin's many pursuits, including his diplomacy, Melville concluded that Franklin, "having carefully weighed the world, . . . could act any part in it." Melville's Franklin was an impostor, then, and though he was naturally curious about the world, his mind was "often grave," but "never serious."

> At times he had seriousness – extreme seriousness – for others, but never for himself. Tranquillity was to him instead of it. This philosophical levity of tranquillity, so to speak, is shown in his easy variety of pursuits. Printer, postmaster, almanac maker, essayist, chemist, orator, tinker, statesman, humorist, philosopher, parlor man, political economist, professor of housewifery, ambassador, projector, maxim-monger, herb-doctor, wit: – Jack of all trades, master of each and mastered by none – the type and genius of his land. Franklin was everything but a poet.[18]

In Melville's hands, Franklin's pragmatism and his appeals to the general population as an emulable American are made fun of, almost precisely to the extent that Franklin did not write about things attractive to intellectuals of the nineteenth century. The bitterness of Melville's portraiture can be taken as an index of the extent to which the author resented his contemporaries' respect and admiration for Franklin's achievements philosophical, pragmatic, scientific, and political.

Franklin and the American Dream in historical context

As the nineteenth century ended, more and more of Franklin's own writings reached print, and general readers and scholars began to reassess Franklin's place in American cultural history. Certainly, Americans' obsession with Poor Richard's dicta short-changed their fuller understanding of Franklin's intellectual life and his impact in global policy. Franklin's very simplicity of expression was taken as a representation of presumed shallow thinking. His rhetorical goal of writing in a plain style so as to be understood by many rather than a few was entirely disregarded. D. H. Lawrence, a novelist of the early twentieth century, once described Franklin as "middle-sized, sturdy, [and] snuff-coloured" and labeled him as "the first dummy American."[19] Few were as vituperative as Lawrence, but several critics did insist that, contrary to the popular assumption that Franklin's model elevated the human condition, his model degraded it by making life seem simplistic and success inevitable.

Criticisms of Franklin are drawn largely from his impact on the social formation and the authors' resentments that his impact was so widespread. If Franklin were so despicable, then it was the presumed American Dream that was being criticized, not the proverbial representative of its ideals. Franklin rose against similar authorities among the intelligentsia in his own time, especially those who professed religious dogmas and admired fixed social stratification, their own above all others. Franklin recognized, however, that individuals in any society were inextricably linked to one another. He therefore promoted doing good for the public, dedicating himself to activities that improved the quality of life for the whole community.

Franklin continues to intrigue even those who believe that they fully understand him. We are now aware that the American Dream image of an honest, frugal, and hard-working Franklin was an invention that began with Franklin himself, an invention that served the purpose, at a most basic level, of fostering individual dignity. The historical Franklin was far more cynical and elusive than unsuspecting readers have surmised. Franklin was a much more complicated man than the one taken to represent the American Dream, and he well understood that the difficulties of life required that one ought to have dreams one believed achievable, for dreams offered hope of a better tomorrow.

Notes

1. Quotations from *Early American Writings*, gen. ed. Carla Mulford (Oxford University Press, 2002), Barlowe, 166; Smith, 172.
2. For Franklin's printing network, see Ralph Frasca, *Benjamin Franklin's Printing Network: Disseminating Virtue in Early America* (Columbia and London: University of Missouri Press, 2006).
3. See Carla Mulford, "Benjamin Franklin, Traditions of Liberalism, and Women's Learning in Eighteenth-Century Philadelphia," in *Educating the Youth of Pennsylvania: Worlds of Learning in the Age of Franklin*, ed. John Pollack (Philadelphia: University of Pennsylvania Press, [2009]).
4. For Franklin's legacy, see Nian-Sheng Huang, *Benjamin Franklin in American Thought and Culture, 1790–1990* (Philadelphia: American Philosophical Society, 1994), and Carla Mulford, "Figuring Benjamin Franklin in American Cultural Memory," *New England Quarterly* 71 (1999): 415–43, and "Benjamin Franklin and the Myths of Nationhood," in *Making America / Making American Literature: Franklin to Cooper*, ed. A. Robert Lee and W. M. Verhoeven (Amsterdam and Athens, GA: Rodopi, 1996), 15–58.
5. Rena L. Vassar, ed., "The Life or Biography of Silas Felton Written by Himself," *Proceedings of the American Antiquarian Society for October 1959* (Worcester, MA: American Antiquarian Society, 1960), 119, 125, 126, 129–30.
6. See Huang, *Benjamin Franklin in American Thought and Culture*, 42–49.
7. The story is told in *Mark Twain's Autobiography*, 2 vols., ed. Albert Bigelow Paine (New York and London: Harper and Bros., 1924) and discussed in Huang, *Benjamin Franklin in American Thought and Culture*, 49.
8. See Huang, *Benjamin Franklin in American Thought and Culture*, 47–49.
9. John L. Blake, ed., *A Biographical Dictionary* (13th edn.; Philadelphia: H. Cowperthwait, 1856), 467.
10. See Mulford, "Figuring Benjamin Franklin," 429–33.
11. *Port Folio*, 1st ser., 1 (February 14, 1801): 53.
12. As discussed and quoted in Huang, *Benjamin Franklin in American Thought and Culture*, 33–35, quotation at 34.
13. For Emerson on Franklin, see William L. Hedges, "From Franklin to Emerson," in *The Oldest Revolutionary: Essays on Benjamin Franklin*, ed. J. A. Leo Lemay (Philadelphia: University of Pennsylvania Press, 1976), 139–56.
14. The quotations are from Emerson's journals of the 1820s, in *The Journals and Miscellaneous Notebooks of Ralph Waldo Emerson*, 16 vols., ed. William H. Gilman, *et al.* (Cambridge, MA: Belknap Press of Harvard University Press, 1960–82), 2: 208. See Hedges, "From Franklin to Emerson."
15. Nathaniel Hawthorne, "Benjamin Franklin," in *Tales, Sketches, and Other Papers*, Riverside Edition (Boston: Riverside Press, 1897), 202.

16. Hawthorne, "Benjamin Franklin," 202.
17. Herman Melville, *Israel Potter: His Fifty Years of Exile* (New York: G. P. Putnam, 1855), 65.
18. *Ibid.*, 81.
19. D. H. Lawrence, "Benjamin Franklin," in *Studies in Classic American Literature* (1923; Garden City, NY: Doubleday, 1951), 19–31.

12

STEPHEN CARL ARCH

Benjamin Franklin's
Autobiography, then and now

Even late in life, after he had become one of the most famous people in Europe and North America, Benjamin Franklin continued to sign himself in letters as "B. Franklin, printer." Over the years, Franklin's *Autobiography* has seemed to many readers to be an analogue to that signature: a simple, unpretentious, and straightforward statement of Franklin's identity. Indeed, Franklin wrote the narrative in a plain style that may have encouraged oversimplified readings. He wrote in unaffected prose, included amusing anecdotes, and admitted to youthful shortcomings and wrong turns, which he called *errata*, using the printer's term for errors. His *Autobiography* displays Franklin's knack for painting a portrait in words, such as the moment when the seventeen-year-old Franklin arrived in Philadelphia and purchased three huge "puffy rolls" with his last few pennies. Indeed, Franklin's *Autobiography* offered iconic pictures that eventually entered American folklore.

Franklin's unadorned prose, iconic pictures, details of his everyday life, and sense of humor have led many readers to see a relatively simple person or idea behind the narrative of the *Autobiography*. Max Weber saw in him the incarnation of the spirit of capitalism. D. H. Lawrence saw an unemotional automaton. Others found the original "self-made man." Yet, then and now, the meaning of Franklin's memoir has been more slippery, more difficult to grasp, than many of those interpretations would admit. We are still learning how to read the *Autobiography*, Franklin's signature text, more than two centuries after he wrote it. The difficulties begin with the physical text itself.

The manuscript and its printings

Franklin's motives for composing a narrative of his life were complicated. In Part One, written in 1771, he says that he suspected that his son, then the 42-year-old Royal Governor of New Jersey, might find it "agreeable . . . to know the Circumstances of *my* Life, many of which [the son was as] yet unacquainted with" (A 43). There is in this an echo of the desire of seventeenth-century Puritans like Thomas Shepard to leave a record for his son "that so [in his father's story] he may learn to know and love the great and most high God, the God of his father."[1] But Franklin was no Puritan; and he was in fact estranged from the son to whom Part One is addressed by the time he came to write Part Two in 1784 and Parts Three and Four in 1788–89. In Part Two, Franklin directed the future printer or editor of the text to insert two letters, one from Abel James and one from Benjamin Vaughan, into the narrative, and those two letters offer many possible motives for Franklin's decision to continue writing his life story, most of which revolve around the "usefulness" of Franklin's example and the "enjoyment" readers would derive from his success. But were those motives Franklin's? They are displaced into the voice of his admirers, and they tell us little about his own thinking. Parts Three and Four offer few direct references to his motives.

Franklin's correspondence sheds some light on his motives for writing, although few epistolary references to the *Autobiography* survive from the years before 1786, fifteen years after he wrote Part One. To the publisher Mathew Carey, in 1786, Franklin reported that Part One is "only some Notes of my Early Life, and finish in 1730. They were written to my Son, and intended only as Information to my Family. I have in hand a full Account of my Life which I propose to leave behind me" (Smyth 9: 534). Two years later, in a letter to the Duke de la Rochefoucauld, Franklin noted that he had "brought the narrative down to my Fiftieth Year" – completed Part Three, presumably – and that "what is done will be of . . . general Use to young readers; as exemplifying strongly the effect of prudent and imprudent Conduct in the Commencement of a Life of Business" (Smyth 9: 675). This motive of "exemplifying" prudent and imprudent conduct for young readers is repeated in several letters in the late 1780s, as is one problem all autobiographers face: how "to speak decently and properly of one's own conduct" (Smyth 10: 32).

Franklin's stated motives in writing his *Autobiography*, then, were several, and they changed over the last nineteen years of his life. Franklin's life and his entire world changed dramatically over those years. Part One of the *Autobiography* was written during a two-week vacation in the English countryside in 1771, during Franklin's tenure as a colonial agent in England. At that time, Franklin still considered himself a colonial, English citizen, and he remained in close contact with the son to whom he addressed Part One. Part Two was written in a small village outside of Paris in 1784, during Franklin's years as a United States envoy and commissioner to France. He was now a US citizen, had sundered all connections to his son, and had by this time spent twenty-four of the previous twenty-seven years living in

Europe. He was hardly a British "colonial." Parts Three and Four were written in 1788 and 1789 in Philadelphia, after Franklin had served in the Constitutional Convention of 1787 and at a moment when the physical frailties of his body were causing him to withdraw from public service and circumscribe his private travel and correspondence.

The varied circumstances of the text's composition and Franklin's mixed motives in writing the narrative present interpretive problems. Can a narrative written at three different moments in time be unified in thesis and theme? Are the several parts of the narrative different in intention and focus? Was the "same" person writing each part of the narrative? Some commentators on the text have proposed that an outline of the narrative, probably written in 1771 (at the same time as Part One), proves that the narrative was unified in concept and design in Franklin's mind as early as 1771.[2] But the extant copy of that outline is not in Franklin's hand, and some schools of literary interpretation deny that such an outline of "events" could control the deeper meaning of the text fifteen years later, no matter how determined the author was to remain true to it. In my opinion the several parts do differ in intention, and Franklin was, in essence, a different person in 1788 from the person he was in 1771. There is meaning *in* the changing design and themes of the narrative as it progresses from Part One to Part Two to Parts Three and Four.

To compound these problems, Franklin never saw his manuscript into print. This fact presents a practical editorial problem. Modern editing practices aspire to present to the reader a version of a text that is as close as possible to the author's intentions. In the case of the *Autobiography*, there is no single moment at which Franklin's "intentions" for the manuscript were authorized. In the late 1780s, he simply assembled all four "parts" into a single manuscript, making some revisions to the earlier parts but never indicating whether those revisions were complete. Did he intend eventually to erase evidence that the four parts were written at different times? Did he intend to revise the manuscript more fully? Did he even intend to publish the manuscript at all? The print history of Franklin's narrative is tormented by our inability to answer such questions definitively.

Franklin wrote the narrative on 230 large folio sized pages which he folded in half, writing on only one half (or column) of each page and leaving the other column blank for possible additions and revisions. Two biographical tributes appeared soon after Franklin's death in April 1790, one by Henry Stuber and the other by Mathew Carey.[3] Both tributes appear to be based on Franklin's manuscript, Stuber's on Part One alone and Carey's on all four parts. Franklin's grandson, William Temple Franklin, had inherited Franklin's holograph (i.e., hand-written) manuscript of the narrative, along with Franklin's other manuscripts, and he took it with him to England in 1790 and then to France in 1791. In France, Temple Franklin exchanged the original manuscript for a copy of the manuscript that his grandfather had sent to a friend in 1789. This seems like a quirky decision to readers today: Temple Franklin traded an extensive, original, handwritten manuscript by one of the most famous people in the world for a *copy* of that same manuscript. But, since his grandfather had left him his papers "to turn them to what profit" he could,[4] Temple Franklin was most concerned with legibility. He wanted to turn a fast buck by publishing his famous grandfather's memoirs quickly.

However, Temple Franklin's edition of the *Autobiography* did not appear in print until 1818, and his reputation suffered because of this long delay: many readers were anxiously awaiting his "authoritative" edition of his grandfather's memoirs. In truth, Temple Franklin was lazy, and he spent part of the 1790s embroiled in confidential real-estate speculation instead of preparing the manuscripts for print. Thus, between 1790, when the two biographical memoirs based on the manuscript appeared in American magazines, and 1818, when Temple Franklin's edition finally appeared, Franklin's *Autobiography* was printed only in incomplete editions or in narrative versions far removed from his original text. A rather free translation into French of Part One appeared in 1791. A re-translation back into English of that edition appeared in London in 1793, published by the Robinson brothers. This "Robinson edition" remained the most popular version of the text until 1818. Another, different re-translation back into English appeared in 1793. And finally, a translation (from the printed English translations) back into French appeared in 1798. These early translations/editions were all derived from Part One of the manuscript and from Mathew Carey's condensation and redaction of all four parts of Franklin's story in his 1790 biographical memoir. Temple Franklin's belated 1818 edition marked the first time that Part Two was made available in print in English and the first time that Part Three was printed in any language.

Temple Franklin's 1818 edition was faulty in many ways, by today's standards. His edition was based on a copy of his grandfather's original manuscript rather than on the original itself. Scholarly investigation reveals that he also "modernized" his grandfather's diction, substituting formal English expressions for Franklin's American colloquialisms. He even introduced errors of fact into the narrative.[5] He meddled with the text and did so with one primary purpose in mind: to make a profitable commodity of his grandfather's memoirs. Not until 1868 did a more authoritative printed version of the manuscript appear. In that year John Bigelow, a former United States minister to France, published a new edition of the *Autobiography* based on the original holograph manuscript Bigelow had tracked down in Europe and purchased. Bigelow revised Temple Franklin's edition by comparing it carefully with the original holograph, printed Part Four for the first time in English, and explained how the original manuscript had passed through several owners' hands in France during the first half of the nineteenth century. Bigelow even gave the narrative its modern title – *Auto-biography* – a neologism that Franklin had probably never heard in his lifetime. Bigelow's edition became the standard edition until twentieth-century editors returned us even more closely, in print, to Franklin's hand-written words.

Bigelow's 1868 edition downplays the fragmented nature of the text. He printed all four parts without designating them as parts, merely retaining Franklin's embedded, transitional comments between the parts and marking those moments with a double or triple line break. Then, too, Bigelow filled out the narrative with a "continuation" of Franklin's life to 1790 derived from his correspondence and from other biographies of Franklin. He made Franklin's fragmented narrative life appear more complete and less disrupted than it had been in the original manuscript version. The two editions that most readers of Franklin's life prior to 1868 might have known – the 1793 Robinson edition and the 1818 Temple Franklin edition – present the first three parts of Franklin's narrative even more seamlessly. The Robinson edition stands at least at three removes from Franklin's manuscript, one half being a translation (into English) of a translation (into French) of a copy of Part One, the other half being a revision (Stuber's) of a biographical memoir (Carey's) that condensed all four parts of the original manuscript.[6] The only textual division in the Robinson edition is marked by the chapter-shift from Franklin's presumed words to Stuber's. For its part, the Temple Franklin edition correctly identifies Part One and Part Two, but it does not identify "Part Three," except (as Bigelow would later do) by retaining Benjamin Franklin's own internal transitional marker.

Before the mid-twentieth century, then, when modern editorial principles were used to bring readers closer to Franklin's manuscript (and to his supposed intentions as author), readers would have encountered Franklin's self-narrated life in versions quite different from today's published editions. As far as we can tell, early readers were unconcerned with the "authenticity" of Franklin's words and voice, and were not very interested in the circumstances surrounding the composition of the text. They read Franklin's life as a record of his lived experience in edited versions of the text(s) that seemed more complete and more unified than the manuscript narrative itself. The *Autobiography* was reprinted over one hundred times before 1860, most often in either the Robinson or Temple Franklin versions. Its reach was international, with translations into German, Italian, Dutch, and most other European languages. One can add to these circulating versions of Franklin's memoirs a number of biographies of Franklin that depended in large part on the early memoirs by Stuber and Carey, and which, though they stand at several removes from his actual writing, offer versions of his life story. When some early readers talk about reading Franklin's "life," we often do not know whether they mean a version of the *Autobiography* or one of those biographies. For example, Mason Locke Weems's very popular *The Life of Benjamin Franklin* (1818) remade Franklin into a moralizing and sentimentalized hero (reminiscent of another Weems creation, the George Washington who "could not tell a lie").[7] In one form or another, and there were very many, Franklin's life story circulated widely in the United States and Europe during the nineteenth century.

Imitation, life's art

One of those many complex and slippery moments in Franklin's narrative occurs in Part Two when Franklin lists the thirteen moral virtues that he intended to "improve" by eradicating his "bad" habits. In his remarks on each of the thirteen virtues, Franklin commented about humility: "Imitate Jesus and Socrates" (A 150). The injunction to imitate is, to my mind, at the heart of Franklin's method throughout the *Autobiography*. From Franklin's youthful method of learning to write well by imitating the *Spectator* papers (A 61–62) to his notion that his "Posterity . . . may find some of [the means of his success] suitable to their own Situations" (A 43) to his attempts to encourage others in Part Three to replicate his successes with the Junto (A 170–71) and *The Pennsylvania Gazette* (A 181), imitation is central to the way in which Franklin imagines both life and art.

Had Franklin told himself to imitate only Jesus, we might be able to read his comment in the Puritan tradition of Thomas Shepard. But the command to imitate Jesus *and* Socrates asks us to consider in what ways those two figures exemplified humility: each humbly submitted at the end of his life to the commands of the state, and each humbly taught his fellow citizens exclusively through the spoken word. The first kind of humility, submission to the general good, helps to explain Franklin's attitude at numerous points in the narrative, as when he is offered a patent for his stove but declines it from the principle that, since he enjoys the inventions of others, he is glad of an opportunity to serve others by offering his invention freely and generously (A 192). If a patent (or, for printed materials, copyright) measures one's pride in and financial control over an invention, Franklin is content to let what we might interpret as a mark of his genius slide into anonymity. Similarly, in describing several of his "projects" in Part Three, he explains that he wrote and published anonymous pamphlets in order to "prepare" the minds of the people for his ideas (A 193). Good ideas, he suggested, belong to no one; they are published anonymously, take hold in the community, and (if successful) work for the good of the people. In the arena of politics, Franklin's tendency to place the community's interest before his own is revealed in his comment that "I shall never *ask*, never *refuse*, nor ever *resign* an office" (A 185). To ask for, refuse, or resign a political office is to impose one's will on the people rather than to submit to theirs. Jesus and Socrates humbly suffered death at the demand of the state; Franklin counsels humility because the larger good of the people or the republic outweighs individual desire.

I do not mean to suggest that Franklin actually succeeded in extinguishing his pride and in effacing his personality in any of these matters; but I do mean to suggest that he participated in the classical and early modern distrust of singularity and individuality and that he employed impersonality and anonymity as strategies to achieve certain goals. This is true both in his life and in the *Autobiography*. Franklin believed in the usefulness of imitation, both as he used it to achieve his own success and as he imagines his narrative affecting other readers. In doing so, he showed that for all practical purposes he valued a common human nature, rather than an original or unique sense of individual identity. Such an attitude relates to my second point about Jesus and Socrates: neither attempted to write down or publish his ideas. Yet Franklin was and has been intimately associated with the world of print since his days as a printer's apprentice in the 1710s. By the 1780s, he was quite literally world famous, in large part because of his writings on electricity, his almanacs, and his political essays. His published papers, in the most authoritative modern collection, will run to nearly fifty volumes! He epitomizes the Enlightenment world of newspapers, journals, novels, encyclopedias, dictionaries, and other printed texts. How does his injunction to imitate Jesus and Socrates square with his own immersion in the world of print?

Anonymous publication was one way for Franklin to deal with this problem. But his *Autobiography* prevented such anonymity. In it, he had to face straightforwardly the problem of how "to speak decently and properly of one's own conduct." The solution to this problem rests in his reiterated concern in the *Autobiography* with the permanence of the printed word. George Whitefield "gave great Advantage to his Enemies," Franklin remarks, because his "Writing and Printing" fixed "Unguarded Expressions and even erroneous Opinions" in print: "*litera scripta manet* [the written word remains]" (A 180). Similarly, Franklin remarks that "the Quakers suffer'd from having establish'd and published it as one of their Principles, that no kind of War was lawful, and which being once published, they would not afterwards, however they might change their Minds, easily get rid of" (A 190). Franklin is telling us in these scenes that in the *Autobiography* he is not spilling secrets of his private self, because to do so would leave them in print for ever. Instead, he is carefully constructing a useful portrait of a successful public man. For this reason, students of Franklin often sense, according to Edmund Morgan, that "for all his seemingly spontaneous openness, [Franklin] kept a kind of inner core of himself intact and unapproachable."[8] To many modern readers, Franklin always seems to be hiding his true inner self in the *Autobiography*.

His *Autobiography* is, in this sense, the antithesis of that other great Enlightenment self-portrait, almost exactly contemporaneous with Franklin's *Autobiography*, Jean-Jacques Rousseau's *Confessions* (wr. 1767–70, pub. 1781). Rousseau initiates the modern tradition in which autobiographical narratives probe the inner, private self. Franklin had continued the classical and early modern tradition in which the individual self is de-emphasized in order to praise God (as in St. Augustine's *Confessions*) or to typify human behavior (in Franklin's case). This is not to say, necessarily, that Rousseau was more innovative or revolutionary than Franklin. Indeed, some readers find in Franklin's piecemeal narrative and adoption of narrative personae a radically modern (or even post-modern) representation of the self as fabricated, a construct both of society and of individual desire.[9] Rousseau expressed a late-Enlightenment commitment to the sentiments and the inner soul, Franklin a late-Enlightenment commitment to the play of the mind.

It is useful, in any case, to remember that neither Rousseau nor Franklin understood his project as an "autobiography" as we now define that term. When John Bigelow first referred to Franklin's narrative as the *Autobiography* in 1868, he retrospectively imposed a specific concept of genre on the narrative. This genre – autobiography – is the narrative expression "of what it is to be a human agent: the senses of inwardness, freedom, individuality, and being embedded in nature," as the philosopher Charles Taylor phrases it.[10] By the mid-nineteenth century, the genre had fully emerged in works by writers like Thoreau, Goethe, and Thomas De Quincey as a way of thinking about individual self expression. The term *autobiography* itself eventually moved from occasional use (sometimes disparagingly) in the early nineteenth century into the mainstream in the twentieth century. Rousseau's narrative has largely escaped the imposition of the term because the force of his title – *The Confessions* – and its echo of Augustine's fourth-century memoir demarcates a singular and defiant project of self-writing: "I have resolved on an enterprise which has no precedent, which, once complete, will have no imitator," Rousseau says.[11] Franklin referred to his narrative as the "history of my life" or as his "memoirs," signaling not a commitment to confess but rather a commitment to explain the observable person in an objective sense. Rousseau initiates the modern autobiographical impulse to reveal the inner or private self. Rousseau claimed to believe his story would have no imitators; Franklin sincerely hoped that his would have many.

The *Autobiography* and its readers

Two oversimplified readings of the *Autobiography* emerged during the early nineteenth century.[12] Variations of both readings continue to be found in biographies of Franklin's life and in critical studies of Franklin's thought. One group of readers considered the *Autobiography* to be the life story of an avuncular, self-made man whose model of financial and social success seemed perfectly suited to meet the demands of a competitive market economy in the early and mid-nineteenth century. In the biographical and critical literature, this interpretation can be found in works like Mason Locke Weems's fictionalized *Life of Benjamin Franklin* and Carl Van Doren's Pulitzer Prize-winning *Benjamin Franklin* (1938). More broadly, it can be found in numerous diaries, journals, and memoirs written by nineteenth-century "self-made men," from the banker Thomas Mellon to the publisher James Harper to the Harvard educator Jared Sparks. In 1827, for example, at the age of fourteen, Mellon reported of himself in his own autobiography, *Thomas Mellon and His Times* (1885), that he was transformed by Franklin's *Autobiography*: "here was Franklin, poorer than myself, who by industry, thrift and frugality had become learned and wise, and elevated to wealth and fame... After [reading his autobiography] I was more industrious when at school, and more constant than ever in reading and study during leisure hours. I regard the reading of Franklin's Autobiography as the turning point of my life."[13] Mellon went on to become a lawyer, judge, real-estate developer, and banking magnate.

From lesser-known figures, like the Massachusetts merchant Silas Felton, we hear the same kind of testimony about upward mobility and business success. Writing in 1801 about having read Franklin's life (perhaps the Robinson edition) in the mid-1790s, Felton remarks: "Doct. Franklin's life and writings fell into my hands. I perused them attentively, and found many valuable precepts, which I endeavoured to treasure up and follow. And I believe I may safely say they kept me from many Errors, for from that time I determined to adhere strictly to Reason, Industry, and good Economy... [and] always to practise reason and truth."[14] Similarly, legend has it that the upwardly mobile Davy Crockett – a man who did not learn to read

and write until the age of eighteen and who (thanks in part to his own strategies of self-promotion) became, like Franklin, a massively symbolic figure in
American history – had a copy of Franklin's *Autobiography* in his pocket
when he died at the Alamo. In the twentieth century, the self-help systems
of both Dale Carnegie and Stephen Covey appear to have been influenced
by this "self-made man" interpretation of Franklin's life, particularly the
emphasis in Part Two of the *Autobiography* on "training" the self in moral
virtues. The "Franklin planner" is not misnamed.

The second early interpretation of Franklin's *Autobiography* saw his life
as a negative commentary on financial success and, more broadly, on capitalism itself. At its extreme, as in D. H. Lawrence's *Studies in Classic
American Literature* (1928), such readers found in the narrative a petty,
conniving, plotting hypocrite whose financial and social success is empty of
emotion or spirit. "And now I, at least, know why I can't stand Benjamin,"
Lawrence wrote. "He tries to take away my wholeness and... my freedom... Benjamin tries to shove me into a barbed wire paddock and make me
grow potatoes or Chicagoes."[15] To Lawrence, the "snuff-coloured" Franklin
he found in the *Autobiography* was a materialistic automaton who had set
America on the road to the robber barons of the late nineteenth century and
the dehumanizing assembly line of Henry Ford in the twentieth. A tempered
version of Lawrence's argument appears in Max Weber's *The Protestant
Ethic and the Spirit of Capitalism* (1904), where Weber finds in Franklin's
writings and life an early statement of the habits and ideas that favored
the rational pursuit of economic gain, as opposed to "traditional" ways of
understanding work (and therefore wealth) as a curse and a burden to be
avoided. Versions of Lawrence's argument also appear more or less straightforwardly in works by a number of well-known American writers, including Edgar Allan Poe ("The Businessman" [1840]), Herman Melville (*Israel
Potter* [1855]), and Mark Twain ("The Late Benjamin Franklin" [1870]).
For this interpretation, too, we can find less-well-known early readers who
found a suspicious character at the heart of the narrative. Alexander Graydon, a minor Pennsylvania lawyer and politician, noted in his own autobiographical narrative, *Memoirs of a Life* (1811), that "the connection between
thrifty youth and respectable age" that Franklin makes in his *Autobiography* did not hold true for him: despite modeling his behavior on Franklin's,
Graydon complains that he did not advance "an inch in the glorious career
of personal aggrandizement."[16]

It is important to note that the memoir's earliest readers did not find
their text in textbooks or anthologies, the places where many readers today
encounter Franklin. The "schoolbooks used in the early years of the republic
betray a great ignorance of the Franklin we know today... [They] do not

really say much at all about Franklin," as Richard Miles pointed out a half-century ago.[17] Before the mid-nineteenth century, readers had to find Franklin's memoirs on their own, and when they did they found the narrative to be useful. Positively or negatively, it spoke to readers like Silas Felton and Alexander Graydon, Thomas Mellon and Herman Melville, similar perhaps to the way that the writings of the Beat poets or the lyrics of Bob Dylan spoke to some people of the latter part of the twentieth century. Some found in them a new way of looking at the world; others saw in them a wrong turn for the civilized world. Franklin's written life seems tame enough to us, but like most great art it has often generated a passionate response from its readers.

Now, Franklin's *Autobiography* is recognized as one of the most significant texts written by any of the men and women associated with the nation's founding. The recent surge of popular interest in Franklin – at least eight full-length biographies have appeared since 2000 – depends in large measure on Franklin's sly self-portrait. For example, Walter Isaacson's bestseller, *Benjamin Franklin: An American Life* (2003), is in its early chapters merely a retelling of Franklin's *Autobiography*: like all of Franklin's biographers, Isaacson finds it difficult to escape the pull of Franklin's plot. This is not a matter of a paucity of resources for the biographers; it is a testament to Franklin's own skill in constructing his narrative. The dozens of in-print editions of the *Autobiography* attest to its wide and continuing readership in all kinds of formats: scholarly texts, coffee-table books, young adult novels, children's stories and games.

Since the mid-twentieth century, scholars have moved the most authoritative version of the text closer to Franklin's words as he wrote them. Max Farrand,[18] Leonard Labaree, J. A. Leo Lemay, and P. M. Zall, among others, have allowed readers to see more clearly Franklin's conception of the project, his revisions to the manuscript, and the related documents that help to shed light on the text. As the scholarly editions corrected (according to modern editing principles) the decisions of earlier editors, critics of Franklin in the fields of literary interpretation, history, political science, and economics have complicated and are still complicating the oversimplified interpretations of earlier readers. The *Autobiography*, now, is understood as a sophisticated literary performance, amenable to all kinds of literary theory, from deconstruction to psychoanalysis to post-colonial studies, and resistant at all turns to any kind of oversimplified reading.

If Franklin hoped and believed his narrative would find readers determined to imitate its stated morals, he surely knew, too, that it would eventually find readers willing to appreciate its ambiguities, its layered complexity, its complicated humor. As any attentive reader could have noticed in Franklin's own account of one of his earliest published literary performances, the "Silence Dogood" letters, he "contriv'd to disguise [his] Hand" from his brother (67) in order to achieve anonymity, and then he apparently managed with great success to imitate the voice of a middle-aged Boston widow who criticized everything from Harvard College to alcohol consumption. These gestures of disguise, anonymity, pseudonymity, and – to use an oxymoron – serious play were from the very beginning hallmarks of Franklin's publications, and there is every reason to think they were in his mind in 1771 when he first sat down to compose the extended signature that is his *Autobiography*.

Notes

1. Thomas Shepard, *God's Plot: The Paradoxes of Puritan Piety Being the Autobiography and Journal of Thomas Shepard*, ed. Michael McGiffert (Amherst: University of Massachusetts Press, 1972), 33.
2. See the commentary on the outline in *Benjamin Franklin's Autobiography: Authoritative Texts, Backgrounds, Criticism*, Norton Critical Edition, ed. J. A. Leo Lemay and P. M. Zall (New York: Norton, 1986), 169.
3. Henry Stuber, "History of the Life and Character of Benjamin Franklin," *Universal Asylum and Columbian Magazine* (May 1790): 268–72; (June 1790): 332–39; (July 1790): 4–9; Mathew Carey, "Memoirs of the late Benjamin Franklin, esq.," *American Museum* 8 (July 1790): 12–20; (Nov. 1790), 210–12.
4. Quoted in John Bigelow, *The Life of Benjamin Franklin, Written by Himself* (Philadelphia: Lippincott, 1874), 38–39.
5. See the excellent "Introduction" to *The Autobiography of Benjamin Franklin: A Genetic Text*, ed. J. A. Leo Lemay and P. M. Zall (Knoxville: University of Tennessee Press, 1981), esp. liii–lviii.
6. The Robinson edition, remember, gives the reader a re-translation back into English of the 1791 French translation of Part One, and then appends to it Stuber's 1790–91 biographical memoir, itself beholden to Carey's memoir.
7. See Carla Mulford, "Benjamin Franklin and the Myths of Nationhood," in *Making America / Making American Literature*, ed. A. Robert Lee and W. M. Verhoeven (Amsterdam: Rodopi, 1996), 50–56; Richard D. Miles, "The American Image of Benjamin Franklin," *American Quarterly* 9 (1957): 126–28; and Nian-Sheng Huang, *Benjamin Franklin in American Thought and Culture, 1790–1990* (Philadelphia: American Philosophical Society, 1994), 67–76.
8. Edmund Morgan, *Benjamin Franklin* (New Haven: Yale University Press, 2002), 30.
9. For a version of this argument, see Jerry Weinberger, *Benjamin Franklin Unmasked: On the Unity of his Moral, Religious, and Political Thought* (Lawrence: University Press of Kansas, 2005).
10. Charles Taylor, *The Sources of the Self: The Making of Modern Identity* (Cambridge, MA: Harvard University Press, 1989), ix.

11. Jean-Jacques Rousseau, *The Confessions*, trans. J. M. Cohen (New York: Penguin, 1953), 17.

12. Gary Carson, "The Romantics' Franklin," *The Markham Review* 7 (1978): 37.

13. Thomas Mellon, *Thomas Mellon and His Times* (1885; rpt. New York: Kraus Reprint Co., 1969), 169–70.

14. Silas Felton, *The Life or Biography of Silas Felton*, ed. Rena Vasser, *Proceedings of the American Antiquarian Society* 69.2 (1959): 129.

15. D. H. Lawrence, *Studies in Classic American Literature* (1923; rpt. New York: Penguin, 1977), 25.

16. Alexander Graydon, *Memoirs of a Life, Chiefly Passed in Pennsylvania* (Harrisburgh: John Wyeth, 1811), 376.

17. Miles, "American Image," 123.

18. Max Farrand, ed., *Benjamin Franklin's Memoirs: Parallel Text Edition* (Berkeley: University of California Press, 1949).

FURTHER READING

Scholarly writings on Benjamin Franklin are abundant. This selective listing includes the better current book-length resources for studying Franklin, along with some of the older standard resources still in use today by those working in Franklin studies. Articles and book chapters on Franklin – too numerous to list here individually – can be found by accessing current databases in most institutional libraries.

Editions of Franklin's collected writings

Benjamin Franklin: Writings. Ed. J. A. Leo Lemay. New York: Library of America, 1987.

Benjamin Franklin's Letters to the Press, 1758–1775. Ed. Verner W. Crane. Chapel Hill: University of North Carolina Press for the Institute of Early American History and Culture, 1950.

The Complete Works of Benjamin Franklin. 12 vols. Ed. John Bigelow. New York and London: G. P. Putnam's, 1904.

The Papers of Benjamin Franklin. 38 vols. to date. Ed. Leonard W. Labaree, *et al.* New Haven and London: Yale University Press, 1959– .

The Works of Benjamin Franklin. 10 vols. Ed. Jared Sparks. Boston: Hilliard, Gray and Co., 1836–40.

The Writings of Benjamin Franklin. 10 vols. Ed. Albert Henry Smyth. New York and London: Macmillan, 1907.

Bibliographies, reference books, critical primary resources

Buxbaum, Melvin H. *Benjamin Franklin, 1721–1906: A Reference Guide.* Boston, MA: G. K. Hall, 1983.

 Benjamin Franklin, 1907–1983: A Reference Guide. Boston, MA: G. K. Hall, 1988.

Ford, Paul Leicester. *Franklin Bibliography: A List of Books Written by, or Relating to Benjamin Franklin.* Brooklyn, NY: [Privately Printed], 1889.

Kalter, Susan, ed. *Benjamin Franklin, Pennsylvania, and the First Nations: The Treaties of 1736–62.* Urbana: University of Illinois Press, 2006.

Lemay, J. A. Leo. *The Canon of Benjamin Franklin, 1722–1776: New Attributions and Reconsiderations.* Newark: University of Delaware Press, 1986.

Miller, C. William. *Benjamin Franklin's Philadelphia Printing, 1728–1766: A Descriptive Bibliography*. Philadelphia: American Philosophical Society, 1974.

Sellers, Charles Coleman. *Benjamin Franklin in Portraiture*. New Haven: Yale University Press, 1962.

Wolf, Edwin, 2nd, and Kevin J. Hayes. *The Library of Benjamin Franklin*. Philadelphia: American Philosophical Society and Library Company of Philadelphia, 2006.

Biographies and biographical studies of aspects of Franklin's life

Brands, H. W. *The First American: The Life and Times of Benjamin Franklin*. New York: Random House, 2000.

Carr, William George. *The Oldest Delegate: Franklin in the Constitutional Convention*. Newark: University of Delaware Press, 1990.

Chaplin, Joyce E. *The First Scientific American: Benjamin Franklin and the Pursuit of Genius*. New York: Basic Books, 2006.

Clark, Ronald William. *Benjamin Franklin: A Biography*. New York: Random House, 1983.

Ford, Paul Leicester. *The Many-Sided Franklin*. New York: Century, 1899.

Huang, Nian-Sheng. *Franklin's Father Josiah: Life of a Colonial Boston Tallow Chandler, 1657–1745*. Philadelphia: American Philosophical Society, 2000.

Isaacson, Walter. *Benjamin Franklin: An American Life*. New York: Simon and Schuster, 2003.

Lemay, J. A. Leo. *Ebenezer Kinnersley, Franklin's Friend*. Philadelphia: University of Pennsylvania Press, 1964.

The Life of Benjamin Franklin, Vol. 1: Journalist, 1706–1730. Philadelphia: University of Pennsylvania Press, 2006.

The Life of Benjamin Franklin, Vol. 2: Printer and Publisher, 1730–1747. Philadelphia: University of Pennsylvania Press, 2006.

Livingston, Luther S. *Franklin and His Press at Passy*. New York: Grolier Club, 1914.

Lopez, Claude-Anne. *Mon Cher Papa: Franklin and the Ladies of Paris*. New Haven: Yale University Press, 1990.

The Private Franklin: The Man and His Family. New York: Norton, 1985.

Morgan, David. *The Devious Dr. Franklin: Benjamin Franklin's Years in London*. Macon, GA: Mercer University Press, 1996.

Morgan, Edmund S. *Benjamin Franklin*. New Haven: Yale University Press, 2002.

Overhoff, Jürgen. *Benjamin Franklin: Erfinder, Freigeist, Staatenlenker*. Stuttgart: Klett-Cotta, 2006.

Randall, Willard Sterne. *A Little Revenge: Benjamin Franklin and His Son*. Boston: Little, Brown, 1984.

Schiff, Stacy. *A Great Improvisation: Franklin, France, and the Birth of America*. New York: Henry Holt, 2005.

Schoenbrun, David. *Triumph in Paris: The Exploits of Benjamin Franklin*. New York: Harper and Row, 1976.

Skemp, Sheila L. *William Franklin: Son of a Patriot, Servant of a King*. Oxford University Press, 1990.

Tourtellot, Arthur Bernon. *Benjamin Franklin, The Shaping of Genius: The Boston Years*. Garden City, NY: Doubleday, 1977.

Van Doren, Carl. *Benjamin Franklin*. New York: Viking Press, 1938.

Jane Mecom: Franklin's Favorite Sister. New York: Viking Press, 1950.

Wood, Gordon S. *The Americanization of Benjamin Franklin*. New York: Penguin, 2004.

Wright, Esmond. *Franklin of Philadelphia*. Cambridge, MA: Harvard University Press, 1986.

Selected monographs

Aldridge, Alfred Owen. *Benjamin Franklin, Philosopher and Man*. Philadelphia: Lippincott, 1965.

Benjamin Franklin and Nature's God. Durham, NC: Duke University Press, 1967.

Franklin and His French Contemporaries. New York University Press, 1957.

Anderson, Douglas. *The Radical Enlightenments of Benjamin Franklin*. Baltimore: Johns Hopkins University Press, 1997.

Arch, Stephen Carl. *After Franklin: The Emergence of Autobiography in Post-Revolutionary America, 1780–1830*. Hanover: University Press of New England, 2001.

Breitwieser, Mitchell Robert. *Cotton Mather and Benjamin Franklin: The Price of Representative Personality*. Cambridge University Press, 1984.

Buxbaum, Melvin H. *Benjamin Franklin and the Zealous Presbyterians*. University Park: Pennsylvania State University Press, 1975.

Campbell, James. *Recovering Benjamin Franklin: An Exploration of a Life of Science and Service*. Chicago: Open Court, 1999.

Carey, Lewis James. *Franklin's Economic Views*. Garden City, NY: Doubleday, Doran, 1928.

Clark, William Bell. *Ben Franklin's Privateers: A Naval Epic of the American Revolution*. Baton Rouge: Louisiana State University Press, 1956.

Cohen, I. Bernard. *Benjamin Franklin's Science*. Cambridge, MA: Harvard University Press, 1990.

Franklin and Newton: An Inquiry into Speculative Newtonian Experimental Science and Franklin's Work in Electricity as an Example Thereof. Philadelphia: American Philosophical Society, 1956.

Conner, Paul W. *Poor Richard's Politicks: Benjamin Franklin and His New American Order*. Westport, CO: Greenwood Press, 1980.

Crane, Verner W. *Benjamin Franklin and a Rising People*. Boston: Little, Brown, 1954.

Delbourgo, James. *A Most Amazing Scene of Wonders: Electricity and Enlightenment in Early America*. Cambridge, MA: Harvard University Press, 2006.

Dippel, Horst. *Individuum und Gesellschaft: Soziales Denken Zwischen Tradition und Revolution: Smith, Condorcet, Franklin*. Göttingen: Vandenhoeck and Ruprecht, 1981.

Dray, Philip. *Stealing God's Thunder: Benjamin Franklin's Lightning Rod and the Invention of America*. New York: Random House, 2005.

Finger, Stanley. *Doctor Franklin's Medicine*. Philadelphia: University of Pennsylvania Press, 2006.

Frasca, Ralph. *Benjamin Franklin's Printing Network: Disseminating Virtue in Early America*. Columbia: University of Missouri Press, 2006.

Granger, Bruce Ingram. *Benjamin Franklin, An American Man of Letters*. Ithaca, NY: Cornell University Press, 1964.

Hall, Max. *Benjamin Franklin and Polly Baker: The History of a Literary Deception*. University of Pittsburgh Press, 1990.

Houston, Alan. *Benjamin Franklin and the Politics of Improvement*. New Haven: Yale University Press, [2008].

Huang, Nian-Sheng. *Benjamin Franklin in American Thought and Culture, 1790–1990*. Philadelphia: American Philosophical Society, 1994.

Jennings, Francis. *Benjamin Franklin, Politician*. New York: W. W. Norton, 1996.

Korty, Margaret Barton. *Benjamin Franklin and Eighteenth-Century American Libraries*. Philadelphia: American Philosophical Society, 1965.

Lopez, Claude-Anne. *My Life with Benjamin Franklin*. New Haven: Yale University Press, 2000.

Middlekauff, Robert. *Benjamin Franklin and His Enemies*. Berkeley: University of California Press, 1996.

Newcomb, Benjamin H. *Franklin and Galloway: A Political Partnership*. New Haven: Yale University Press, 1972.

Nolan, J. Bennett. *Benjamin Franklin in Scotland and Ireland, 1759 and 1771*. Philadelphia: University of Pennsylvania Press, 1938.

Olson, Lester C. *Benjamin Franklin's Vision of American Community: A Study in Rhetorical Iconology*. Columbia: University of South Carolina Press, 2004.

Pace, Antonio. *Benjamin Franklin and Italy*. Philadelphia: American Philosophical Society, 1958.

Sappenfield, James. *A Sweet Instruction: Franklin's Journalism as a Literary Apprenticeship*. Carbondale: Southern Illinois University Press, 1973.

Seavey, Ormond. *Becoming Benjamin Franklin: The Autobiography and the Life*. University Park: Pennsylvania State University Press, 1988.

Skemp, Sheila L. *Benjamin Franklin and William Franklin: Father and Son, Patriot and Loyalist*. Boston and New York: Bedford Books of St. Martin's Press, 1994.

Smith, Jeffrey A. *Franklin and Bache: Envisioning the Enlightened Republic*. Oxford University Press, 1990.

Stourzh, Gerald. *Benjamin Franklin and American Foreign Policy*. University of Chicago Press, 1954.

Waldstreicher, David. *Runaway America: Benjamin Franklin, Slavery, and the American Revolution*. New York: Hill and Wang, 2004.

Walters, Kerry. *Benjamin Franklin and His Gods*. Urbana: University of Illinois Press, 1999.

Weinberger, Jerry. *Benjamin Franklin Unmasked: On the Unity of His Moral, Religious, and Political Thought*. Lawrence: University Press of Kansas, 2005.

Zall, Paul M. *Franklin's Autobiography: A Model Life*. Boston: Twayne Publishers, 1989.

Collections of essays

Balestra, Gianfranca, and Luigi Sampietro, eds. *Benjamin Franklin: An American Genius*. Rome: Bulzoni, 1993.

Barbour, Brian M. *Benjamin Franklin: A Collection of Critical Essays*. Englewood Cliffs, NJ: Prentice-Hall, 1979.

Buxbaum, Melvin H., ed. *Critical Essays on Benjamin Franklin*. Boston: G. K. Hall, 1987.

Lemay, J. A. Leo., ed. *The Oldest Revolutionary: Essays on Benjamin Franklin*. Philadelphia: University of Pennsylvania Press, 1976.

Reappraising Benjamin Franklin: A Bicentennial Perspective. Newark: University of Delaware Press, 1993.

Oberg, Barbara B., and Harry S. Stout, eds. *Benjamin Franklin, Jonathan Edwards, and the Representation of American Culture*. Oxford University Press, 1993.

Pollack, John, ed. *Educating the Youth of Pennsylvania: Worlds of Learning in the Age of Franklin*. Philadelphia: University of Pennsylvania Library, forthcoming.

Talbott, Page, ed. *Benjamin Franklin in Search of a Better World*. New Haven: Yale University Press, 2005.

Tise, Larry E., ed. *Benjamin Franklin and Women*. University Park: Pennsylvania State University Press, 2000.

INDEX

Académie Royale des Sciences 20 (*see also* Royal Academy of Sciences, Paris)

Academy of Philadelphia 4, 52, 105

Adams, John 60–61, 80

Adams, Matthew 52

Adanson, Michel, as author of *Voyage to Senegal* 16

Addison, Joseph 37, 59
  as author of *Cato* 25
  as co-creator, with Richard Steele, of *The Spectator* 38–39, 58

Adorno, Theodor W. 87

Aepinus, Franz Maria Ulrich Theodor Hoch 72–73

Aitken, Robert 19

Albany Plan of Union (1754) 4, 6

d'Alembert, Jean le Rond, as co-compiler of the *Encyclopedia* 134–35

Almanac tradition 1

American Academy of Arts and Sciences 20, 73

American Philosophical Society 4, 14–15, 20–22, 51, 52, 57, 72–73, 105
  Transactions of 15, 73

American Revolution 9, 15, 30, 45, 63, 73, 80, 117–20, 123, 129, 135

American Society, *see* American Philosophical Society

Andrews, Jedediah 32

Aquinas, Thomas 134

Aristotle 134
  as natural philosopher 66

Art of Making Money Plenty in Everyman's Pocket, The 150

Articles of Confederation 6

Associates of Dr. Bray 59

Associators, Pennsylvania 123

Augustine 166–67

Bache, Benjamin Franklin 18, 153

Bache, Sarah ("Sally") Franklin 117, 119, 125–29

Bache, William 129

Bacon, Francis 66, 71, 91

Banks, Joseph 63

Barlowe, Arthur 145

Bartram, John 14

Batavian Society, Holland 57

Behrends, Johann Adolf 50

Benjamin Franklin Institute of Technology 138

Bentham, Jeremy 82–83
  as author of *Introduction to the Principles of Morals and Legislation* 82

Berkeley, George, Bishop 59

Bible 28, 32, 41, 47
  as King James version 32

Bigelow, John 162–64, 166

Blackmore, Richard 33

Blake, John L. 152

Boerhaave, Hermann 17

Bond, Thomas 14–15

Bowdoin, James 16

Bowle's Moral Pictures; or, Poor Richard Illustrated . . . 150

Boyle, Robert 64
  London lectures by 64

Braddock, Edward, Gen. 4

Brientnall, Joseph 55

Brillon de Jouy, Anne-Louise Boivin d'Hardancourt 60

British Empire 9, 51, 124

Brownrigg, Mary 17